THE DARK SIDE OF THE IVORY TOWER

A cursory reading of the history of U.S. colleges and universities reveals that violence, vice, and victimization – campus crime – has been part of collegiate life since the colonial era. Not until the late 1980s – some 250 years later – did campus crime suddenly become an issue on the public stage. Drawing from numerous mass-media and scholarly sources and using a theoretical framework grounded in social constructionism, *The Dark Side of the Ivory Tower* chronicles how four groups of activists – college student advocates, feminists, victims and their families, and public health experts – used a variety of tactics and strategies to convince the public that campus crime posed a new danger to the safety and security of college students and the ivory tower itself, while simultaneously convincing policy makers to take action against the problem. Readers from a range of disciplinary interests, campus security professionals, and informed citizens will find the book both compelling and valuable for understanding campus crime as a newly constructed social reality.

John J. Sloan III is Associate Professor of Criminal Justice and Sociology and Chair of the Department of Justice Sciences at the University of Alabama at Birmingham. He has authored or coauthored more than 100 scholarly articles, book chapters, research reports, and presentations and coedited two previous books on campus crime. Professor Sloan has been a Research Assistant at the Institute for the Study of Children and Families at Eastern Michigan University, as well as Visiting Professor of Criminal Justice at the universities of Alabama and West Florida.

Bonnie S. Fisher is Professor in the School of Criminal Justice and a Research Fellow at the Center for Criminal Justice Research at the University of Cincinnati. She has authored or coauthored more than 150 scholarly publications and has coedited four volumes that focus on victimization issues. Professor Fisher was an honorary visiting scholar at University of Leicester, Scarman Centre, in the United Kingdom; a visiting scholar in the Division of Prevention and Community Research at the Consultation Center at Yale University School of Medicine; and a visiting professor in the Department of Sociology at John Jay College of Criminal Justice.

The Dark Side
of the Ivory Tower

Campus Crime as a Social Problem

John J. Sloan III

University of Alabama at Birmingham

Bonnie S. Fisher

University of Cincinnati

CAMBRIDGE
UNIVERSITY PRESS

CAMBRIDGE UNIVERSITY PRESS
Cambridge, New York, Melbourne, Madrid, Cape Town, Singapore,
São Paulo, Delhi, Dubai, Tokyo, Mexico City

Cambridge University Press
32 Avenue of the Americas, New York, NY 10013 2473, USA

www.cambridge.org
Information on this title: www.cambridge.org/9780521124058

© John J. Sloan III and Bonnie S. Fisher 2011

First published 2011

Printed in the United States of America

A catalog record for this publication is available from the British Library.

Library of Congress Cataloging in Publication data
Sloan, John J.
 The dark side of the ivory tower : campus crime as a social
 problem / John J. Sloan III, Bonnie S. Fisher.
   p. cm.
 Includes bibliographical references and index.
 ISBN 978-0-521-19517-1 (hardback)
 1. College students – Crimes against – United States. 2. Crime
 prevention – United States. 3. Safety education – United States.
 I. Fisher, Bonnie, 1959– II. Title.
 HV6250.4.S78S55 2010
 364–dc22   2010006614

ISBN 978-0-521-19517-1 Hardback
ISBN 978-0-521-12405-8 Paperback

Contents

Preface

On February 14, 2008, 27-year-old former graduate student Steven P. Kazmierczak killed 5 people and wounded 16 others after he opened fire in a lecture hall at Northern Illinois University using a shotgun and three handguns. That shooting came almost a year to the day after the worst mass shooting ever on a U.S. college campus occurred at Virginia Polytechnic Institute and State University (Virginia Tech), when 23-year-old Seung-Hui Cho, a senior there, shot and killed 32 students and professors and wounded dozens of others in two separate on-campus incidents before taking his own life. Media reports of shootings, rapes, serious sexual and physical assaults, stalking, and other heinous crimes occurring on college campuses have become common, appearing in news outlets such as the *New York Times*, the *Washington Post*, and the *Boston Globe* and trade publications such as the *Chronicle of Higher Education*. These publications have also widely reported that alcohol abuse among college students is rampant and has been linked to many deaths from alcohol poisoning or serious injuries suffered while intoxicated. If media reports are to be believed, a "dark side" of the ivory tower of academe has emerged, which threatens the health and safety of millions of college students in the United States.

What is interesting is this: violence, vice, and victimization have occurred on college campuses dating back to the origins of higher education in America. Historical evidence indicates that during the 17th, 18th, 19th, and 20th centuries, murders, lynchings, rapes, violent assaults, serious vandalism, hunger strikes, and riots were not uncommon on college campuses. What is also interesting is that beginning

in the 1980s, and continuing to the present, alarm bells started ringing as a variety of sources – including government agencies such as
the U.S. Department of Education and the U.S. General Accounting
Office – expressed mounting concern about crime and safety on
American college campuses. Claims began appearing in mass-media
outlets that college students were *routinely* being murdered, raped,
and otherwise victimized on college campuses. Reporters described
a "rape culture" that had apparently developed on college campuses.
According to these reports, the campus rape culture encouraged college men, enabled by alcohol use or by the provision of drugs such
as GHB or Rohypnol ("roofies") to unsuspecting women, to sexually
victimize college women on campus. Student offenders appeared to
be committing these types of assault with relative impunity. Parents of
student victims claimed to the press that security on college campuses
was either lax or nonexistent, which created many opportunities
for on-campus victimizations. Students also appeared to be drown-
ing themselves in a sea of alcohol, engaging in dangerous "binge
drinking" with far-too-frequent fatal consequences. Finally, claims
were leveled by a variety of sources – including student victims, their
parents, counselors, and campus officials – that postsecondary administrators, in a cynical effort to maintain the images of their institutions, denied there was a crime problem on their campuses, did little
to prevent on-campus victimizations, failed to respond adequately to
the needs of campus crime victims, and failed to punish adequately
known student offenders.

It thus appears that over the past 20 years, "campus crime" – an
umbrella term we use to refer to a variety of illegal or deviant behaviors occurring on college and university campuses – moved from a
private problem involving victims, their families, and individual postsecondary institutions to a large-scale social problem to which policy
makers, including Congress and the state legislatures, have repeatedly
responded.

What events contributed to the apparent change in how media portrayed the dark side of academe? Were specific groups or individuals
responsible for the apparent sea change in how mass media depicted
crime occurring on college campuses? If yes, then what strategies
did these groups or individuals use? How did policy makers become

convinced that campus crime was a problem deserving of their attention? What steps did policy makers take to address crime on college campuses?

In this book, we argue that since the late 1980s campus crime in the United States has been *socially constructed* as a new social problem. What this means is that campus crime came to be labeled a social problem not necessarily because of some objective level of threat it posed to the public welfare but because groups of activists *made claims* about the problem and used a variety of strategies and tactics to convince the public and policy makers that the problem posed a "real" threat to the collective well-being.

In analyzing how campus crime was socially constructed as a new social problem, we identify the major parties involved in its construction, including the claims they made about campus crime. We also examine the strategies they used to package, and then disseminate to the public, information about the problem. Finally, we examine policy responses that activists were able to shape and have mandated to address the problem. In so doing, we draw upon extant literature that examines how only some problems, under certain conditions, come to be selected, identified, and responded to as social problems.

In Chapter 1, we present a brief history of violence, vice, and victimization on American college and university campuses to illustrate that the dark side of the ivory tower has always had a presence on college campuses and that recent claims about the threat it poses are nothing new. Chapter 2 presents the theoretical framework that guided our examination of the social construction of campus crime. Here, we not only discuss the applicability of the framework to understanding campus crime as a social problem and provide examples but also identify four groups we believe were instrumental in helping to construct campus crime as a new social problem. We then devote the next four chapters to examining these groups and analyzing their individual contributions to socially constructing campus crime. Chapter 3 is devoted to analyzing the role played by Security On Campus, Inc. (SOC), a nonprofit, grass-roots lobbying organization that was founded by the parents of a student slain in her dorm room at Lehigh University in 1986. The chapter reveals the claims of SOC that college and university campuses are "unsafe and violent" places and the instrumental role SOC played in getting Congress to first consider and ultimately to pass new federal laws designed to reduce campus crime. Chapter 4 analyzes the contributions of campus feminists to constructing campus crime through their claims that "date" or "acquaintance" rape was rampant on college campuses. Campus feminists also identified not only the causes of this form of sexual victimization of college women but the consequences for victims of this crime as well. Chapter 5 explores how victims of campus crime – primarily students and their families – helped construct campus crime as a social problem by making claims to the media based on lawsuits they had filed against postsecondary institutions. In their suits, they alleged that postsecondary administrators failed to take necessary steps to prevent their on-campus victimizations from occurring. These claims resulted in postsecondary institutions not only being forced by Congress to address security and safety issues on college campuses but also being held liable in multiple state courts for the victimizations. Chapter 6 examines how public health researchers also assisted in socially constructing campus crime as a new social problem by making claims about the extent and nature of collegiate alcohol abuse. In particular, these researchers created a new term, "binge drinking," that defined how college students were abusing alcohol and from which serious negative consequences, both direct and indirect, arose. In Chapter 7, we examine commonalities among the claimsmakers and their legacy to the social construction of campus crime as a new social problem.

We have several goals for this book. First, we seek to describe and explain how campus crime came to be elevated to the status of a new social problem. Specifically, we show how several disparate groups of activists, both individually and collectively, were able to bring the problem to the public's attention, to use mass media to disseminate their claims, and to shape policy responses to the problem. Second, we show how these groups of activists, despite representing different interests, ultimately became loosely coupled around sets of claims each group was making about campus crime and security, ranging from who were the perpetrators to what they perceived as appropriate policy responses. Third, we seek to make a contribution to the existing literature on the social construction of social problems. Finally, we seek to educate readers about how social forces, rather than objective levels of danger or threat, often work first to create and then to help institutionalize social problems.

The book can serve as a resource for those concerned about campus crime and safety issues and is directed to both academic and nonacademic audiences. For the academic audience, the book could be used as a main or supplemental text in various courses in sociology, social problems, criminology, criminal justice, victimology, or public policy in which discussion about crime in specific social contexts occurs. The book could be used in a "first-year experience" or "freshman experience" class for college students, where freshman critically examine a topic that is salient to their campus experiences. A senior capstone course could also be designed to use the book to bring together the experiences of college students' tenure and critically compare these to the themes developed in the chapters. The universal appeal of the topic of campus crime most certainly would pique students' interest at any stage of their college years. For the nonacademic audience, the book could serve as a resource to help readers understand better how social problems and related policy responses are not necessarily grounded in the objective threat the problem poses but rather in how skillfully activists are able to bring the problem to the forefront of public discourse.

Acknowledgments

This book could not have been finished without the help and support of many. We thank both Ed Parsons, our Editor at Cambridge University Press, for his guidance during the production of the book and the reviewers of previous drafts of the manuscript for their helpful comments. We also thank the editorial team at Cambridge University Press whose careful work considerably improved the manuscript. Further, we thank our colleagues at the University of Alabama at Birmingham and the University of Cincinnati, as well as the hundreds of students at our respective universities who have attentively listened to each of us talk endlessly about campus crime – both inside and outside our classes. Our students provided us with valuable insights from a new perspective, and that insight has informed the writing of this book. We gratefully acknowledge the University of California Press for permission to quote extensively from Joel Best's *Random Violence: How We Talk about New Crimes and New Victims* (Berkeley: University of California Press, 1999).

John thanks the University of Alabama at Birmingham for granting him a sabbatical leave that provided release from his administrative and teaching duties so he could work on the book. He also thanks Professor John O. Smyla and the University of West Florida Department of Criminal Justice and Legal Studies for allowing him access to its library holdings and providing him an office and support staff while on sabbatical. Most of all, he thanks his wife, Tavis, for her understanding and support during the writing of the book.

Bonnie expresses her heartfelt appreciation to her husband Nick, and their daughters, Olivia and Camille, for their love, support, and good humor during the writing of this book.

THE DARK SIDE OF THE IVORY TOWER

CHAPTER ONE

Violence, Vice, and Victimization on American College and University Campuses
A Brief History Lesson

Despite...numerous warnings...[19th-century] college students continued to consume alcohol, play cards, bet on horse races, and pursue sexual liaisons. They also used violence to settle conflicts among themselves and to protest college discipline. College students' persistent reputation for rowdiness and debauchery reflects the influence of the "code of honor" which allowed, and even encouraged, drunkenness, gambling, sexual license, and fighting.[1]

Since the 1980s, a shift in thinking about college and university campuses has occurred in the United States. No longer is the "ivory tower" of academe perceived as a place of retreat for scholarly inquiry. Nor is college perceived as a time for growth, where students "find themselves" and their place in the world. Rather, when talk turns to life on college campuses, that talk is often about crime, especially violence. In particular, the recent mass shootings at Virginia Tech and Northern Illinois University are often used to illustrate just how dangerous college campuses have apparently become.[2] Besides mass shootings occurring on campus, date rape, sexual assault, and other forms of violence against women seem commonplace.[3] In fact, a recent

---

[1] Evelyn D. Causey, "The Character of Gentleman: Deportment, Piety, and Morality in Southern Colleges and Universities 1820–1860" (Ph.D. dissertation, University of Delaware, Newark, 2006), p. 30.

[2] Since 1960, for example, there have been 13 officially recorded mass shootings on American college or university campuses resulting in 88 people killed and 106 others wounded. See Lauren Smith, "Major Shootings on American College Campuses" (2007), retrieved July 16, 2008, http://chronicle.com/free/2007/04/2007041610n.htm.

[3] See Joetta Carr, *American College Health Association Campus Violence White Paper* (Baltimore: American College Health Association, 2005).

report on the sexual victimization of college women published by the
U.S. Department of Justice indicated that approximately 3 percent of
college women experience either an attempted or a completed rape
during a typical nine-month academic year.[4] According to one *New York
Times* story, violence has "become a way of life for college students,"[5]
and some researchers suggest that media reports on campus violence
have "created the impression that college and university campuses are
increasingly dangerous places."[6]

During the past 20 years, individuals and their families who have
been affected by violence on campus have often responded to these
events by successfully suing postsecondary institutions over these incidents. In their lawsuits, student victims or their families have claimed
that colleges and universities were liable for damages arising from
these incidents because campus security was lax at best and nonexistent at worst. The legal basis for victims' claims was the argument that
postsecondary institutions *owed a legal duty of care* to students and campus visitors to protect them from harm, especially when such harm
was foreseeable.[7]

Finally, researchers have repeatedly warned about a new public
health problem on America's college campuses, "binge drinking,"
where several times a week college students consume large amounts
of alcohol in a single sitting. Binge drinking is symptomatic, according to researchers, of a larger "party culture" that characterizes many
U.S. colleges and universities and which not only condones alcohol
abuse but encourages it. High levels of alcohol abuse, in turn, have
been linked with such grave consequences for students as poor academic performance, serious physical injury, sexual victimization,

---

[4] Heather Karjane, Bonnie S. Fisher, and Francis T. Cullen, *Sexual Assault on
    Campus: What Colleges and Universities Are Doing about It,* National Institute of Justice
    Research for Practice, NCJ 205521 (December) (Washington, DC: National
    Institute of Justice, 2005), retrieved June 1, 2009, http://www.ncjrs.gov/pdffiles1/
    nij/205521.pdf.
[5] Nadine Joseph, "Campus Couples and Violence," *New York Times,* June 23, 1981, sec.
    A, p. 20.
[6] Bonnie S. Fisher, "Crime and Fear on Campus," *Annals of the American Academy of
    Political and Social Science* 539 (1995): 85–101.
[7] Phillip Burling, *Crime on Campus: Analyzing and Managing the Increasing Risk of
    Institutional Liability,* 2nd ed. (Washington, DC: National Association of College
    and University Attorneys, 2004).

and even death from alcohol poisoning or drunken driving-related traffic accidents.[8]

RAISING THE SPECTER OF THE DARK SIDE OF THE IVORY TOWER

A steady stream of media reports has emerged over the past 20 years that could lead the average person to believe that postsecondary institutions in the United States have fallen prey to the "dark side" of the ivory tower – that "violence, vice, and victimization" have become the norm on campus rather than the exception. Indeed, if these reports are to be believed, parents should be rightfully reluctant to send their 17- and 18-year-old children off to college, where, at best, they might escape with their lives after four or five years on campus.

Yet most of the public is unaware that claims about widespread violence and other forms of crime on college campuses are not new. Indeed, when examining the history of American higher education, one is quickly struck by how consistently postsecondary institutional administrators, parents of college students, faculty members, and popular media sources – both electronic and print – of the day raised similar claims that this dark side was jeopardizing the very foundations of American higher education.

What makes the past two decades apparently different from previous eras is that claims about the threats to the health and well-being of the nation's college students became institutionalized with the assistance of 24-hour news cycles, cable television outlets, and the Internet. Now, a serious incident occurring on a college campus such as a shooting or a sexual assault is almost certain to receive near saturation coverage from various electronic and print media sources. Such coverage, in turn, helps elevate campus crime to the level of a new social problem in America.

In response, postsecondary institutions have undertaken a host of efforts to address the "new problem" that violence, vice, and

---

[8] See, for example, Henry Wechsler, Alan Davenport, George Dowdall, Bruce Moeykens, and Stephen Castillo, "Health and Behavioral Consequences of Binge Drinking in College: A National Survey of Students at 140 Campuses," *Journal of the American Medical Association* 272 (1994): 1672–1677.

victimization are allegedly posing to them. Many colleges and universities are now allocating significant resources to educate incoming students about the safety risks they may face while on campus, especially when drinking alcohol. Several states and the Congress have passed laws mandating, among other things, that postsecondary institutions report annually how much crime is occurring on their campuses. The courts have also held colleges and universities liable under civil law for on-campus victimizations involving their students. Consequently, a steady stream of claims has arisen over the past 20 years alleging that college students face major dangers from various forms of violence, vice, and victimization while on campus. These claims, in turn, have resulted in significant changes in how various social institutions – colleges and universities, the courts, and legislative bodies – respond to campus crime.

How did this situation develop during the late 1980s and the 1990s? What were the claims being made, and which parties were making them? How were these parties able to construct a new reality of college life rife with violence, crime, and alcohol abuse? What processes were involved? How did college students and their families, government institutions, and colleges and universities themselves respond to the claimed threat that on-campus violence, vice, and victimization posed to higher education?

This book addresses these questions by critically examining how campus crime came to be socially constructed as a new social problem. In the chapters that follow, we show how four groups, individually and collectively, came forward and made largely anecdotal claims that college students not only were at high risk of becoming the victims of various forms of crime, especially violent crime, but were also involved in unprecedented levels of alcohol abuse occurring on campus. These claims were then repeated by both electronic and print media and ultimately convinced concerned parents of college students, as well as the American public more generally, that college students faced serious dangers. As a result, something had to be done immediately to protect our young people from the grave consequences this threat posed to their futures. Ultimately, campus crime become elevated to the status of a new and growing social problem worthy of significant policy intervention at the highest levels of government.

As we show in later chapters that focus on specific claims made about campus crime and the groups making them, much of what was being said inferred that the tripartite problem of violence, vice, and victimization occurring on postsecondary campuses was somehow "new," "unprecedented," or "startling" in both its scope and magnitude. In other words, the claims being made during the 1980s and into the 1990s indicated that campus crime was *new*; that it *posed a serious threat to every college student* and his or her family; and, because the threat was imminent, *significant policy resources had to be allocated to fight it*. As we show in the remainder of this chapter, however, claims about the threat posed to students by violence, vice, and victimization occurring on college campuses are not new. Rather, concerns about the threat posed by the dark side of the ivory tower to the physical and psychological health of college students and to their safety have existed since the establishment of the first U.S. institutions of higher learning during the 17th and 18th centuries. In contrast to previous historical periods, in recent years several groups – the parents of a student murdered as she slept in her college dormitory, the courts, campus feminists, and public health advocates – came forward and helped convince the public, the courts, and legislators of the chronic, ubiquitous, and imminent threat that campus crime posed to the nation's college students. Only large-scale changes in how postsecondary institutions both proactively and reactively dealt with the threat could address the problem.

A BRIEF HISTORY LESSON

Institutions of higher learning have existed in America since the mid-1600s.[9] From the humble beginnings of nine colleges founded in New England during the colonial era to recent Carnegie Foundation estimates of 4,391 postsecondary institutions operating in the United

[9] There is no consensus among scholars of the history of higher education concerning which school can be officially deemed as the first college in the United States. Likely candidates include the College of William and Mary and Harvard University, both of which were founded in the late 1600s, while Yale University came into existence in the early 1700s. See Arthur M. Cohen, *The Shaping of American Higher Education: Emergence and Growth of the Contemporary System* (San Francisco: Jossey-Bass Publishers, 1998).

States during the fall of 2004, American colleges and universities have undergone a metamorphosis.[10]

One of the biggest changes occurring in American colleges is their evolution from male-only, liberal-arts-focused, church-affiliated institutions whose primary mission was to train men to enter the clergy[11] into an astonishing variety of largely coeducational institutions designed to educate students from many disciplines for entry into an assortment of careers. Further, as they evolved, colleges (and eventually universities) have taken different forms, including technical, junior, or community colleges; large state and private research universities, both sectarian and nonsectarian; and schools serving specific subgroups of students (e.g., women or African Americans). Recent years have even seen the emergence of "virtual" universities, including those operating on a for-profit basis such as the University of Phoenix and Argosy University.[12] Finally, as colleges evolved over the next three centuries,[13] they became an increasingly indispensable part of the social and economic fabric of America.

Beyond the evolutionary aspects of postsecondary institutions, what is also interesting when exploring the history of U.S. colleges and universities is that only some 300 years *after* their creation has the violence, vice, and victimization occurring there – what we refer to as campus crime – generated near the level of attention recent years have witnessed. While there have been occasional outcries over perceived

---

[10] These figures are available at the Carnegie Foundation for the Advancement of Teaching Web site, retrieved September 16, 2008, http://www.carnegiefoundation. org/classifications/index.asp?key=785.

[11] Frederick Rudolph, *The American College and University* (Athens: University of Georgia Press, [1962] 1990).

[12] According to the most recent Carnegie Foundation information from the fall of 2004, there are 34 subclasses of postsecondary institutions operating in the United States organized by several categories, including public and private non- and for-profit "associate's colleges," where less than 10 percent of all degrees awarded are bachelor's degrees; "baccalaureate colleges," where baccalaureate degrees represent at least 10 percent of all degrees awarded and less than 50 master's degrees or 20 doctorates are awarded annually; and "doctorate universities," which award at least 20 doctoral degrees each year. Retrieved September 16, 2008, http://www. carnegiefoundation.org/classifications/index.asp?key=798.

[13] John S. Brubacher and Willis M. Ruby, *Higher Education in Transition: A History of American Colleges and Universities, 1636–1976* (New York: Harper and Row. 1976); Christopher J. Lucas, *American Higher Education: A History*, 2nd ed. (New York: Palgrave Macmillan, 2006).

lawlessness on college campuses – particularly over the civil unrest, protests, and demonstrations of the 1960s and early 1970s – much of the campus crime that apparently has been routine on college campuses for most of their history did not trigger in the public, advocacy groups, or researchers any sense of alarm or urgency. Nor was there anywhere near the large-scale, coordinated response by elected state and federal officials or campus administrators to these behaviors similar to what has occurred in recent years.[14] This lack of systematic response to the historical problem of campus crime sharply contrasts with the historical response of America to its crime problem more generally, especially since the 1960s and in its largest cities.[15]

The Early Years: The 17th and 18th Centuries
The earliest postsecondary institutions in America took the form of small, usually church-affiliated liberal arts colleges, purposely nestled in rural settings to avoid the perceived problems associated with the burgeoning cities of the time.[16] As the historian of American higher education Christopher Lucas described it:

> Going to college meant four years spent...under close supervision by college officials, far from the temptations of city life. Virtually all were residential boarding schools serving *in loco parentis* – which is to say, colleges accepted full responsibility for the social, recreational, and spiritual development of the young men entrusted to their care.[17]

While a complete history of deviant and criminal behavior occurring on the campuses of the earliest American postsecondary institutions

---

[14] One coordinated response that *did* occur during the 1960s and early 1970s was states' passing laws authorizing colleges and universities to create campus police departments staffed by sworn law enforcement officers. See Diane C. Bordner and David M. Peterson, *Campus Policing: The Nature of University Police Work* (Lanham, MD: University Press of America, 2001).

[15] Consider that during the 20th century trillions of dollars in resources were invested by the federal government to solve "the crime problem," often with unintended consequences. See Jonathan Simon, *Governing through Crime: How the War on Crime Transformed American Democracy and Created a Culture of Fear* (New York: Oxford University Press, 2007).

[16] Christopher Lucas, *Crisis in the Academy: Rethinking Higher Education in America* (New York: St. Martin's Press, 1996), p. 51; Brubacher and Rudy, *Higher Education in Transition*, pp. 39–58.

[17] Lucas, *Crisis in the Academy*, p. 51.

is not available,[18] the existing historical record nonetheless reveals an important dichotomy occurring at these schools. On the one hand, because early colleges operated *in loco parentis*, literally "in the place of the parents," they were largely left to regulate the conduct of students in any manner they saw fit.[19] As a result, school administrators believed themselves to be largely removed from or even *above* the law and were far more likely to use an iron fist than a velvet glove when it came to disciplining their students.[20] Against this backdrop, students faced harsh rules of discipline designed to "make them men." Required chapel and scripture readings were a routine part of the academic program of study, and conservative Protestant theology served as the basis for the discipline that students faced, which emphasized a "spare the rod, spoil the child" orientation.

On the other hand, the historical record also contains well-documented accounts of students at these earliest colleges engaging in a variety of improper, if not downright illegal behavior. For example, underclassmen often had to act as "servants" for upperclassmen. Students also engaged in vandalism of college facilities and theft from one another and from faculty members. Students routinely got drunk and rowdy and engaged in hazing one another.[21] There are also many accounts chronicling students engaging in serious assaults of fellow students, including stabbings and shootings, and even murdering not only each other but faculty members as well, often over relatively trivial matters.[22]

---

[18] One might argue that one reason a consistent historical record does not exist is because violence, vice, and victimization were *normal behaviors* on many campuses and thus did not necessarily warrant detailed record keeping. Additionally, much of the historical record tends to focus mostly how early colleges operated, from an administrative standpoint, as well as on curricular matters.

[19] For recent discussion of late 20th-century and early 21st-century trends in higher education relating to *in loco parentis*, see Britton White, "Student Rights: From *In Loco Parentis* to *Sine Parentibus* and Back Again? Understanding the Family Educational Rights and Privacy Act in Higher Education," *Brigham Young University Education and Law Journal* 2 (2007): 321–350.

[20] Michael C. Smith, "The Ancestry of Campus Violence," pp. 5–16 in J. M. Sherill and D. G. Siegel (Eds.), *Responding to Violence on Campus* (San Francisco: Jossey-Bass, 1989), p. 7.

[21] Cohen, *The Shaping of American Higher Education*; Lucas, *American Higher Education*.

[22] Cohen, *The Shaping of American Higher Education*; Lucas, *American Higher Education*; Brubacher and Rudy, *Higher Education in Transition*.

The problem that school administrators faced was that "the system of discipline...failed to achieve its...specific purpose."[23] The breakdown in discipline was evidenced both through individual cases of deviance and crime and through planned and organized large-scale resistance to the rules. In fact, the disorders and riots that occurred on American college campuses during the 1960s were predated by at least 200 years by similar disorders that struck Harvard, Princeton, and other colleges in New England.[24]

In short, emerging postsecondary institutions aspired to achieve the lofty educational goals that came to be defined as the ivory tower of academe[25] through rigid codes of student conduct and harsh discipline. Simultaneously, however, they were also dealing with an emerging student culture that condoned drunkenness, rowdiness, hazing, and criminality – the dark side of the ivory tower. This "culture of deviance" would, as we show here, remain a hallmark of student life at postsecondary institutions as they grew in size and stature and spread throughout the nation.

The Unfolding Years: The 19th Century

Accounts, both media-based and institutional, of illegal and deviant behavior on the part of college students continued during the 19th century. As colleges first became entrenched in the East and then followed westward expansion of the United States, "the student body was [increasingly] made up of youth accustomed to the individualistic ways of frontier existence [and] the problem of discipline was an ever-present source of difficulty" for college administrators.[26] In turn, college administrators complained at great length about the indifference students expressed toward their academic studies, while also expressing strong frustration at their inability to enforce their schools'

---

[23] Rudolph, *The American College and University*, p. 104.

[24] Ibid.

[25] Although the term "ivory tower" originated in the biblical *Song of Solomon*, beginning in the 1800s the term became a pejorative description of a world where faculty and students engaged in pursuits of the mind, disconnected from the practical concerns of everyday life. Retrieved June 1, 2009, http://www.statemaster.com/encyclopedia/Ivory-tower#_ref-WWW_0.

[26] Donald G. Tewksbury, *The Founding of American Colleges and Universities before the Civil War* (New York: Columbia University Press, [1932] 1965), p. 27.

"moral standards" with students. Both lore and officially recorded lamenting by college and university presidents testified to the persistence of students who never seemed to accept academic rigor or high achievement and bragged of never having "cracked a book."[27]

Although they were apparently disinterested in academic pursuits, college and university students of the 19th century *were* apparently interested in other sorts of activities. For example, students at the University of North Carolina at Chapel Hill, on learning that prayers had been canceled one summer evening in 1849, "whooped and hollered on the campus and in a nearby hotel for much of the night," to the chagrin of university administrators.[28] In the South, "despite numerous warnings college students continued to consume alcohol, play cards, bet on horse races, and pursue sexual liaisons."[29] Both college authorities and members of the academy noted that "alcohol abuse, gambling, and promiscuity flourished in institutions of higher learning," and in a speech at the College of William of Mary, one of its professors claimed that postsecondary institutions had "subjected...youth to strong temptations" and led young men into "dissipation and vice."[30] During the 1832–1833 academic year, the faculty at Dartmouth met 68 times to sanction instances of delinquency by students enrolled there, while during the 1851–1852 academic year 282 cases of student delinquency came before a faculty disciplinary board at the University of North Carolina at Chapel Hill from a student body of just 230 men.[31] One young man enrolled at Furman University in 1854 wrote to his parents that he was thankful he had the maturity to withstand "the ensnaring temptations of college life which have seduced many a youth... [into] the most degrading of habits and vices."[32] College students in the South developed a general reputation as being rowdy and for pursuing debauchery; such behavior was apparently influenced by a code of honor of the time that allowed (and even encouraged) drunkenness, gambling, sexual

[27] Lucas, *American Higher Education*, pp. 93–94.
[28] Causey, "The Character of Gentleman," pp. 71–72.
[29] Ibid., p. 30.
[30] Ibid., p. 200.
[31] Rudolph, *The American College and University*, p. 106.
[32] Ibid., pp. 202–203.

promiscuity, and other deviant behaviors to flourish openly.[33] Thus, despite administrators' threats of sanction, including dismissal from school, students continued engaging in various forms of deviant and illegal behavior.

Beyond students' persistence at pursuing various vices, the historical record reveals that college campuses during the 19th century were violent places. Young men engaged in acts of sabotage that resulted in injury and death to students and faculty members. They brawled with one another on a regular basis to resolve conflicts and rioted to express their grievances against the administration, not only in the South but elsewhere.[34] As Causey described it,

> Students generally expressed regret over their use of violence only if someone was killed in the altercation. After a student fatally shot University of Virginia professor John A. G. Davis during a riot in 1840, the young men of the university published resolutions conveying their regret over the incident and declaring the shooter deserved the... contempt of the students.[35]

One young man enrolled at the University of North Carolina at Chapel Hill in 1853 revealed in a letter to his parents that he had narrowly avoided killing another student who had offended him: "I have made a most fortunate escape, not from the hands of my antagonist, but an escape from crime and probably disgrace."[36]

Historical evidence from the 19th century also reveals that student residential dormitories apparently contributed to the violence that was flourishing on many college campuses of the time. The historian Frederick Rudolph notes that "young men were brought into close proximity under the harshest of conditions, and on whose time the intellectual purposes of college placed too few demands."

---

[33] Ibid., p. 30. As discussed in Chapters 4 and 6, similar codes of honor are claimed to exist today that justify sexual violence perpetrated against college women by college men and the serious abuse of alcohol by college students. See Martin D. Schwartz and Walter S. DeKeseredy, *Sexual Assault on the College Campus: The Role of Male Peer Support* (Thousand Oaks, CA: Sage Publications, 1997).

[34] Rudolph, *The American College and University*, pp. 202–205. See also John R. Thelin, *A History of American Higher Education* (Baltimore: Johns Hopkins University Press, 2004), p. 65.

[35] Causey, "The Character of Gentleman," p. 241.

[36] Ibid.

Dormitories "created an environment in which residents were … capable of being whipped into an explosive rebellion." The rebellions were expressed, more often than not, in the form of strikes orchestrated by undergraduate students against faculty members and administrators, protesting some real or imagined wrong. Between 1800 and 1830, for example, Princeton experienced six student-led strikes; between 1800 and 1875, violent rebellions were staged by students at, among others, Amherst, Brown, the University of South Carolina, Georgetown, and DePauw.[37]

The social conditions of students' dormitories – overcrowding, poor food, significant class differences among those living in them, and lack of administrative oversight – created an atmosphere in which frustration, argument, and crime were common. Dormitories were places where "in quiet desperation, plots [against other students] were hatched," and where "what may have begun in innocence often ended in tragedy and misfortune." Historians of higher education even implicitly linked dormitory conditions of the time to on-campus murders of students and faculty members that were committed by college students at such schools as Miami of Ohio, South Carolina College, the University of Virginia, Illinois College, the University of Missouri, and the University of North Carolina at Chapel Hill.[38]

While apparently uninterested in their academic studies, many students of the time were *immensely* interested in drinking, fighting, duels, and sexual liaisons and were ready to engage in these activities at a moment's notice. They hatched plans for and carried out strikes and other forms of rebellious behavior against school administrators and engaged in various forms of delinquency serious enough to warrant a formal response by faculty disciplinary boards. Dormitory life apparently subjected residents to harsh living conditions and at least implicitly contributed to the violence and victimization that was occurring among students. Yet the bad reputations that college students developed apparently had little impact on changing their behavior. College administrators could only bemoan students' attitudes about their classes and their mischievous and sometimes illegal behavior.

[37] Rudolph, *The American College and University*, pp. 96–98.
[38] Ibid., pp. 96–97.

Given the historical picture of campus life during the 18th and 19th centuries, did these patterns of deviant and illegal behavior continue into the 20th century? Or did a sudden surge in levels of illegal behavior occurring on college campuses warrant recent alarms about students' behavior and the policy initiatives directed at the behavior? During the 20th century, did campus crime rise to such levels as to warrant it being labeled a new and pressing social problem?

The Modern Years: The 20th Century

As American colleges and universities entered the 20th century, at least one prominent historian of higher education has suggested that not much changed regarding students' illegal and deviant behavior.[39] As early as 1905, President Henry Seidel Canby of Yale University described American universities as an "unheard of combination of sporting resort [and] beer garden...that left everyone's minds as confused as a Spanish omelet."[40] During the first decades of the 20th century, historians described American college campuses as a kind of "play world," where young, primarily middle- and upper-class men occupied themselves with hoops and marbles, experimented with nonsensical slang and pig Latin, and pulled pranks on faculty members and other students during class. According to President Woodrow Wilson in a speech given at Princeton in 1909, students were "preoccupied with extracurricular pursuits," which included the "release of their social gifts" and "training in give-and-take [with one another]."[41]

During the first decades of the 20th century, on-campus alcohol consumption by students (and alumni) became a highly regarded tradition. Indeed, excessive drinking before, during, and after collegiate football games was a major weekly highlight on many campuses during the fall each year.[42] Drunken brawls also followed football games,

[39] Much of the discussion in this section is based on Calvin B. T. Lee, *The Campus Scene: 1900–1970* (New York: Van Rees Press, 1970). Lee was dean of the School of Liberal Arts at Boston University; some of the book chronicles Lee's personal experiences with students over a career as a postsecondary administrator that spanned several decades.

[40] Lucas, *Crisis in the Academy*, p. 101.

[41] Lucas, *American Higher Education*, p. 201.

[42] While women were on many campuses, men still constituted a majority of the students at postsecondary institutions until the 1940s. Thus, most of the misbehavior involved college men and was directed at other college men.

either as expressions of celebratory victory or as mechanisms to dull the pain of defeat. For example, according to Lee, a 1913 story in the *Washington Star* reported that after one football game between Georgetown University and the University of Virginia, local District of Columbia police had to work overtime to gather up and jail nearly 100 young drunks, most of whom were students.[43] Lee describes students at the University of California at Berkeley rolling kegs of beer to the top of a hill for an all-night annual "beer bust" and holding "wet celebrations" off campus that often resulted in the destruction of public property and arrests by local authorities. At Stanford University, the administration banished liquor from its campus after one drunken student entered the wrong fraternity and was shot by a resident who feared the intruder was a burglar. Lee notes that a 1903 investigation of an "eastern university center" found that "90 percent of students drank during their freshman year and 95 percent their senior year; that 35 percent drank heavily; and that 15 percent became 'drunkards.'" At Yale University, social clubs of students reserved tables at local New Haven bars and engaged in the "charming ritual" of carving their names or initials into the tables. Perceived levels of campus debauchery relating to alcohol abuse became so great that some schools even took to advertising *they* had been able to reduce levels of drinking among students, in some cases by as much as 50 percent.[44] Beyond worries over collegiate drinking, popular concerns of the day also arose over college students' apparent distractions with beauty pageants and beauty queens, popularity contests, and the adulation of football heroes – all of which supplanted their interest in academic pursuits.[45]

During the 1920s, college students continued their apparent march toward ruination, only they appeared to be heading there more quickly with the advent of the mass-produced automobile.[46] The sexes continued to mingle, although constraints on that behavior had somewhat loosened. For example, some sororities relaxed a few of their strict

[43] Lee, *The Campus Scene*, pp. 9–10.
[44] Ibid.
[45] Lucas, *Crisis in the Academy*, p. 202.
[46] Lee, *The Campus Scene*, pp. 28–47. In 1927, for example, the University of Michigan banned students from having a car on campus because many students had been killed in automobile accidents. Ibid., p. 29.

rules concerning male visitors and sorority residents' consumption of liquor.[47] Male-female relations became such an issue of discussion that 800 college women met at a conference to discuss the role of "petting" in romantic relationships. In fact, among the generation of students attending college in the 1920s, the word "neck" ceased to be a noun and instead became a verb, while among students "necking" entered the popular lexicon as a "leisure sport" or an acceptable form of "recreation" for them. In 1920 the University of North Dakota banned "cheek-to-cheek dancing" and "unnecessary clinging or cuddling" among coed couples attending on campus dances or similar events. One institutional historian at the University of Rhode Island proudly proclaimed that URI students had not "descended to the depths of depravity" that allegedly characterized social life at some of the Ivy League institutions, where bare-knee kissing was *en vogue*. School administrators instituted campaigns not only against modern dancing but against perceived influences on students that "pertained to the lust of the flesh, the lust of the eye, and a pride of life."[48]

At Yale University during Prohibition, while *overall* consumption of alcohol declined, consumption of hard liquor increased significantly. Increases also occurred in both the number and level of seriousness of public disorders related to students' excessive drinking.[49] At Princeton, frequent drunkenness on weekends coincided with big on-campus events such as "House Party weekend," football games, and dances. One Princeton student wrote an op-ed piece in the student newspaper in which he said that Prohibition "is altogether wrong and has a distinctly detrimental effect on the colleges...the undergraduate will not observe the law." The student went on to state that "70 percent of his classmates" drank alcohol.[50]

In the May 20, 1925, edition of the *Nation* magazine, results were published of polls conducted by the magazine of students at the universities of Texas, Chicago, Kansas, Wisconsin, and Colorado between 1919 and 1921 to determine "what was a sin for college students." The

---

[47] Fraternities apparently made moves in that direction but ultimately did not vigorously pursue them.

[48] Lee, *The Campus Scene*, p. 32.

[49] Ibid., p. 34.

[50] Ibid., p. 44.

results showed that among male and female students "sex irregularity" ranked first, followed (in order) by stealing, cheating, lying, drinking and gambling.[51] One popular press article of the time described the college generation of the 1920s:

> We held the romantic of faiths – salvation by sex. Freud was our high priest, Lawrence the god who thrust us toward an escape from the bald daylight of current rationalism. Through Lawrence, we beheld man crouched at the pitiful circle of light, around him all the horror of the dark...we were still pretty adolescent and sexually incompetent.[52]

The popular press also took to describing students with metaphors suggesting a congenial collective experience likened to "colts romping in a pasture."[53] As historian John Thelin described it,

> If colleges became famous between the world wars for their magnifi-cent architecture and big-time sports, they also became notorious for the hedonistic behavior of their students. Most major campus events – homecoming celebrations, commencement week reunions, proms, and year-round fraternity gatherings – all were associated with alcohol. Bathtub gin, speakeasies, gambling on college sports... dominated the popular images of campus life.[54]

Hints of high levels of promiscuity among college students, reported in the popular press or on the radio, titillated the public at large. One report on campus life at Dartmouth during the 1920s suggested that the university, which had been founded to "Christianize the hea-thens," had now degenerated into "heathenizing the Christians."[55]

Lee summed up the typical college campus of the 1920s:

> The collegiate mood of the 1920s was affected not only by expansion of the pre–World War I traditions of big-time college football and fraternity life, but also by a freer attitude toward the opposite sex and more open use of alcohol....Alumni supported construction of lavish new fraternity houses and filled the stadiums on Saturdays as the fervor for collegiate football reached its highest. And afterwards,

[51] Ibid., p. 53.
[52] Ibid., p. 46.
[53] Thelin, *A History of American Higher Education*, p. 158.
[54] Ibid., p. 211.
[55] Ibid., p. 217.

alumni as well as students would retire to enjoy fraternal camarade-
rie and revelry. Although the amount of liquor consumed and the
extent of sexual activity may have been over-exaggerated, the campus scene of this college generation was nevertheless typified by fraternity and sorority houses, dances, and parties.[56]

During the 1930s, and in spite of the Great Depression and rising
international tensions following Hitler's ascent to power in Germany,
college campus "fads and fashion were as outlandish as ever, replete
with fraternity dances and parties."[57] According to Lee, with the end
of Prohibition in 1933, drinking became somewhat less fun for students now that alcohol was again legal.[58] Students continued to find
diversion from their studies via card playing (bridge was especially
popular), while the board game *Monopoly* became hugely popular on
campus. Fraternities held "radio dances" featuring Big Band, swing,
or sweet music as an inexpensive way for the sexes to mix on a weekly
basis under the socially acceptable guise of "pre-courtship." Hoaxes
and pranks were common, with many of them having a distinctly political edge. "Lonely Hearts Clubs" sprang up on campuses, beginning
at Princeton in 1937 with an ad that appeared in the Vassar College
student newspaper saying:

> Hundreds of men are lonely at Princeton. Are you lonely too?
>
> Find your post box lover by writing to the Lonely Hearts Club, 121
> Little Hall, Princeton, New Jersey. Everything confidential.[59]

Perhaps the fad most associated with college students and campuses
during the 1930s was goldfish swallowing.[60] The practice apparently
began in March 1939 in Boston and quickly spread as newspaper
reporters filed their stories on the "amazing feats" of students who
would swallow as many as two dozen of the creatures at one time.
Eventually schools banned the practice, beginning with Boston
College. Kutztown State Teachers College even suspended one of its
students for "conduct unbecoming a student in a professional course

---

[56] Ibid., p. 47.
[57] Lucas, *Crisis in the Academy*, p. 202.
[58] Lee, *The Campus Scene*, pp. 48–72.
[59] Ibid., p. 57.
[60] Ibid., pp. 57–58.

[of study]" after he swallowed 43 goldfish in just under one hour's time. An editorial appearing in the *New York Herald Tribune* remarked that "if [college] students are not swallowing goldfish, they are up to something else just as foolish."[61]

Sexual relations among students became an issue when some of the Ivy League schools loosened their rules about dormitory visiting protocol by members of the opposite sex, including in residents' rooms.[62] At Dartmouth University, for example, students could receive their dates unchaperoned until 11:00 P.M. At Yale, male students were allowed to receive female visitors in their rooms until 6:00 P.M. *if* the females received written permission from the dean of students. At Harvard, male students were allowed to entertain their "current flames" from 1:00 to 7:00 P.M. in their dormitory rooms without a chaperone. Although this practice did not become widespread, and was in fact soundly criticized outside of New England, it nonetheless showed a liberalizing of sexual mores on college campuses, and "sex on campus" remained relevant not only to students but to parents and school administrators as well. *Fortune* magazine "investigated" sex on campus in 1936 and reported that "sex on college campuses was still with us" but that college campus administrators were targeting the regulation of sexual relationships among students "more casually" than they had in previous years. One study of students at 46 colleges and universities that was published in 1938 found that one-half of college men and one-quarter of college women engaged in premarital sexual intercourse while in college.[63]

The 1940s, especially during the Second World War, did not reveal the level of major fads, crazes, or other peculiarities among students that previous decades had witnessed. When huge numbers of students volunteered for service in the armed forces, enrollment at most postsecondary institutions plunged. Veterans returning from World War II, who often constituted a considerable portion of the student body, were older, more mature, often married, and had children living with them on campus. More studious and less given to participate in the party scene that had characterized college campuses during the

61 Ibid., p. 58.
62 Ibid., pp. 58–62.
63 Ibid., p. 60.

1920s and 1930s, returning veterans wanted to finish their education quickly, improve their economic prospects, and move on with their lives.[64]

The 1950s saw its share of illicit activities by students. Several fads became popular among college students, including piano wrecking, goldfish swallowing (again), and telephone booth stuffing, but none was more prominent than the panty raid. Panty raids became a staple of the rites of spring on thousands of campuses across the United States and typically involved mass assaults on both female-only and co-ed dormitories by male students seeking to procure women's lingerie. To illustrate the scale of some of these assaults, at the University of Missouri in the spring of 1952 more than 2,000 male students invaded not only the women's dormitories on *their* campus but those at nearby Stephens College.[65] Similar large-scale panty raids occurred at the universities of Michigan, Nebraska, and Iowa and at Miami University of Ohio, among other locations. At the University of Massachusetts at Amherst, male students not only invaded dormitories to collect lingerie souvenirs from dresser drawers but also collected them from *live* female bodies as well. Eventually the men were stopped by local police. At the University of California at Berkeley, one such raid resulted in $10,000 damage to one of the dormitories, and some of the women who lived there were "knocked around, assaulted, and carried outside in pajamas or in the nude" by male intruders. One local newspaper carried an editorial that condemned the raid as a "night of debauchery" on the part of student participants.[66] Police in Athens, Ohio, were forced to use tear gas to break up a large-scale panty raid that occurred at Ohio University. Lee observes that "no one has counted how many students were arrested, jailed, put on probation, or expelled as a result of such activities."[67]

Besides panty raids, there was also the piano wrecking craze. The object of this particular activity was to see which student could, in the shortest amount of time, smash a piano into pieces that were small

[64] Ibid., pp. 73–87.
[65] Ibid., pp. 88–107.
[66] Ibid., p. 97.
[67] Ibid. Lee notes that on some campuses, female students living in dormitories were punished by their institutions for inciting the raids or for encouraging male students to continue their activities once a raid had begun.

enough to pass through a hole just under eight inches in diameter. Telephone booth jamming also became a major fad, while the number of national fraternity chapters doubled between the end of World War II and 1956.

The now familiar annual exit of masses of college students and the affiliated rituals of spring break also became institutionalized during the 1950s. Beginning in the mid-1950s, students began converging on Ft. Lauderdale during spring vacation, where they were both unsupervised and ready to satisfy their thirst from sunrise to sunset with various alcoholic concoctions. Indeed, the novel *Where the Boys Are* depicted the hedonism of spring break in Ft. Lauderdale during the 1950s.[68]

The 1960s brought to U.S. postsecondary institutions "commitment, involvement, relevance, and pot,"[69] not to mention mass takeovers of campus buildings, bombings, and even deadly clashes on some campuses between students and not only local police but National Guard troops as well. The decade saw students "drive college administrators, faculty members, state legislators, Congress, and even the President of the United States to the point of distraction with the chaos, bloodshed, and disruption [that was] occurring."[70] Students organized classmates and peers to protest a host of institutional and social issues ranging from how professors taught classes to the war in Vietnam. While representing a large but vocal minority of students, protestors and their activities managed to capture a stunned public's attention. Riots and public demonstrations supporting "liberal" political ideology and demands for social change occurred on many college campuses across the nation.[71] At campuses such as the University

---

[68] Ibid. For humorous but enlightening examples of various rites of spring activities on American college campuses, see Simon J. Bronner, *Piled Higher and Deeper: The Folklore of Campus Life* (Little Rock: August House Publishers, 1990), pp. 93–97.

[69] Lee, *The Campus Scene*, p. 108. For popular-press-based sources on the college students of the 1960s, see the following: Editors of the Atlantic Monthly, *The Troubled Campus* (Boston: Little, Brown, 1966); and Esther Lloyd-Jones and Herman Estrin (Eds.), *The American Student and His College* (Boston: Houghton-Mifflin, 1967). For the "official" results of the federal government's investigation into the campus unrest of the 1960s, see the United States President's Commission, *Report of the President's Commission on Campus Unrest* (Washington, DC: U.S. Government Printing Office, 1970).

[70] Lee, *The Campus Scene*, p. 109.

[71] Smith, "The Ancestry of Campus Violence," pp. 8–9.

of Michigan, the University of California at Berkeley, and Columbia University, students expressed their rage at "the system" by burning draft cards and bras, by taking over campus buildings and engaging in sit-ins, by raising money for the Viet Cong, and by protesting the presence of ROTC programs on college campuses.

Student protests also had a tendency of turning into violent confrontations, resulting in the deaths and injuries of both students and local police officers and National Guard troops sent to quell the disturbances.[72] In 1968 for the first time in history, felony indictments were returned against students who had participated in student-led campus riots.[73] A protest in 1970 at Kent State University in Ohio turned lethal when Ohio National Guard troops fired on a group of student protestors, killing 4 and wounding 9 others. A few days later, lethal violence erupted when local police officers fired into a dormitory at Jackson State College (now University) in Mississippi, killing 2 students and wounding 12 others.[74] Blanket media coverage of such events propelled the "campus movement" into the mainstream of American news "with a force that was both wrenching and riveting," and some state governors, including those of California and Ohio, used campus unrest to launch "get tough" reform campaigns directed at college presidents and deans whom the governors perceived to have not done enough to maintain law and order or curtail unrest on campus.[75]

Finally, the decade of the 1970s revealed a continuation of the violence, vice, and victimization witnessed on campus during the 1960s. Journalist Lansing Lamont's *Campus Shock* described the typical college campus of the 1970s as overcrowded, experiencing relaxed sexual mores and violence, combined with fierce competition for grades, epidemic levels of cheating, and where students' anxiety levels were acute.[76] Students at elite universities went to previously unheard of

[72] See, for example, Immanuel Wallerstein and Paul Starr (Eds.), *The University Crisis Reader: Confrontation and Counterattack*, vol. 2 (New York: Random House, 1971).
[73] Smith, "The Ancestry of Campus Violence," p. 9.
[74] Ibid., p. 8.
[75] Thelin, *A History of American Higher Education*, p. 310; Cohen, *The Shaping of American Higher Education*, pp. 202–203.
[76] Lansing Lamont, *Campus Shock* (New York: E. P. Dutton, 1979). Lamont's book is a practicing journalist's account of college life during the late 1970s at a dozen

lengths to thwart their competitors, including one Columbia pre-med student who reset his classmates' alarm clocks so they would oversleep and miss an important examination.[77] Fights among dormitory roommates or suitemates arising from overcrowding were not uncommon during the 1970s, and it appeared that cooperation among students was no longer the norm on many campuses.[78] Students vandalized campus buildings, including an incident at Yale where students smeared excrement and foul-smelling acid around the dining hall of their dormitory in a low-level but nonetheless targeted protest over conditions in their dormitory. Thefts, assaults, and even homicides were occurring on many campuses, including at elite institutions such as Harvard, Yale, and the University of Michigan.[79] The "new" sexual morality of the 1960s had become institutionalized among college students and was difficult to avoid even for those who wished to do so, as students were often housed in an ever-expanding number of co-ed dorms.[80]

As students took advantage of the opportunities created by relaxed campus rules, they also paid a price for them. One such area involved relaxed rules involving conjugal visits occurring in on-campus dormitories. While live-in girlfriends or boyfriends were common in dormitories, so too were "one-night-stands," broken hearts, and sexually transmitted diseases.[81] Cheating by students had apparently reached epidemic proportions – even at elite Ivy League schools, where centuries-old honor codes and systems broke down under the pressure of student ambivalence about whether cheating was immoral.[82] Students rarely apologized when they were caught, and instead rationalized

"elite" public and private postsecondary institutions of the day, using interviews with unscientifically selected groups of students who were attending those schools.

[77] Ibid., p. 8.
[78] Ibid., p. 9.
[79] Yale allegedly spent $100,000 upgrading building security during the late 1970s, which included placing new locks on all campus buildings and gates, on dormitory entryways, and on the doors to dormitory suites and bathrooms. The school's 34-person campus police department donned uniforms for the first time and officers were issued .38 caliber revolvers and were required annually to qualify with their weapons using standards that were established and administered by the City of New Haven Police Department. See Lamont, *Campus Shock*, pp. 15–16.
[80] Ibid., pp. 33–44.
[81] Ibid.
[82] Ibid., pp. 71–86.

their behavior by arguing they were simply doing "what everyone else was doing."[83]

When viewed through the lens that recent history can provide, college campuses during most of the 20th century continued to experience levels of violence, vice, and victimization similar to what their counterparts of previous eras encountered. Students rioted and engaged in other forms of violence. They cheated on examinations and course assignments. They drank and engaged in illicit sexual liaisons. Campus officials, media outlets, and the public, while apparently alarmed by these behaviors, did not undertake concerted efforts to address either their on-campus presence or their underlying causes. Critics of higher education, some from inside the academy itself, railed about the threat posed by the dark side of the ivory tower. In response, college or university administrators responded with minimal changes in schools' operations, while federal and state policy makers were largely silent about campus violence, vice, and victimization until the 1980s.

CHANGING PERCEPTIONS: THE 1980s AND 1990s

The Media Portrayal

During the 1980s and into the 1990s against a backdrop of the Reagan Revolution, the demise of disco, and the mass transformation of electronic and print media and how social problems were marketed by these entities,[84] public perceptions about violence, vice,

---

[83] Ibid., p. 73.

[84] For a fascinating discussion of the transformation of America during the 1970s and 1980s, see Philip Jenkins, *Decade of Nightmares: The End of the Sixties and the Making of 1980s America* (New York: Oxford Press, 2006). In the book, Jenkins chronicles, among other topics, the transformational change in mass media that occurred during the 1970s and 1980s beginning with Rupert Murdoch's purchase of the *New York Post* in 1976 and Ted Turner's launch of the Cable News Network (CNN) in 1980. Jenkins makes a crucial point (pp. 197–199) that "the presentation of broadcast news placed a new premium on immediacy, as satellite, video, and other new technologies allowed immediate access to news sites, without the need for traditional bulky film cameras and their attendant crews. *Electronic news gathering radically changed both the operations of journalism and the expectations of viewers.... Together these developments marked a trend toward sensational coverage, immediate presentation of news and simplistic stories encapsulated within a short time frame*" (emphasis added). This transformation helped foster "outlandish productions about child abuse and kidnapping, serial murder, poorly substantiated drug menaces, and Satanism scares" that occurred during the 1980s.

and victimization on college campuses changed, as did the lack of an organized, large-scale response to the "problem" of campus crime. Electronic and print journalists began routinely issuing reports suggesting the dark side of the ivory tower had become a serious and ongoing threat not only to the future of higher education in America but to the safety and well-being of millions of college students of the time. Stories carried by the *New York Times, Washington Post, Time* and *Newsweek* magazines, and the major television networks and the burgeoning cable news industry all suggested there were "unprecedented," "startling," or "heretofore unimagined" levels of criminal victimization occurring on college campuses. Regular reports of murder and other forms of serious interpersonal violence, such as rape and sexual assault, occurring not only at large state universities and smaller liberal arts colleges but at "elite" colleges and universities became common. Reports also emerged of serious hazing incidents resulting in the deaths of, or significant injuries to, students pledging collegiate fraternities. Reports also pointed to the presence of guns on campus as a new threat. During the late 1990s, reports also emerged that technology was contributing to new forms of campus deviance, which included illegal downloading and sharing of copyrighted materials, downloading prewritten papers, and various forms of online victimization including cyberstalking and bullying. Finally, according to the reports, large numbers of college students were abusing alcohol and literally drinking themselves to death as well. One 1986 poll conducted by *Newsweek* magazine showed that student concerns about the violence, vice, and victimization of the time were rising, when more than one-third (38 percent) of student respondents indicated they worried "a great deal" or "a fair amount" about crime on or near their campus.[85]

During the 1980s and 1990s, mass-media portrayal of the new reality of the ivory tower suggested that unprecedented levels of danger now confronted college students, be it from violence or involvement with alcohol abuse, and no student attending a postsecondary institution in the United States was safe. If journalistic reports were to be believed, the ivory tower had finally succumbed to its dark side, and

[85] Smith, "The Ancestry of Campus Violence," p. 9.

dramatic action was needed to rescue not only the campus experience but the millions of students whose lives were so thoroughly wrapped up in its image and culture.

Responses to Media Reports

Beginning in the late 1980s, an initial response to the call that "something needs to be done" occurred. First, state courts began holding postsecondary institutions liable under existing tort or contract law for student victimizations occurring on college campuses.[86] In 1990 Congress passed the groundbreaking *Student-Right-to-Know and Campus Security Act of 1990*[87] (hereafter, the *Campus Security Act*), which, among other reforms, mandated that *all* postsecondary institutions eligible to participate in federal financial aid programs (i.e., all Title IV–eligible schools) would publicly report their campus crime statistics on an annual basis. Further, pressure from parents and other groups during the late 1980s and 1990s saw colleges and universities implement new orientation programs for first-year students to reduce the problems of collegiate alcohol abuse and sexual victimization.[88] The period also saw student advocates organize Take Back the Night, an annual candlelight event, and the Clothesline Project, both of which were designed to raise awareness about violence occurring against college women. The 1980s and 1990s also saw postsecondary institutions invest in "target hardening" activities, including installing computer-controlled or key-card access to campus buildings and closed-circuit television (CCTV) surveillance systems in parking decks, as well as upgrading existing security in an effort to make campuses safer. Security officials routinely began meeting to discuss and then establish "best practices" relating to crime prevention, community-oriented policing, and related activities on college campuses.[89]

[86] Burling, *Crime on Campus.*
[87] 20 USC 1942.
[88] Burling, *Crime on Campus.*
[89] Charlie Johnson, "Mental Health, Northern Illinois Tragedy to Be the Focus of UCO Hosted National Campus Security Summit," retrieved September 20, 2008, http://campus securitysummit.ucok.edu/media_release_03–19–2008.htm. See also Kelly Cobiella, "Rethinking Campus Security," *CBS Evening News with Dan Rather,* April 4, 2007, retrieved September 23, 2008, http://www.cbsnews.com. stories/2007/04/16/eveningnews/main26 92132.shtml.

Finally, during the latter part of the 1990s Congress passed amendments to the *Campus Security Act* that included guarantees that victims of on-campus sexual assaults retained certain rights if they chose to pursue student disciplinary proceedings against their alleged attackers. College and university administrators also began providing student victims and substance abusers on-campus medical and mental health services.[90]

The late 1980s and 1990s thus saw high levels of mass-media interest in, and reporting on, campus crime. The reports painted a highly troubling picture that showed that the dark side of the ivory tower had become an ongoing serious threat to present and future generations of college students. In turn, social institutions – including the legislative and judicial branches of government – pursued courses of action designed to both control and prevent deviant and illegal behavior on U.S. college campuses. Postsecondary institutions undertook various initiatives to make their campuses safer, while simultaneously educating students about reducing their risk of experiencing a criminal victimization or becoming a substance abuser while in college.

CAMPUS CRIME: THE SOCIAL CONSTRUCTION OF A NEW REALITY?

Scholars' analyses of the history of higher education clearly indicate that violence, vice, and victimization have been part of the landscape of postsecondary education almost since the first colleges were created in America during the 17th century. Murder and other forms of violence occurring on campus were well documented, as was drinking, student hazing, and sexual promiscuity. The question, however, is this: What was different during the 1980s and 1990s that explained

[90] For discussion, see Angela Amar and Susan Gennaro, "Dating Violence in College Women: Associated Physical Injury, Healthcare Usage, and Mental Health Symptoms," *Nursing Research* 54 (2005): 235–42. See also Michael Williams, "Comparisons in Date Rape/Sexual Assault Prevention Programs on College Campuses: What Works, What Doesn't, and What's Promising," paper presented at the annual meetings of the American Society of Criminology, Atlanta, Georgia, November 13, 2007; and Patti LaSalle, "Task Force Offers Comprehensive Recommendations Aimed at Alcohol and Drug Abuse Prevention," retrieved October 13, 2008, http://smu.edu/newsinfo/stories/taskforce-report-release-2-feb2008.asp.

such large-scale interest in, and activism toward, campus crime? How did this interest quickly translate into policy responses by the judiciary, Congress, and multiple states?

In the chapters that follow, we answer these questions by analyzing how Security On Campus, Inc., campus crime victims and their families, campus feminists, and public health researchers all played major roles in changing public perceptions about campus crime and, in so doing, prompted policy makers to respond swiftly and repeatedly to it. We explain and illustrate how, during the late 1980s and through the 1990s, these groups – individually and then collectively – began making significant claims about the extent, nature, and causes of campus crime. We also document how these groups created their own definitions of specific aspects of campus crime in which they were most interested. We then show that they undertook large-scale, targeted efforts to "educate" parents of current and prospective college students and the public more generally about the crisis that threatened *every college and university campus in the United States.* The impending dangers campus crime posed to every college student could no longer be overlooked. The time was now ripe for action by policy makers and accountability for campus administrators.

By labeling on-campus violence and victimization as the newest "crisis" that was facing society, we show how the groups were able not only to create public recognition of the problem but to convince the public to accept *their interpretation* of the scope and causes of the problem on the basis of anecdotal evidence and occasionally questionable scientific investigations that national and local electronic and print media helped publicize. We then argue that these groups' efforts ultimately resulted in widespread public acceptance of campus crime as a new social problem not only worthy of their attention and concern but also worthy of action by Congress, the judiciary, and college or university administrators.

Once these groups convinced the public of the legitimacy of their claims, the four then mobilized *other* interest groups, including victims' rights advocates; the therapeutic community, including counselors and medical doctors; and security and law enforcement professionals, who turned *their* attention to the "crisis" of campus crime and collegiate substance abuse. Activists and their allies ultimately joined

forces and pressed legislators and college or university administrators to develop new responses designed to reduce the problem.[91]
Congress, the states, the judiciary, and college administrators then
responded to the call to action by creating new policies designed to
reduce the impact of the dark side of the ivory tower on the lives of
American college students.

Thus, in contrast to previous historical eras, four groups – a public
advocacy group created by the parents of a student murdered in her
dormitory room at Lehigh University, campus feminists, campus
crime victims and their families, and public health researchers – were
able to convince both the public and policy makers that campus crime
posed a new and serious threat not only to societal well-being but to
the physical and academic well-being of millions of college students
and that action was needed to address that threat. *What* these groups
claimed and, using those claims, *how* they were able to successfully
construct campus crime as a new social problem is the focus of the
remainder of the book.

---

[91] S. Daniel Carter and Catherine Bath, "The Evolution and Components of the *Jeanne
Clery Act*: Implications for Higher Education," pp. 27–44 in Bonnie S. Fisher and
John J. Sloan III (Eds.), *Campus Crime: Legal, Social, and Policy Perspectives*, 2nd ed.
(Springfield, IL: Charles C. Thomas, 2007). See also Jonathan Kassa, "Security
On Campus, Inc. (SOC): Our Mission Is Safer Campuses for Students," pp. 191–
194 in M. Paludi (Ed.), *Understanding and Preventing Campus Violence* (Westport,
CT: Praeger Press, 2008); and Magnus Seng, "The *Crime Awareness and Campus
Security Act*: Some Observations, Critical Comments, and Suggestions," pp. 38–52
in Bonnie S. Fisher and John J. Sloan III (Eds.), *Campus Crime: Legal, Social, and
Policy Perspectives* (Springfield, IL: Charles C. Thomas, 1995).

CHAPTER TWO

Constructing Campus Crime
as a New Social Problem

On April 5, 1986, the whole Clery family fell victim to the medieval myth that college campuses that look safe are safe and the policy of a lot of college campuses, if it's negative to their image, what you don't know can't hurt you.[1]

Beginning in the late 1980s, mass-media sources were not the only ones focusing on the apparent emergence of a dark side of the ivory tower. Elected officials, government agencies, and academic researchers also began focusing their attention on it as well. In the late 1980s and early 1990s several states – including Pennsylvania, California, and Tennessee – passed "campus crime legislation" designed, among other goals, to ostensibly force postsecondary institutions to publish their crime statistics annually. In the 1990s Congress also passed federal campus crime legislation, which it then amended several times, including most recently in 2008. This legislation, originally known as the *Student Right-to-Know and Campus Security Act of 1990*, mandates all postsecondary institutions eligible to participate in federal financial aid programs to, among other requirements, compile an annual report on security policies and crime statistics for their campuses and make it available to the public, including prospective and current students and employees.

Additionally, throughout the 1990s a small but relatively prolific group of researchers from a range of disciplines began conducting

---

[1] Howard Clery. Quote from U.S. Congress, Hearing of the House Subcommittee on Postsecondary Education, March 14, 1990. Transcript from Federal Information Systems Corporation Federal News Service. Available on LexisNexis® Congressional; accessed April 16, 2010.

social scientific studies into the extent and nature of crime on college campuses and published that work in both academic and popular press outlets. In the late 1990s the U.S. General Accounting Office expressed its concerns over "a steady rise in violent crime [being] reported on some college campuses,"[2] while news outlets including the *Chronicle of Higher Education* and the *New York Times* frequently reported that "heinous crimes" were routinely occurring on (or near) college and university campuses in the United States.[3]

Reports of disorder on college campuses following athletic teams' successes – such as a school winning a national championship in football or basketball – or in celebratory events such as Halloween or Cinco De Mayo – seemed to occur with shocking frequency.[4] Underage drinking and recreational drug use, coupled with drug-induced sexual assaults, were also apparently common at colleges and universities around the nation if mass-media reports were to be believed.[5] Fraternity hazing received its share of coverage, particularly when death or injury was involved.[6] As the Internet increasingly

[2]   U.S. General Accounting Office, *Campus Crime: Difficulties Meeting Federal Requirements*, Report to Congressional Requesters, March (Washington, DC: U.S. General Accounting Office, 1997).

[3]   For example, see Douglas A. Lederman, "Colleges Report 7,500 Violent Crimes on Their Campuses in First Annual Statements Required under Federal Law," *Chronicle of Higher Education*, January 20, 1993, pp. A32–A42; Douglas A. Lederman, "Weapons on Campus? Officials Warn That Colleges and Universities Are Not Immune from the Scourge of Handguns," *Chronicle of Higher Education*, March 9, 1994, pp. A33–A35; and Ann Matthews, "The 'Ivory Tower' Becomes an Armed Camp," *New York Times Magazine*, March 7, 1993, pp. 38–47.

[4]   For a recent discussion of how colleges and universities have responded to these events, see Laura Davis, "Has 'Big Brother' Moved Off Campus? An Examination of Colleges' Responses to Unruly Student Behavior," *Journal of Law and Education* 35 (2006): 153–198.

[5]   A report by the National Institute of Alcohol Abuse and Alcoholism estimated that "a half million [college students] suffer unintentional injuries [while] under the influence of alcohol. Another 600,000 are assaulted by fellow drinking students and more than 70,000 are sexually assaulted. The data on academic achievement, damage to facilities, and health problems are equally alarming." College Task Force of the National Advisory Council on Alcohol Abuse and Alcoholism, *A Call to Action: Changing the Culture of Drinking at U.S. Colleges* (Washington, DC: National Institute of Alcohol Abuse and Alcoholism, 2002), p. vii. See also Tamara Madensen and John Eck, *Student Party Riots*, Problem Oriented Guides for Police Problem Solving, Specific Guides, Series No. 39 (Washington, DC: U.S. Department of Justice Office of Community Oriented Policing Services, 2006).

[6]   For example, CNN, "Taming the Animal House," *Crossfire*, April 12, 1990; John Larrabee, "College Suspends Fraternity Members," *USA Today*, September 20,

became a staple of life in modern society, student involvement in various forms of cybercrime emerged, such as illegally downloading and sharing music or video files, or downloading prewritten papers for their classes from various Web sites. Reports also emerged of students being stalked or harassed in cyberspace.[7] Finally, interest in and concerns over college students bringing guns onto campus – concealed or otherwise – and the ramifications of such behavior for campus safety and security burgeoned during the 1990s.[8]

Over the past 20 years, "campus crime" – a term we use to refer to various forms of violence, vice, and victimization involving students as offenders and victims and occurring primarily on college and university campuses – moved from what was, in essence, a private problem involving victims, their families, and a particular postsecondary institution in which the victim had enrolled or was visiting to a large-scale social problem in need of policy attention. We argue that since the late 1980s campus crime has been *socially constructed* as a new social problem in the United States, despite the fact that campus crime has existed on college and university campuses since they were first founded during the colonial era.

1990, p. A1; "Seven Members of College Fraternity Face Murder Charges for Hazing Death of Fraternity Pledge," *CBS Evening News with Dan Rather* February 17, 1994; and "When Hazing Becomes Torture," *The Geraldo Rivera Show*, April 30, 1997. See also Barbara Hollman, *Hazing: Hidden Campus Crime* (San Francisco: Jossey-Bass, 2002), and Hank Nuwer, *Wrongs of Passage: Fraternities, Sororities, Hazing, and Binge Drinking* (Bloomington: Indiana University Press, 1999).

7   See James Davis, "Graphic 'Cyber-Threats' Land Student in Court," *USA Today*, February 10, 1995, p. 3A; Samson Mulugeta, "Students Held in $100G Cyber Theft," *New York Daily News*, March 18, 1995, p. 18; Associated Press, "Fraudulent Card Company Agrees to Pay Students and Parents," *Christian Science Monitor*, July 14, 1998, p. B3; and George E. Higgins and David A. Makin, "Does Social Learning Theory Condition the Effects of Low Social Control in Students' Software Piracy?" *Journal of Economic Crime Management* 2 (2004), retrieved December 4, 2009, http://www.utica.edu/academic/institutes/ecii/publications/articles/BA3526A1-F840-F4FD-3CE8AFBA74AEB151.pdf.

8   For example, Carol Innerst, "Colleges Fret about Guns, Fights," *Washington Times*, May 15, 1991, p. A5; Associated Press, "College Student Sprays Campus with an Assault Rifle, Killing Two," *New York Times*, December 16, 1992, p. A1; DaNeen L. Brown, "Violence Muscles Its Way onto Campus: Norfolk Shooting Shows That Colleges Are No Longer Sanctuaries," *Washington Post*, February 15, 1994, p. 2; Janofsky, Michael, "Johns Hopkins Student Held in Fatal Shooting," *New York Times*, April 12, 1996, p. A3; Judy Woodruff and Gene Randall, "Study Links Gun Ownership and Alcohol Abuse among Students," *CNN Worldview*, July 2, 1999.

If we are correct and campus crime was socially constructed as a new social problem, questions arise as to how this happened. What were the social forces and processes involved? How was the public moved to accept campus crime as a social problem and to demand that policy makers address it? Which groups were making claims about campus crime, and what sorts of claims were they making? What role did the media play in helping to bring campus crime to the center of the public stage? What role did academic researchers play in helping to socially construct campus crime as a new social problem?

We answer these questions using a theoretical framework that is grounded in what sociologists call "social constructionism."[9] This perspective suggests a particular social problem – whether it be annual scares about tainted candy given to youngsters at Halloween, the 1980s epidemic of so-called crack babies, or campus crime – is not created because of the objective threat it may pose to members of the public but rather because certain groups *make claims* about the problem and use a variety of tactics to convince the public the problem poses a threat to the collective well-being.

Using this framework as our guiding perspective, we examine how campus crime was created as a new social problem during the late 1980s and 1990s and ultimately became institutionalized. We identify the major parties involved in its construction and the claims they made. We also examine the devices they used to package and disseminate information to the public about the problem. Finally, we examine the policy responses the parties were able to shape to address the problem. In so doing, we draw upon and apply the work of Joel Best[10] and his analysis of how only certain problems or conditions,

---

[9] See the following for early statements on how social problems are socially constructed: Howard Becker, *Outsiders: Studies in the Sociology of Deviance* (New York: Free Press of Glencoe, 1963); Herbert Blumer, "Social Problems as Collective Behavior," *Social Problems* 18 (1971): 298–306; Peter Berger and Thomas Luckman, *The Social Construction of Reality* (London: Penguin, 1976); and Malcolm Spector and John Kitsuse, *Constructing Social Problems* (Menlo Park, CA: Cummings, 1977). For more recent examples of social constructionism, see Joseph Gusfield, *The Culture of Social Problems* (Chicago: University of Chicago Press, 1989), and Joel Best, *Random Violence: How We Talk about New Crimes and New Victims* (Berkeley: University of California Press, 1999).

[10] We rely on a framework outlined in Best, *Random Violence*. Other examples of his work in social constructionism include Joel Best, "Endangered Children and Anti-Satanist Rhetoric," pp. 95–106 in J. Richardson, J. Best, and D. Bromely (Eds.),

rather than others, come to be selected, identified, and responded to as social problems.[11]

This chapter presents the theoretical framework that guided our analyses of the social construction of campus crime as a new social problem. Best's framework explores how various groups come forward and make claims about a particular issue. Then, with the help of mass media, the groups activate various processes that ultimately result in policies intended to address the new and pressing problem. In subsequent chapters, we return to key elements of the framework to illustrate how four major groups helped construct campus crime as a new social problem. The groups we identify as crucial include Security On Campus, Inc., a grass-roots lobbying operation founded by the parents of a slain Lehigh University student; campus crime victims or members of their families, who brought their plight to the media and filed lawsuits against postsecondary institutions, seeking compensation for damages they suffered as a result of on-campus victimizations; feminists, outraged over apparent extreme levels of sexual violence being perpetrated against women on college campuses; and academic and public health researchers, who sounded alarm bells about connections between levels of college students' alcohol abuse and dire consequences arising from that behavior. These groups, individually and then collectively, helped orchestrate the social construction of the new social problem of campus crime.

After presenting an overview of this theoretical framework,[12] we discuss the specifics of the framework that we use to unravel, document,

The Satanism Scare (Edison, NJ: Aldine Transaction, 1991); and Joel Best, *Threatened Children* (Chicago: University of Chicago Press, 1990).

[11] An excellent review of social problems theory is found in Stephen Hilgartner and Charles L. Bosk, "The Rise and Fall of Social Problems: A Public Arenas Model," *American Journal of Sociology* 94 (1988): 53–78.

[12] Best's work should be considered but *one example* of the application of a social constructionist framework for understanding how social problems are created; it is by no means the *only* such framework. Our purpose in this research was to use Best's framework – originally developed to examine the evolution of random violence in society as a new social problem – to describe and explain the evolution of campus crime as a new social problem during the past 20 years. Social constructionism as a theoretical framework for studying social problems has continued to develop well after Best's work during the late 1990s. Examples of recent works in the area of social constructionism include, but are not limited to, the following: Philip Jenkins, *Mystics and Messiahs* (New York: Oxford University Press, 2000); Michael Welch,

and describe the processes involved in creating this new social problem. We then apply the framework to inform subsequent chapters of the book devoted to each of the four parties we argue were responsible for constructing campus crime as a large-scale social problem. In each of those chapters, we present key parts of the framework and then "fill in the blanks" by chronicling how the parties contributed to that process, including the claims they made and actions they took.

CONSTRUCTING SOCIAL PROBLEMS

Herbert Blumer, one of the first scholars to argue that social problems are socially constructed, observed that social problems were created through a *process of collective definition* involving several interrelated activities.[13] That is, social problems arise from "projections of collective sentiments, rather than [serve as] simple mirrors of objective conditions" involving some level of harm associated with the condition.[14] By itself, level of harm cannot explain *why* some conditions ultimately are defined as social problems, whereas others of equal or potentially greater harm are not. Instead, social problems are "embedded within a complex institutionalized system of...formulation and dissemination."[15]

The processes of collectively defining some condition as a social problem, in effect, involve a winnowing down of a huge number of potential problems to a small number that actually become identified social problems.[16] The process begins when social activists identify

Flag Burning: Moral Panic and the Criminalization of Protest (Piscataway, NJ: Aldine-Transaction, 2000); Joel Best, *Damned Lies and Statistics* (Berkeley: University of California Press, 2001); Elizabeth M. Armstrong, *Conceiving Risk, Bearing Responsibility: Fetal Alcohol Syndrome and the Diagnosis of Moral Disorder* (Baltimore: Johns Hopkins University Press, 2003); Nancy S. Berns, *Framing the Victim: Domestic Violence, Media, and Social Problems* (Piscataway, NJ: Aldine-Transaction, 2004); Joseph E. Davis, *Accounts of Innocence: Sexual Abuse, Trauma, and the Self* (Chicago: University of Chicago Press, 2005); and Karen M. Staller, *Runaways: How the Sixties Counterculture Shaped Today's Practices* (New York: Columbia University Press, 2006).

[13] Blumer, "Social Problems as Collective Behavior"; Spector and Kitsuse, *Constructing Social Problems*.

[14] Hilgartner and Bosk, "The Rise and Fall of Social Problems: A Public Arenas Model," p. 54.

[15] Ibid., p. 55.

[16] Ibid.; Best, *Random Violence*.

a particular social or economic condition they perceive as posing a threat to the public welfare.[17] Using mass media and, more recently, such mechanisms as the Internet and blogs, individuals and groups then make overt claims about the pressing nature and characteristics of a particular condition. These claims are made partly to mobilize members of various social movements to support them, as well as to gain the public's attention.[18] Once a critical mass of attention has been generated, activists then seek endorsement of their claims from a broad-ranging coalition of others. These coalitions often, but not always, include fellow activists, journalists, academics, and members of the medical and mental health professions. Activists seek endorsement by others – especially experts in a particular field – that the condition is, in fact, a *problem* in need of immediate action by policy makers. In other words, those making the claims ("claimsmakers") seek to *legitimize the problem*, and if successful, the problem receives a recognized place in the larger arena of public discourse.[19] Once legitimation is achieved, activists and their allies work to *secure the public's interest* and encourage the public to make demands on policy makers to address the condition. If the process is successful, the public is now convinced that the problem has reached crisis levels. Finally, those helping to create the new social problem lobby for policies to address the problem via new legislation, judicial remedy, or administrative change.

THE CONTEXT FOR NEW SOCIAL PROBLEMS

Building on earlier work by social constructionists, Joel Best developed an alternative framework for analyzing the construction of social problems, which we adopted in our analysis of how campus crime became a recognized social problem.

[17] Blumer, "Social Problems as Collective Behavior."
[18] This suggests there is an interpretative process involving mass media through which media serve as filters to vast amounts of incoming information and ultimately choose to focus on a small portion of that information. For examples and discussion, see the following classic statements: Herbert Gans, *Deciding What's News* (New York: Pantheon, 1979); and Todd Gitlin, *The Whole World Is Watching* (Berkeley: University of California Press, 1980).
[19] Best, *Random Violence*.

Naming the Problem

In constructing a social problem such as campus crime, the problem must first be *named*, set apart from other problems, and pointed to as a condition we have not previously experienced. As Best described it, "naming is a key moment in the history of any social problem."[20] Interestingly, the name given the problem is often deliberately vague and lacks a precise definition.[21] Instead, what occurs is that claimsmakers provide what Best calls a *typifying example* of the problem through mass-media outlets, with no effort to provide a proper definition or domain scope for the example.

Best argues that activists prefer broad-based and vague definitions for the very reason that precise definitions not only invite controversy but threaten the attention from the public that activists seek in making their claims.[22] Thus, the new social problem of "campus crime" has come to mean anything from relatively minor thefts to mass murders occurring on college campuses, with activists providing enough examples not only to give the public, especially the parents of college-age children, a visual picture of the problem but to solicit an emotional response from them. For example, consider the following excerpts, voiceovers from a CBS News story discussing "campus violence":

> In the green and hilly peace of Lehigh University in eastern Pennsylvania, it is hard to imagine that 10 years ago this campus was the scene of a brutal murder.

> Nineteen-year-old Jeanne Clery was a freshman when a fellow student, someone she did not know, broke into her dormitory room and killed her. After 10 years, her parents, Connie and Howard, are still haunted by the crime.[23]

Or this excerpt from a National Public Radio story, narrated by Bob Edwards:

---

[20] Ibid., p. 166.
[21] Ibid., pp. 29–31. Best used "wilding" as an example. Wilding was a term associated with random acts of violence perpetrated by groups of young males against women. The term arose from a particularly heinous assault of a female jogger in Central Park, which generated a firestorm of outrage and dominated the news for weeks. Wilding, however, never rose to the level of a new social problem.
[22] Ibid.
[23] CBS News, *Sunday Morning*, September 14, 1997.

Last week a freshman at Purdue University in Indiana shot and killed a graduate student who worked as a resident assistant in his campus dormitory. He then shot himself.

It was at least the fourth incident of fatal student-against-student violence on American college campuses this year. University administrators ...are trying to come to terms with the role of their idyllic campuses in a violent world.[24]

Domain Expansion and Elaboration. Naming the problem also involves expanding and elaborating its domain. Domain expansion occurs when activists tack new claims onto an existing problem so that the problem's domain now includes the new condition. For example, "hate crimes" originally described violence perpetrated against individuals because of their race or their ethnic origin. However, in recent years the scope of hate crimes has expanded and now includes criminal victimization directed at people not only because of their race or ethnicity but also because of victims' religious beliefs, sexual orientation, or physical or psychological disability.[25]

Domain elaboration allows activists to elicit support from potentially powerful allies, such as those in the fields of medicine, education, academe, and law. Best argues that activists "gradually extend the problem's domain, arguing the other, less melodramatic, cases in another form are really no different than, are the moral equivalent of, or just the same as the original typifying example(s) and the problem is complex, with facets demanding attention."[26] Activists use domain expansion and elaboration to argue that "the cause" needs sustained support from the public and to offer a fresh "angle" to the media, which encourages print and electronic outlets to keep the problem visible. As a result, the problem is kept continually before the public.

Diffusion. Naming new social problems also involves activists showing that the problem has crossed geographic or temporal boundaries.

---

[24] NPR, *Morning Edition*, October 24, 1996.
[25] Best used the example of post-traumatic stress disorder (PTSD), which originally was applied to returning veterans of the Vietnam War to describe a host of symptoms including sleeplessness, inability to concentrate, and other problems. PTSD gradually expanded to include similar symptoms experienced by crime victims, victims of domestic violence, and child abuse. See Best, *Random Violence*, pp. 168–169.
[26] Ibid., p. 199.

Geographic diffusion involves activists taking examples of the new problem occurring in one place, finding similar examples in another place,
and connecting those occurrences. Claimsmakers then argue the
problem has spread across what are sometimes large geographic dis-
tances. For example, between 1996 and 2000, the U.S. Department of
Education initiated "program reviews" of 117 colleges and universities
to determine if the schools had failed to comply with *The Student Right-
to-Know and Campus Security Act*, which mandated public reporting by
postsecondary institutions of their crime statistics and security policies.
Security On Campus, Inc., then used the "117 schools" figure to argue
that the problem of institutional noncompliance with the law was
"widespread" and involved a "host of different types of institutions" –
both two- and four-year schools as well as public and private colleges
and universities.[27] What is interesting here is the fact that what activists failed to note was that among the 117 schools investigated by the
government, only 8 of them (roughly 6 percent) were actually *found*
to be in noncompliance with the requirements. Activists also failed
to note that more than 4,000 postsecondary institutions were operating in the United States during the period in question, so the 117
that had been identified as *potentially* noncompliant constituted about
3 percent of *all* postsecondary institutions in the United States (not
all of which were required to follow the mandates of the legislation).
Finally, activists failed to note that none of the 8 noncompliant schools
received any kind of formal sanction from the U.S. government.

Temporal diffusion, on the other hand, involves activists searching the
historical record for evidence that the problem had actually existed
long before now but for a variety of reasons had not been addressed.
Activists then propose that the public now has the responsibility of
doing something about the problem, either because attitudes have
changed or because society finally has the ability to affect the problem. To illustrate, consider the following information we found at
the Millsaps College campus police Web site, describing how that
department is using "innovative measures" to address campus crime

---

[27] This information is available from the Security On Campus, Inc., Web site, retrieved
September 18, 2008, http://www. securityoncampus.org/schools/cleryact/index.
html.

and "stay ahead of crime trends." The implication is that the Millsaps College police department – with enough institutional support – can actually *do* something about campus crime:

> One question that is standard among those who observe our operations is: "Why have so much security on a small to medium sized campus?" The answer is that we, through innovation and forward thinking, attempt to actually stay ahead of crime trends. Innovative measures have many associated costs. It is to our college administration's credit that it is willing to perceive new and additional security measures as investments in our students, rather than counting such hardware and programs as drains on resources.[28]

Taking Ownership and Achieving Social Recognition of the Problem

One of the most important dynamics in the process of creating social problems is that some entity – a group or social movement – takes ownership of the condition it wishes to bring to the public's attention. By taking ownership, claimsmakers help culminate a process of elevating the condition to the status of a new "social problem."[29] To illustrate, under ordinary circumstances the murder of one student in her dormitory room by another student at the same university, while tragic, does not itself constitute a social problem. Only when a claimsmaker defines that murder as *emblematic* of the larger condition of concern (unsafe and violent college campuses) and identifies the target group affected by the problem (millions of college students and, by extension, their families) does that murder become something else entirely – the *new* problem of violent and unsafe college campuses.

When taking ownership, activists seek to move the problem from the periphery to the center of the public stage. In the case of campus crime, this was accomplished when various claimsmakers focused on college campuses and "demonstrated" how violent and unsafe they were by using the testimony not only of victims but also of various "authorities," some of whom were academics. Best argues that claimsmakers' use of testimony is but one of several strategies they developed to help achieve their ends. Also included is claimsmakers' use of

---

[28] Retrieved December 4, 2009, http://www.millsaps.edu/safety.
[29] Best, *Random Violence.*

rhetoric that identifies new victims and villains that are associated with the condition of interest.[30] Claimsmakers likewise identify members of a target group of prospective victims (e.g., college students) and go to great lengths to show that members of this group are not only at great risk *but at equal risk* of experiencing the problem. Claimsmakers may even argue the problem is "patternless, pointless, and getting worse" and use other emotionally charged language to incite fear rather than to promote understanding of the condition.[31]

Once claimsmakers have obtained public recognition of the problem, they then work to convince the public that the problem threatens *them* by making claims about it. Activists might, for example, claim that the murder of a particular college student illustrates how the "violence that has plagued our cities" has now "invaded the peace and tranquility of the college campus." Melodramatic examples are used both to typify the condition and to impress upon the audience the seriousness of the threat posed by the condition.[32] For example, a claimsmaker arguing that college campuses have become unsafe and violent will take the story of the murder of a student at one college or university and combine it with the stories of murders of students at other schools to illustrate the "growing menace" of "random campus violence." Best suggests that claimsmakers will thus take an *incident* and turn it into an *instance* of the new problem to press the point that the public should be concerned about what is going on.[33] By turning incidents into instances, claimsmakers *problematize events*, such that isolated instances of particular criminal acts are turned into repeated examples of a larger condition or problem.[34] To illustrate, a 1990 *USA Today* story claimed that American colleges and universities were "no longer safe havens from the violence." That claim was reinforced by the newspaper's chronicling a series of gun-related assaults that occurred between May and October 1990 on disparate

---

[30] For example, Donileen Loseke, *The Battered Woman and Shelters: The Social Construction of Wife Abuse* (Albany: SUNY Press, 1992); Donileen Loseke, *Thinking about Social Problems: An Introduction to Constructionist Perspectives* (Edison, NJ: Transaction Books, 2003).

[31] Best, *Random Violence*, pp. 10–20.

[32] Ibid.

[33] Ibid., p. 35.

[34] Ibid., p. 36.

campuses such as Montana State University, Alabama A&M University, the University of Oklahoma, Catholic University in Washington, D.C., and Utah State University.[35]

Establishing an Orientation

All claims about social problems establish a particular orientation, a specific way of thinking about the condition. Once a problem is named and claimed by a group, the group presents itself as an authority on the problem and as a spokesperson for it. In doing so, the group "frames" the problem. That is, the group defines an appropriate orientation toward it, which becomes *the* way to understand the problem.[36] Framing is important because it is around a particular orientation that claimsmakers create that media outlets will "wrap" a story and broadcast messages about it. Policy makers will also develop responses to the problem that are based on an orientation often impressed on them by claimsmakers. Thus, if the stalking of divorced or separated college women by their ex-husbands is framed as a new form of "domestic violence," it can then be presented as yet *another* example of how men victimize their partners and spouses. As Best suggests, establishing ownership of a problem creates a single, dominant orientation toward that problem, what he calls "collective action frames," which are then broadcast to the public and which specify the nature of the problem, provide examples of it, and indicate how activists believe the problem can be solved. Ultimately, creating a dominant orientation toward the problem encourages the public to alter its thinking about the problem, so that its thinking is now in line with the "master frame" the activists created.[37]

Legitimizing the Problem

Once the public has recognized the problem, claimsmakers then work to get the condition legitimized or acquire large-scale social endorsement as a new social problem. To accomplish this goal, claimsmakers typically rely on experts, including academic researchers, victims or

---

[35] Denise Kalette, "Dangerous Lessons: Campuses No Longer Safe Haven," *USA Today*, November 29, 1990, p. 1.
[36] Best, *Random Violence*, p. 173.
[37] Ibid., p. 174.

their families, and government agencies (e.g., the U.S. Department of Justice or the Centers for Disease Control and Prevention) to come forward and agree with them that the condition is "a problem" about which the public should be concerned. In 1991, for example, Representative Jim Ramstad (R-MN) and two other members of the House of Representatives called a press conference to announce they were introducing the *Campus Sexual Assault Victims Bill of Rights* that "addresses the *growing epidemic* of rape on college campuses."[38]

Claimsmakers also rely on experts to further legitimize their assertions. Sometimes the experts are "celebrities" working in a particular field, such as public health, who have accumulated impressive professional credentials and whose writings or public statements to media sources agree with the claims made by activists. Other times claimsmakers will identify academic researchers whose routine work may implicitly agree with the claims being made about a particular problem, and therefore this body of work helps legitimize those claims. For example, a researcher may publish results from his or her study showing that college women experience high levels of sexual victimization.[39] The results are picked up by electronic and print journalists, who then interview the author about the incidence of sexual victimization among college women. Claimsmakers then use the study's results or statements made by the researcher to print journalists to argue the researcher's findings echo the claim they are making. Finally, legitimacy can also be achieved when the expert is employed by a federal government agency, such as the U.S. Department of Education, the Centers for Disease Control and Prevention, or the U.S. Department of Justice. When an expert employed by a federal agency expresses concerns over the problem, the claimsmaker can now argue the federal government is agreeing with the claims being made, and it too is concerned with the problem.

Claimsmakers also use the experiences of victims or their families, broadcast through mass-media outlets, to legitimize the condition as a "real" social problem. Grieving parents who speak of the loss of

---

[38] Federal News Service, "Press Conference on the Introduction of and the Need for the *Campus Sexual Assault Victims Bill of Rights*," May 14, 1991 (emphasis added).

[39] See, for example, Eugene J. Kanin, "Date Rape: Unofficial Criminals and Victims," *Victimology: An International Journal* 9 (1984): 95–108.

their son or daughter to "senseless violence" at a college or university or strain to explain the impact of an on-campus sexual assault on their daughter are powerful images of the crisis posed by the problem and its negative impact on people's lives. For example, a 2005 story reported by NBC News included an interview with Stacy Bogart, who discussed her alleged rape by a fellow student on the Ohio State University campus and the university's alleged mishandling of her complaint, over which she sued. She was quoted in the story as saying, "I was victimized once by the rapist and again by the university's inaction. Throughout all of this, I realized that it takes a lot of pain to make change. I believe it is my obligation to stand up against the injustice and fight for...the victims that OSU administrators have ignored, neglected, or silenced."[40] In sum, legitimacy is achieved because credentialed experts, representatives of the government, or victims *declare* that the condition is a large-scale problem and speak with authority about it, while mass-media outlets repeatedly broadcast the messages and the powerful images that often accompany them.

Best further suggests that claimsmakers not only are familiar with the role of mass media in helping create new social problems but depend on media assistance to further their cause to a broader audience.[41] Because claimsmakers are familiar with the workings of mass media, they fit their claims into a template commonly used by media, which is to graphically describe the problem, explain its causes, and interpret its meanings.[42] Media representatives then involve experts, victims, or other interested parties who "give legs" to the story. Additionally, because claimsmakers realize that once legitimacy is achieved it must be *maintained*, they work toward keeping the media interested in the problem by presenting it as increasingly serious and getting worse, knowing the press will continue to cover it. Claimsmakers can then say "See, we *told* you it is a problem! Look at its impact on these poor victims and their families! Look at what the experts say about it. We need legislative action *now* to address this problem!"

[40] NBC News, *Dateline*, December 11, 2005.
[41] Best, *Random Violence*.
[42] Ibid., p. 37.

Once the condition is legitimized as real, Best argues that claims-makers then mobilize and obtain public support for the goal of convincing the public to take a stand, get involved, and demand that policy makers or other officials, such as college or university administrators, take action.[43] Here, claimsmakers again enlist mass-media sources or other entities such as lobbying groups to "get the message out" that a crisis is brewing and requires emergency measures be taken. The point is to get the public to think about how this "new" problem (e.g., unsafe and violent campuses) actually ties into a larger, well-known, and pressing problem (e.g., random violence) about which a large number of people have great concern. Doing so helps get the condition or problem *institutionalized*, what Best describes as the "amassing of public support for the claims made about the new problem."[44]

Institutionalizing Social Problems
How does the institutionalization of social problems occur? Best argues that institutionalization is contingent on the contributions of four major entities: mass-media, activists, the government, and experts.[45] Media are important to institutionalizing social problems through their typifying of disparate incidents into examples of the larger problem. They also, using specific language, describe the condition in compelling terms – "widespread," "growing," or "significant" – while also helping to explain the potential cause of the condition, along with its meaning and significance. Further, as long as the condition can be approached from fresh angles, such as reports of new incidents, the media continue to broadcast emotionally charged images and rhetoric about the problem.

Activists are crucial to institutionalization, because they have assumed ownership of the problem and have helped maintain attention to it. They also have influenced how media interpret the problem by encouraging media sources to frame the condition according to activists' own ideology. The government is likewise important to

---

[43] Ibid.
[44] Ibid., p. 47.
[45] Ibid., pp. 63–69.

institutionalization through the passage of laws; through establishment of enforcement procedures; through political gains accompanying campaigns addressing the new problem; and through opportunities for additional media coverage via reporting on hearings, interviews with key legislators, and reporting on floor debates. Finally, experts often offer their endorsement of particular ideologies about the problem and thus lend support to the claims made by activists. As Best describes it, experts "reaffirm the nature of the new [problem], track progress toward controlling it, and offer more refined ways of thinking about the issue."[46]

Cultural Resources

Best further suggests that a new social problem such as campus crime must "gain recognition, generate concern, and mobilize action" and that "some claims succeed while others get ignored."[47] Why do only some claims succeed? Among the key reasons Best cites are *cultural resources* and the *novelty of the new*. Best describes cultural resources as collections of ideas that are invoked by individuals to help them make sense of events, and which social movements and activists tap into, using specific rhetoric to help make their claims persuasive. Claimsmakers will thus tell people about what sort of problem is significant, the reasons they ought to worry about it, and the sorts of policies that should be developed to address the problem.

Claimsmakers must "package" the new problem and typically do so by describing the motivations of offenders, such as how their behavior (e.g., stalking) leads to other behavior (e.g., murder), and the qualities of victims (e.g., innocent), as well as the particulars for how the problem should be addressed. They also use melodramatic imagery to provoke attention, create worry, and help develop policies to address the problem by presenting it in stark terms – "evil" villains versus "innocent" victims – combined with descriptions of the outrages perpetrated by the offenders. Such strategies are designed to elicit from the public strong feelings against the villains and favorable attitudes toward the "new" victims. As Best suggests, each time

[46] Ibid., p. 68.
[47] Ibid., p. 72.

claimsmakers borrow the language, familiar orientations, and tactics relating to other social problems, they are ultimately borrowing cultural resources used previously to describe *other* problems, such as random violence occurring in major cities, and applying those resources to the *new* problem.[48]

The Novelty of the New

Another key to why some claims succeed is that claimsmakers use the novelty of the new in their efforts to help construct a social problem. As Best describes it, "novelty" is a central theme in our culture.[49] As a result, new problems are more interesting than old problems; new problems also command crucial media attention and inspire activists to rally around the new cause. In effect, because of a cultural affinity for novelty, the public implicitly demands the creation of new social problems, particularly those relating to crime. Thus, for campus crime to succeed as a new social problem, it had to be projected not only as a new type of *crime* but also as one that had the potential to touch millions of young people and their families. The issue thus becomes personalized – it is no longer a college or university issue. It becomes "my" issue because "I have children of college age."

The Ideology Surrounding New Victims

In creating a new social problem, activists also create new types of victims and introduce them to the public. Best suggests that activists achieve this by tapping into cultural resources and by making dramatic claims about the new form of victimization they have "discovered."[50] They document victims' suffering and impress on the public the idea that what happened to the victims actually had a long history, but nevertheless their suffering had gone largely ignored. The public then develops a sympathetic and supportive perception of these new victims. In other words, activists create a *new ideology* that involves several core ideas that help push their agenda onto the public's consciousness.

[48] Ibid.
[49] Ibid., pp. 86–92.
[50] Ibid., pp. 103–117.

First, activists usually argue the new victimization is widespread. Joanne Belknap and Edna Erez, for example, writing about apparently rampant sexual violence perpetrated against college women on campus, cited a recent study that found that "over one-quarter...of college women reported an unwanted sexual experience...with African American women reporting a higher rate (36%) than white women (26%)."[51] Activists justify their estimates of the scope of the problem – which are almost always large – by promoting the broadest possible definition of what constitutes "victimization" by the new problem, using domain expansion and elaboration. For example, "sexual violence against women" encompasses a very wide range of behaviors, but because the definition of the condition is so broad, "big numbers" can be easily produced that will grab the public's attention when publicized by electronic or print media outlets.

Activists also work to show this new form of victimization is straightforward and unambiguous – there are two actors, a victimizer and a victim, and the "evil" victimizer "takes advantage" of the "innocent" victim. Thus, two students on a date where the male is alleged to have drugged the female and sexually victimized her sends a powerfully unambiguous message: date rapists – evil offenders – exploit the trust of the innocent victim, resulting in serious consequences for her. If date rape is also presented as being widespread by using multiple instances described in graphic detail, the "crisis" of date rape is vividly seared on the public's consciousness. Best suggests that "claiming that victimization is clear-cut stakes out the moral high ground; it lets activists defend good victims beset by evil victimizers."[52] Beyond alleging new victims and villains associated with the problem, activists also claim that these new forms of victimization, despite being widespread, actually remain publicly unrecognized, because of either a general lack of awareness or victims' reluctance to discuss their experiences. Regardless of why the new form of victimization remains hidden, the failure by the public to recognize the plight of victims

[51] Joanne Belknap and Edna Erez, "Violence against Women on College Campuses: Rape, Intimate Partner Abuse, and Sexual Harassment," pp. 188–209 in Bonnie S. Fisher and John J. Sloan III (Eds.), *Campus Crime: Legal, Social, and Policy Perspectives*, 2nd ed. (Springfield, IL: Charles C. Thomas, 2007).

[52] Best, *Random Violence*, p. 109.

is a serious situation that must be addressed through legislative or administrative actions.

Beyond illustrating the rampant, straightforward, but somewhat hidden nature of the new victimization, activists also focus on ensuring the public is aware of the *consequences* of this new form of victimization. Activists often claim that, even in its most minor form, this new kind of victimization can have potentially lifelong psychological or emotional consequences for the victim. They then document those consequences as uncovered by therapists working with victims. Doing so invites the "medicalization of victimization" and creates opportunities for experts, including nurses, medical doctors, and mental health professionals, to further legitimize the condition by documenting its devastating psychological, physical, or financial effects on victims.[53]

Activists argue that people need to be taught to recognize this new form of victimization, mainly through an educational process developed by them. Best cites several examples of such programs, including sexual abuse or date or acquaintance rape prevention programs offered to college freshman as part of new student orientation. Activists then use mass-media sources – newspapers, magazines, television talk shows, and other outlets – to help "educate" the public on recognizing the new form of victimization. Importantly, this coverage typically incorporates a particular ideology about the new form of victimization along with activists' substantive claims about the widespread nature of the problem, its possible consequences, and need for the public to stop overlooking the suffering of victims. Activists also educate the public that *all* claims of victimization involving the new problem must *always* be respected, regardless of whether there is evidence to support them. To question victims' claims, according to the claimsmakers, is to engage in "victim blaming," which subjects victims to further psychological or emotional trauma and reinforces efforts to try to keep the problem hidden. Activists also make the point that, by definition, some claims of victimization are true – why would a woman falsely accuse a man whom she knows of raping her?

Finally, Best argues that in recent years, the label of "victim" has slowly been replaced with a more positive connotation, such as

[53] Ibid., p. 106.

"survivor."[54] These more "empowering" terms are designed not only to affirm the claim that the new form of victimization has occurred and has consequences but also to reduce an individual's reluctance to define himself or herself as a victim, a response that helps keep the problem hidden from the public and may discourage the victim from seeking medical or mental health services.

In total, these propositions about new victims form what Best calls a virtually incontrovertible ideology that encourages identifying and labeling victims: it defines victimization as common, consequential, and clear-cut yet unrecognized; it justifies helping individuals identify themselves as victims; it delegitimizes doubts about victims' claims; and it provides, new, nonstigmatizing labels for those who have suffered. It is, in short, a set of beliefs that makes it easy to label victims, and very difficult to dispute those labels.[55]

Each form of victimization that is associated with the new social problem has its advocates who make claims about their particular form of victimization; wholesale application of these propositions to all forms of victimization does not occur. Interestingly, however, each group staking a claim about a new form of victimization tends to use these same propositions to make their point about the widespread nature of the victimization *they* have discovered; to show there are significant consequences associated with the victimization they discovered; and to argue that the victimization they discovered is unambiguous yet hidden and that victims' claims must be respected.[56] Thus, whether the new claims relate to the frequency of sexual assaults of college women occurring at fraternity parties or student rowdiness at athletic events fueled by alcohol abuse, there is little difference in how the new victimization is described and, ultimately, how it is elevated to the center of public discourse.

Responding to New Victims
Until or unless major institutions in society – political, economic, educational, legal, media – accept and adapt their behavior to claims about

---

[54] Ibid., pp. 116–117.
[55] Ibid., p. 117.
[56] Ibid.

new victims, the ideology surrounding new victims will not take hold with the public. According to Best, each of these institutions must, in its own way, accept activists' claims about new victims and victimizations and favorably respond to these claims.[57] For example, when state legislatures began passing "rape shield laws" during the 1970s, the stated goal of the legislation was to reduce the "revictimization" of rape victims during cross-examination at trial by preventing defense counsel from asking about the victims' past sexual behaviors, and thus blaming them for their predicament.[58] The statutes were passed not because elected officials believed the legislation would matter, but rather because they *knew* that regardless of the actual effect of the laws, they would earn political points from victims and victim advocates by taking the lead in addressing the problem and therefore protecting helpless rape victims.[59] Best also suggests that law reviews and academic journals often provide sympathetic commentaries on the plights of the new victims and may even recommend legal steps that should be taken to address the condition. Further, mental health professionals – including counselors and social workers – have adopted the "medical model" (e.g., uncovering symptoms, labeling the condition, diagnosing its cause, and delivering treatment) in response to the "needs" of new victims. Because the model is based in medicine, and is therefore legitimate, adopting it also gives legitimacy to those professionals – social workers or counselors – working with the new victims of the social problem.

In the present case, the "need" to educate the public about campus crime mobilized postsecondary institutions to help educate students, parents, faculty members, and staff about the problem. Faculty members even produced scholarship about the problem, including recommendations about how it should be addressed, which was

---

[57] Ibid., pp. 113–118.

[58] Susan Estrich, "Rape Shield Laws Aren't Foolproof," *USA Today*, July 27, 2003, retrieved April 30, 2010, http://www.usatoday.com/news/opinion/editorials/2003–07-27-estrich_x.htm. See also "Rape Shield Laws: Can They Be Fair?" retrieved April 30, 2010, http://law.jrank.org/pages/9643/Rape-Rape-Shield-Laws-Can-They-Be-Fair html.

[59] Retrieved December 4, 2009. An excellent discussion of rape shield laws, including their history and the different categories into which they fit, is available at http://www.naesv.org/ Resources/Articles/UnderstandingRapeShieldLaws.pdf.

shared at professional conferences. Mass media also identified these threads and wove them together into stories favorable to the ideology of the activists who were pushing the new form of victimization.[60] Because these institutions enjoy positions of relative power in society, they turn the ideology surrounding new victims into a common frame of reference that cuts across a host of contexts: legal, educational, therapeutic, and media. In turn, this furthers the interests of activists whose goal is to convince the public about the legitimacy of their claims about the new social problem. Once these powerful institutions are mobilized and accept the ideology of activists, the status of the new victim is solidified and legitimated and, perhaps most important, becomes accepted by the general public.

CONCLUSION

The construction of new social problems such as campus crime involves a variety of processes, where claimsmakers connect together component parts of the "new" problem and present those connections to the public with a particular frame of reference. The claimsmakers name and take ownership of the new problem. They package the problem for public consumption using cultural resources, such as melodramatic images. Claimsmakers then legitimize the problem and work toward institutionalizing it. They create a powerful ideology relating to the new form of victimization, the victims it touches, and villains engaging in the behavior. They seek to influence powerful institutions in society first to adopt the ideology they create about the problem and then to respond with policy initiatives that contain the melodramatic images and rhetoric associated with the ideology. In the chapters that follow, we apply this framework to crime for the purpose of describing and explaining how crime came to be socially constructed into a new social problem.

[60] Best, *Random Violence.*

CHAPTER THREE

Constructing Unsafe and Violent College Campuses

The impact of crime on college and university campuses has increased dramatically. The Columbine High School tragedy confronts all educational institutions with the previously unimaginable possibility that members of our campus communities are capable of planning and carrying out...a brutal massacre of students, faculty and administrators.[1]

While the spree murders that occurred at Virginia Tech and Northern Illinois University raised serious public concerns over the safety of college and university students in the United States, campus violence is hardly new. With some exceptions during the 1960s, media coverage of violence on college campuses during the 20th century generally took a matter-of-fact tone. That is, the facts of these incidents were reported – who, what, where, and when – along with observations from various commentators on both sides of the larger gun control debate. However, claims about these incidents serving as a harbinger of bigger problems were largely absent.

Beginning in the 1980s and continuing into the 1990s, however, a change occurred in the tone of mass-media coverage of campus violence. What had been relatively routine reports of serious criminal incidents on college campuses now began including language hinting that something alarming was occurring that put millions of college students at risk of becoming the victims of serious violence – including murder. For example, a 1981 story appearing in the *New York Times* indicated that "violence was *becoming a way of life* for students" and that

---

[1] Phillip Burling, *Crime on Campus: Analyzing and Managing the Increasing Risk of Institutional Liability*, 2nd ed. (Washington, DC: National Association of College and University Attorneys, 2004), p. 1.

"large numbers" of students involved in romantic relationships were "physically abusing their partners."[2] Similarly, a 1984 *New York Times* story indicated that rioting by college students after athletic contests or when large parties were broken up by police was becoming common on college campuses.[3]

As the 1990s unfolded, media reports of college campuses as increasingly "unsafe and violent" places continued at a stronger pace, and such claims become more common. Warnings about an "epidemic of violence" on college campuses were even being echoed on Capitol Hill in testimony before the House Subcommittee on Postsecondary Education in 1990, where it was revealed that "every ten days a murder occurs on a college campus" and that "one...of six women students is sexually assaulted on college campuses."[4] Stories of murder and murder-suicides, rape and sexual assault, gun-related assaults, and other serious forms of violence occurring on college campuses not only became more common but began being peppered with claims by activists that serious violence on college campuses was *not* a rare event and that postsecondary institutions were covering up that fact. Thus, the stories that were appearing sounded alarm bells for the public as claims about the extent and nature of such violence became far more common.

To illustrate, a 1995 story in the *Guardian* (London), which chronicled the murder-suicide of two students then enrolled at Harvard University, made the point that, even in the "hallowed halls of the Ivy League," violence on campus was rearing its ugly head.[5] The *Chronicle of Higher Education* carried stories with sobering headlines – "Weapons on Campus?" and "400,000 Undergraduates in the U.S. Own a Handgun, Study Finds" – suggesting that the presence of weapons

---

[2] Nadine Joseph, "Campus Couples and Violence," *New York Times*, June 23, 1981, sec. A, p. 20 (emphasis added).

[3] UPI, "Around the Nation: Kansas State Students in Melee with Police," *New York Times*, October 15, 1984, sec. A, p. 12.

[4] Statement by Howard Clery in 1990 testimony before the House Subcommittee on Postsecondary Education on the murder of his daughter in 1986 at Lehigh University where she was a student. Retrieved November 24, 2009, http://www.securityoncampus.org/Congress/ 03131990.html.

[5] Christine Nifong, "Tragedy Underlines Foreign Student Challenges," *Christian Science Monitor*, June 2, 1985, United States Section, p. 3; Jonathon Freedland, "Blight Hits Ivy League," *Guardian* (London), Features Section, June 12, 1995, p. 27.

on college campuses had become an "alarming" problem.[6] A Student
Press Law Center handbook for journalists covering crime on college
campuses revealed that campus crime statistics "can be alarming,"
adding that "one in five women will be sexually assaulted while in college" and "one in six students will be victimized [by violence] during
their college life."[7] As Philip Burling put it,

> The longstanding public perception that college and university cam-
> puses offer safe havens from crime lasted into the early 1990s; there-
> after, that perception began to give way to a suspicion, among at least
> some opinion makers, that educators had conspired to hide the fact
> that campuses are dangerous hang-outs, where the laws are rarely
> enforced, and where the risk of violence and crime is covered up to
> increase [schools'] enrollment.[8]

By the end of the 1990s, journalists' accounts of campus violence,
combined with increasingly troubling claims about campus violence
being made by various activists, succeeded in convincing the public
that violence on college and university campuses had become *such*
a problem that it threatened the peace and tranquillity of the ivory
tower and jeopardized the safety and security of millions of U.S. college and university students.

Thus, during the late 1980s and through the 1990s, media reports of
campus violence sounded increasingly ominous warnings. What were
once relatively routine reports of campus violence, slowly adopted
more of an alarmist tone. Campus violence – including gun-related
incidents, student riots, murders, and rape – had apparently reached
epidemic proportions. No longer were college campuses idyllic oases
that isolated students and faculty members from larger social ills. In
this new world, violent elements had officially invaded the ivory tower
and now posed a serious threat to its stability.

---

[6] Douglas Lederman, "Weapons on Campus? Colleges Face Gun Problems," *Chronicle
of Higher Education*, March 9, 1994, pp. A33–A35. In the article, Lederman characterized guns on college campuses as a "growing menace" and suggested that
"gun violence [was] becoming more prevalent." See also Leo Reisberg, "400,000
Undergraduates in the U.S. Own a Handgun," *Chronicle of Higher Education*, July 16,
1999, p. A40.

[7] Student Press Law Center, *Covering Campus Crime: A Handbook for Journalists*, 3rd ed.
(Arlington, VA: Student Press Law Center, 2000).

[8] Burling, *Crime on Campus*, p. 1.

The process of constructing a new social problem – that college campuses had become unsafe and violent places – had thus begun in earnest. Activists who stepped forward during the 1980s and 1990s were largely responsible for expediting that process. They began making claims about violence on college campuses and, in the process, named the problem and took ownership of it. They engaged in activities that helped to legitimize campus violence as a new social problem and, ultimately, helped institutionalize it. They developed an orientation for understanding the problem and identified both new victims and new villains associated with it. In short, they were involved in all of the processes that Best's theoretical framework suggests are crucial to constructing a new social problem.

SECURITY ON CAMPUS, INC.

A key party in helping to construct campus crime as a new social problem was Security On Campus, Inc. (SOC). A grass-roots lobbying operation, SOC was founded in 1988 by Howard and Connie Clery after their daughter was brutally murdered in her dorm room at Lehigh University in 1986. SOC then spent the late 1980s and the 1990s convincing the public and policy makers that postsecondary institutions were unsafe and violent places; college or university administrators, in a cynical effort to maintain the images of their schools, were allowing students to be victimized rather than "coming clean" about how unsafe and dangerous their campuses were; and, because of the scope, magnitude, and seriousness of the problem, congressional intervention was needed to start holding schools responsible for student safety.

The strategies that SOC used resulted in the social construction of unsafe and violent college campuses as a new social problem. By viewing its actions and strategies through the lens of the theoretical framework discussed in Chapter 2, we show how SOC named, took ownership, and made a series of claims about college campuses being unsafe and violent. We illustrate how SOC and its representatives created an ideology about campus violence, which included identifying new victims and offenders, and how colleges and universities were inadequately responding to both. This ideology helped SOC to develop informal alliances with other activists, such as victims' rights proponents, not to mention alliances developed with various government agencies, including the U.S. Department of Education and the U.S. Department of Justice's National Institute of Justice, to help design policy that would respond to on-campus violence. SOC helped institutionalize the problem using various strategies that ultimately influenced policy makers in taking action. These activities resulted in the passage of new legislation, first in the state of Pennsylvania, then in other states, and finally by the U.S. Congress, that addressed SOC's claims that college campuses had become such unsafe and violent places that the safety and well-being of millions of college students were being threatened.

The Founding of SOC

In the early morning hours of April 5, 1986, Lehigh University sophomore Jeanne Ann Clery, then 19, slept in her dormitory room, unaware that fellow student Josoph Henry had gained entry into her dormitory through a series of unlocked and propped open doors. Henry, 20, whom Ms. Clery did not know, apparently had intended to commit burglary when he came upon her unlocked room and entered it. When Ms. Clery awoke to find him there, Henry then brutally raped, tortured, and strangled her to death in her own bed. He was later arrested, convicted, and sentenced to death. During his trial, evidence showed that "three doors, each equipped with automatic locks, had been propped open with empty pizza boxes for the convenience of the resident students."[9] Evidence at the trial also showed that between 1984 and the date of the murder there had been 181 reported security lapses at the dormitory where Ms. Clery lived, mostly doors being propped open or left unlocked; and that 38 incidents of violence, including robberies, rapes, and assaults that had occurred either in or near to Ms. Clery's dormitory, had been reported to campus authorities. Perhaps most damaging for Lehigh was evidence showing that college officials *knew* about these problems but took no

---

[9] Karen Gross and Andrew Fine, "After Their Daughter Is Murdered at College, Her Grieving Parents Mount a Crusade for Campus Safety," retrieved December 4, 2009, http://www.people.com/people/archive/article/0,,20116872,00.html.

steps to address them, including alerting dormitory residents about the incidents that had occurred.[10]

At the completion of the criminal trial and on the basis of evidence presented there, the Clerys filed a $25 million lawsuit against Lehigh University claiming the university was liable for negligence in the death of their daughter because it failed to notify Jeanne Ann, other residents of the dormitory, or the larger campus community about security lapses and criminal incidents occurring in or near the dormitories. Although the suit was eventually settled out of court, it was to be "the first round in a campaign that would touch state legislatures, colleges, and concerned parents across the country. The Clerys had...ignited a cause."[11] The Clerys used a reported $2 million settlement from the lawsuit to found Security On Campus, Inc., a 501(c)(3) nonprofit corporation.[12] After establishing an office in their home as SOC headquarters, the Clerys enlisted volunteers and a few paid assistants to create data banks and mailing lists they used in their effort to "fight back" against the forces they believed had caused their daughter's murder.[13] In 1989 the *Philadelphia Inquirer* described the Clerys and SOC as *the* "driving force" in efforts to "make colleges safer."[14]

The Clerys' initial objective was to create a guide for college students and their parents that would provide information on the level of security (or lack thereof) on college campuses. The goal of this guide was to raise awareness of the problems that security lapses could cause, including serious criminal victimization like that which took their daughter's life.[15] The organization's mission, however, soon

---

[10] Daniel Carter and Catherine Bath, "The Evolution and Components of the *Jeanne Clery Act*: Implications for Higher Education," pp. 27–44 in Bonnie S. Fisher and John J. Sloan III (Eds.), *Campus Crime: Legal, Social, and Policy Perspectives*, 2nd ed. (Springfield, IL: Charles Thomas, 2007).

[11] Gross and Fine, "After Their Daughter Is Murdered at College."

[12] Exact terms of the settlement were not made public. See Denise Kalette, "Campus Crime Fighters: New Law Ends Parents' Tragic Battle," *USA Today*, November 12, 1990, p. 1.

[13] Ibid.

[14] Sheila A. Downey, "He Turned Grief into Security Law for Campuses," *Philadelphia Inquirer*, January 6, 2008, p. B08. The article describes Howard Clery's two-decade-long effort to make college campuses safer.

[15] David Smith, "Campus Security Challenges Colleges," *Christian Science Monitor*, January 8, 1990, p. 18.

expanded to include additional activities including advocating on the need for changes in campus security policies to address the violence and victimization that SOC claimed was rife on college and university campuses.

SOC's Mission

According to its Web site, SOC's mission is to "prevent violence, substance abuse and other crimes on college and university campus communities" and "compassionately assist victims."[16] SOC representatives, in testimony before Congress, listed three points as part of the group's mission:

> Forewarn prospective students, their parents, and the campus community about the prevalence of crime on our nations' college and university campuses;

> Assist student-victims and their families with compassion and resource guidance pertaining to Federal and State laws, Victims' Advocacy Organizations and Legal Counsel, as well as providing access to our paper files and database;

> And foster security improvements through campus community initiatives and legislative initiatives that will ultimately restore a safe learning environment for... students.[17]

Soon after its founding, SOC hired Frank Carrington as its chief legal counsel.[18] Carrington had previously devoted his entire professional life to addressing crime victims' rights and needs. He served on President Reagan's Task Force on Victims of Crime; he authored the 1975 publication *The Victims*; he cofounded the Crime Victims' Legal Advocacy Institute; and he had served as executive director and president of Americans for Effective Law Enforcement.[19] He was

---

[16] http://www.securityoncampus.org.

[17] Benjamin F. Clery (President of Security On Campus, Inc.), Testimony on "Campus Crime and the *Accuracy in Campus Crime Reporting Act of* 1997 (HR715) before the Hearing of the House Education and Workforce Committee" (July 17, 1997). Transcript from *Federal Document Clearing House Congressional Testimony*. Available from LexisNexis® Congressional; accessed September 26, 2008.

[18] Carter and Bath, "The Evolution and Components of the *Jeanne Clery Act*."

[19] AELE was created in response to the successes of the American Civil Liberties Union and other civil rights groups in representing defendants in state courts and before the U.S. Supreme Court. Retrieved December 4, 2009, http://www.aele.org/About.html.

even honored in 1991 by President George H. W. Bush for his service to crime victims. Carrington soon became SOC's driving force and, along with the Clerys, the face of SOC, especially in Washington, D.C., as SOC began making claims about the "new" problem of violent and unsafe college campuses.[20]

Given the wording of SOC's mission statement, it was not surprising that the organization would assert that violence and crime were widespread on college campuses but that information relating to such incidents was being withheld from the public; that postsecondary institutions were mistreating campus crime victims and not responding appropriately to their needs; and that security arrangements or policies at postsecondary institutions were wanting, resulting in an increased risk to students of experiencing the same fate as Jeanne Ann. Through these claims, SOC and its representatives helped construct campus crime as a new social problem and ultimately influenced policy actions designed to reduce its threat.

THE SOCIAL CONSTRUCTION OF VIOLENT AND UNSAFE COLLEGE CAMPUSES

Best argues that claimsmakers, when naming a problem, rely on *typifying examples* rather than on *concise definitions* of the problem, which helps them achieve public recognition of the problem as a new social problem.[21] Recall also that a typifying example is where the claimsmaker takes an incident and transforms it into an instance of the new problem. The purpose of doing so is to impress on members of the public that they should be worried about the problem and convince them something should be done immediately to address it. This is exactly what SOC did: it routinely used Jeanne Ann Clery's murder as a typifying example of the unsafe and violent nature of college campuses in this country. SOC also used the incident to support its claim that postsecondary institutional administrators were apathetic toward the problem. Both of these situations, in turn, should

---

[20] Mr. Carrington was tragically killed in a fire at his residence in January 1992. See Carter and Bath, "The Evolution and Components of the *Jeanne Clery Act.*"

[21] Joel Best, *Random Violence: How We Talk about New Crimes and New Victims* (Berkeley: University of California Press, 1999), pp. 130, 167–169.

alarm the parents of college-age children. SOC, Frank Carrington, and the Clerys then connected Jeanne Ann's murder to murders and violent assaults perpetrated against other college students on campuses around the nation. They also connected the behavior of Lehigh University officials involving security lapses and coverups in their daughter's case with the behavior of institutional officials at other colleges and universities nationwide. In effect, SOC expanded the scope and seriousness of campus violence beyond Lehigh to include *all* postsecondary institutions and their campuses in the United States.

Making the Claims
To understand the claims SOC and the Clerys were making about unsafe and violent college campuses, consider the following examples. In a 1990 interview on the *CBS Morning News*, Connie Clery commented to reporter James Hattori that "we know there's *one murder every 10 days* on a college campus – that's pretty violent."[22] That same year, in a prepared statement read before the House Subcommittee on Postsecondary Education of the Committee on Education and Labor, Howard Clery stated that "*one out of five students* is a victim of crime."[23] In a *Boston Globe* story published in 1990, Howard Clery was quoted as saying: "We found there were *hundreds and then thousands of students being victimized* on their own college campuses, and without exception, the *colleges were not telling anybody about it.*"[24] Further, according to Connie Clery, "there is no way that campuses and their students can be safe *unless institutions tell the truth about campus crime.*"[25]

These and similar statements allowed SOC and its representatives to ultimately tie together unrelated events. They took the victimization of their daughter and tied it to what they claimed was the victimization of

[22] James Hattori, "Violent Crimes Increase on U.S. College Campuses," CBS, *Morning News*, October 11, 1990 (emphasis added).
[23] Statement of Mr. and Mrs. Howard Clery, Security on Campus, Inc., before the Subcommittee on Postsecondary Education of the Committee on Education and Labor, House of Representatives, Washington, DC, March 14, 1990 (emphasis added), retrieved November 1, 2008, http://www.securityoncampus.org/congress/03141990.html.
[24] Anthony Flint, "Bill OK'd Requiring Campus Crime Statistics," *Boston Globe*, October 25, 1990, Metro Section, p. 1 (emphasis added).
[25] Carter and Bath, "The Evolution and Components of the *Jeanne Clery Act*," p. 27 (emphasis added).

"hundreds and thousands of students" allegedly occurring on college campuses around the nation. They also took the knowledge that Lehigh officials had done nothing to warn their daughter about security lapses in her dormitory and tied *that* behavior to the behavior of other college or university administrators, who were "not telling anybody about" campus violence and security lapses. In doing this, SOC created a framework, which it then presented to the American public via mass media and congressional testimony. SOC named the problem and helped establish ownership over it. SOC also turned incidents of campus violence into instances of the new problem. Doing so showed just how big the issue of unsafe and violent college campuses had become.

The claims made shaped SOC's guiding ideology. Repeatedly, the message sent was that college campuses were violent and unsafe places. This situation was because callous college or university administrators were unwilling to publicly share their crime data and take the necessary steps to address the problem because they wanted to protect their schools' images. The Clerys repeatedly "pitched" this ideology to the mass media during the late 1980s and 1990s and punctuated their claims by identifying both the new victims and the perpetrators that were associated with the problem. The new victims included unwary college students, whose lack of knowledge about campus violence increased their risk for victimization, while the new villains were not the perpetrators of the victimizations but were postsecondary officials desperate to maintain their institutions' images and willing to do almost anything to achieve that goal.[26]

SOC and its representatives then spent the late 1980s and most of the 1990s publicizing the new problem of unsafe and violent college campuses and uncaring postsecondary institutional administrators. They appeared on national television talk shows and were interviewed by reporters for both print and electronic media outlets.[27] They

---

[26] A classic illustration of this claim is found in a documentary on campus security produced by the A&E Network. The report presents a case study of the lengths taken by officials at the University of Minnesota to keep the public from learning about rapes and assaults allegedly committed by student-athletes enrolled at the school. See Arts & Entertainment Television Network, *Investigative Reports: Campus Insecurity* (New York: New Video, 1998).

[27] For example, the Clerys appeared at least three different times on CNN's *Larry King Live* in the mid-1990s.

also testified before House and Senate committees that held hearings about campus violence.[28] Further, they distributed press releases to media outlets around the nation. According to one account, the Clerys' media appearances and testimony before legislative committees were for the purpose of raising "awareness about campus safety issues" and providing "information to the public that postsecondary institutions were hiding their crime information."[29]

The Clerys also spoke at professional conferences, such as the First National Conference on Campus Violence held at Towson State University in 1987. Their appearances at professional conferences were designed not only to "get the message out" by using yet another venue from which to speak but also to generate support for their efforts from academic researchers, victims' advocates, and law enforcement or security professionals attending these conferences.

It was not unusual for the mass media or legislative committees to portray the Clerys as the "aggrieved parents reaching out to other parents and their children" to ensure *they* would never have to experience the same loss and grief the Clerys had experienced. All of these activities helped move the problem of unsafe and violent campuses to the center of public and postsecondary institutional attention.[30] The Clerys' credibility came from the fact they had tragically lost their daughter at an "unsafe and violent campus" and, by default, had become "experts" on the problem. They were perceived as sympathetic figures fighting to ensure Jeanne had not "died in vain." As one CBS News reporter described them,

> Here on the Lehigh campus there is a plaque dedicated to the memory of Jeanne Clery. It says that we must protect one another so that her death will not have been in vain. And to that end, *her parents have devoted their lives to campus security, making it not only an issue of personal grief, but also a matter of public policy.*[31]

[28] Testimony of Benjamin Clery, 1997.
[29] Carter and Bath, "The Evolution and Components of the *Jeanne Clery Act*," p. 29.
[30] Ibid., p. 42.
[31] Rita Braver, "Campus Crime: Safety Issues on American College Campuses and One Couple's Fight to Keep Their Murdered Daughter's Memory Alive by Fighting for Campus Security," CBS News, *Sunday Morning*, September 14, 1997 (emphasis added).

The Clerys and SOC had thus named a new problem: unsafe and violent college campuses and callous campus administrators, who, through inaction, allowed students to be victimized. Initially the Clerys, and then later various SOC representatives, were able to take ownership of the problem because of the tragic circumstances surrounding the death of their daughter. In effect Jeanne Clery, her parents, and by extension SOC itself became the public face of the problem of unsafe and violent college campuses and unresponsive postsecondary officials. Using the media, SOC and its representatives effectively spread the gospel according to Security On Campus, Inc. Doing this allowed SOC's claims to gain traction with the public and permitted SOC to capture the attention not only of the parents of college-age children but of college or university administrators as well.

Domain Expansion, Elaboration, and Diffusion

As Best suggests, naming a new social problem also involves expanding and elaborating its domain – the scope of the problem and those being touched by it – and showing the public that the problem has crossed geographic or temporal boundaries (i.e., it is not isolated).[32] Best argues that domain expansion occurs when activists attach new claims to an existing problem, so the two become intertwined. In the current context, SOC took the new problem of unsafe and violent college campuses and tacked it onto the existing problem of societal violence more generally. SOC and its representatives also took the claim that colleges and universities "were more concerned with preserving their own images than with the safety of their students" and linked it with public distrust of and cynicism toward large-scale social institutions, such as the federal government and public education.

When expanding the domain of the new problem, activists argue that other, less dramatic cases are really no different from the original typifying example and, thus, that the problem is complex and multifaceted and demands attention.[33] Recall the message from SOC was that the murder of Jeanne Clery illustrated how unsafe and violent college campuses were. In a 1990 story appearing in *USA Today*, reporter

---

[32] Best, *Random Violence*, pp. 168–170, 172.
[33] Ibid.

Denise Kalette wrote: "The Clerys present a chilling portrait of the irreparable harm campus violence can cause... [as scores] of students are killed during their college years. But thousands are assaulted and raped. A 1989 study shows that 21,000 students fall victim to violent crimes each year. That's 57 violent acts each day."[34] SOC, along with various media, was ultimately equating Jeanne Clery's murder with *all other forms of violence perpetrated against college students around the nation.* College students who were being murdered were no different from college students who were being assaulted or raped – they were all part of the *same* problem: violent and unsafe campuses.

Domain elaboration, beyond allowing activists to show how "all encompassing" the problem is, allows them to solicit support from potentially powerful allies, such as those in the fields of law, medicine, education, and academe.[35] SOC and the Clerys were able to find allies from a range of groups, especially those working with crime victims and, in particular, those working with the victims of on-campus sexual assault. For example, during the mid-1990s, SOC developed what would become a long-standing relationship with the U.S. Department of Justice's Office of Victims of Crime.[36] Ties to law, academe, medicine, and activist groups can also be seen in the makeup of SOC's board of directors for 2008, which consisted of a local prosecutor with the reputation for stressing victims' rights in criminal prosecutions of sexual assault cases; the president of a nonprofit foundation in Philadelphia that provides financial assistance to families facing catastrophic medical bills arising from the treatment of their children; a professor from St. Joseph University, whose research has focused on linkages between alcohol abuse by college students and criminal victimization; a personal injury attorney from the greater Philadelphia area; and a neurologist. Thus, SOC had successfully fostered ties to government, law, medicine, academe, and the nonprofit foundation sector and could muster resources from those sectors if or when needed.

---

[34] Denise Kalette, "Campus Crime Fighters: New Law Ends Parents' Tragic Struggle," *USA Today*, November 12, 1990, p. 1D.

[35] Best, *Random Violence*, pp. 67–70.

[36] The Office of Victims of Crime Web site lists SOC as a resource for "rights and services afforded campus crime victims" and provides visitors with a link to the SOC Web site. Retrieved September 21, 2008, http://www.ojp.usdoj.gov/ovc.

Formal or informal ties by SOC to other activist organizations included College Parents of America, which its Web site describes as "the only national membership association dedicated to advocating and to serving on behalf of current and future college parents";[37] the Rape, Abuse, and Incest National Network, which provides counseling to rape victims via a 24-hour-a-day hotline;[38] the It Happened to Alexa Foundation, which provides grants to eligible individuals to cover the expenses of a support person or persons to accompany the sexual assault victims to court;[39] and Take A Stand Against Violence!, a victims' support network.[40]

Activists constructing a new social problem also show how diffuse the problem is. They do this by taking a single example of the new problem and finding similar examples of it occurring in another place or at another time. This is illustrated by the claims made by SOC about how disparate incidents of campus violence and institutional reluctance to publicly report crime data were actually connected. The Clerys' repeated claims, such as a student "is murdered on campus every 10 days" or that "hundreds and thousands of students are victimized on college campuses each year," showed that the violent victimization of college students was, literally, occurring *everywhere on a routine basis.*[41]

Establishing an Orientation

Claims by activists seeking to construct a new social problem help to establish an orientation, a way of thinking about the problem. Once a problem is named, ownership is established, and public recognition

---

[37] Retrieved December 4, 2009, http://www.collegeparents.org/cpa/about-cpa.html.
[38] Retrieved December 4, 2009, http://www.rainn.org.
[39] Retrieved December 4, 2009, http://www.ithappenedtoalexa.org.
[40] Retrieved December 4, 2009, http://www.tkastnd.org.
[41] In a "fact sheet" on campus crime that SOC authored in 2004, SOC included the following information: "A total of 86 homicides, 7,486 sex offenses, 9,649 aggravated assaults, and 3,590 arsons were reported 'on campus' from 2000–2002." There is, however, no *context* for these figures, other than they represent aggregate, reported, on-campus incidents over a three-year period. Considerations such as on how many college or university campuses these incidents were reported or how many students were enrolled at these schools were not discussed in the report. As a result, there was no unit of comparison (e.g., the number of reported offenses per 10,000 students nationally) against which one might assess the apparently impressive magnitude of SOC's figures. Retrieved December 4, 2009, http://www.securityoncampus.org.

of the problem is achieved, activists then frame the problem – that is, they work to create an orientation toward the problem that becomes *the* way to understand it. This process of "framing the condition" is important because it is often around a particular orientation that mass media will "wrap" a story and policy makers will tailor their responses.[42]

In framing the problem, activists specify its nature, provide examples of it, and indicate how the problem can be addressed. Activists do this to bring the public's way of thinking about the problem in line with their own. SOC and the Clerys thus framed the new problem of campus violence as one in which innocent students were being victimized because the students were not aware of the unsafe and dangerous places that college campuses had become, and because campus administrators denied crime information to the public in an effort to protect the college's or university's image. According to SOC, the solution was legislation at the state and federal level that would *force* postsecondary institutions to routinely and publicly release their campus crime statistics, because college administrators were apparently unwilling to do so on their own.

SOC's framework is perhaps best illustrated by testimony given in 1997 by Benjamin Clery, Jeanne Ann Clery's older brother, before the House Education and Workforce Subcommittee on Postsecondary Education, Training, and Life-Long Learning:

> The reality of violent crimes and property crimes at our nation's colleges and universities is alarming, and administrative tactics to distort campus crime statistics is scandalous…[when crime] is a common problem plaguing campuses across the nation…. Many college campuses in suburban and rural areas are the high crime neighborhoods in their communities, contrary to public relations spins that school administrators derive from their corrupted crime statistics. Homicides, whether murder or manslaughter, are no longer "aberrations" on the college scene…. For the sake of law-abiding students and the entire campus community, I implore members of the committee to work toward bipartisan passage of the *Accuracy in Campus Crime Reporting Act* (HR715).[43]

---

[42] Best, *Random Violence*, pp. 177–178.
[43] Testimony of Benjamin Clery, 1997.

Media reports of campus violence followed along these lines as well, first describing the magnitude of the problem, providing examples of it, and then suggesting how the problem might be solved. A classic illustration of how media followed the SOC framework is seen in this 1990 story that appeared in *USA Today*:

> Every 2 hours and 12 minutes, seven days a week, a violent crime pierces the quiet at the nation's college campuses. A freshman at Montana State University picks up a shotgun and kills two fellow students in May. At Alabama A&M University in Huntsville (AL) in July, an argument at a dance erupts in gunfire and a young man dies. At the University of Oklahoma days later, an engineering student walking across an isolated stretch of campus is stabbed; police arrest a 15 year-old boy. A *USA Today* investigation shows knifings, rapes and even murder are part of the college experience.... Colleges are under pressure ... to do a better job of warning students [while] court cases, too, are pressuring colleges to warn and protect [students].[44]

The particular story thus describes the apparent magnitude of the problem and provides emotionally charged yet effectively moving examples. The story also suggests how the problem might be successfully addressed – putting legislative (Congress) and judicial (the courts) pressure on postsecondary institutions to do a better job of warning students about how violent and unsafe college campuses are. According to SOC, this pressure would result in students becoming more aware of their risks of victimization, while schools would implement necessary security to reduce the level of such victimizations occurring at postsecondary institutions.

Legitimizing and Institutionalizing the Problem

Getting the public to *recognize* the new social problem is not enough for it to rise to the level of a new social problem. Activists must also work to acquire large-scale social endorsements or *legitimization* of their claims.[45] To do so, claimsmakers encourage experts, victims or their families, or government agencies to come forward and agree there is a problem about which the public should be concerned and about which something must be done. Once the problem is acknowledged,

---

[44] Kalette, "Campus Crime Fighters."
[45] Best, *Random Violence*.

activists then work toward getting the problem institutionalized – amassing public support for their claims through contributions by mass print and electronic media, the government, other activists, and a variety of so-called experts.

Because SOC had framed the new problem as that of "unsafe and violent college campuses" resulting from college or university administrators caring more about their schools' images than about the safety of their students, getting experts to echo these sentiments would move the problem toward legitimization. In effect, if enough experts, victims or their families, and representatives of government agencies came forward to echo SOC's framing of the problem, SOC could then claim the problem was legitimate.

To illustrate, consider the following quotes in the 1990s from experts, victims, and representatives of government that echo the framework SOC established for the new problem of violent and unsafe college campuses and uncaring campus administrators. In 1990 Mike Young, director of campus safety at Rollins College, in describing the situation on his campus to the *St. Petersburg Times* admitted that "crime is out there. Bad guys are out there. There are people who are going to steal your stuff, hold you up, do drugs, or whatever. This is the real world."[46] Teresa Awalt, the marketing director for the National Campus Violence Prevention Center at Towson State University, wrote in a letter to the editor of the *New York Times* that parents were becoming more "sensitive" to the issue of campus safety when looking at prospective colleges for their children.[47] Officials with Safe Campuses Now! told the *New York Times* that "crime at rural and suburban campuses was a real and present threat,"[48] while Frank Carrington testified to a congressional subcommittee that postsecondary institutions were "more concerned with protecting their images than with seeing justice done for victims."[49] A story on CNN-Money.com claimed that "trying to determine a college's crime rate

[46] Wire Reports, "Reports Says 5,270 Crimes Were Committed at Colleges Last Year," *St. Petersburg Times*, May 1, 1990, State Digest, p. 4B.
[47] Kimberly McLarin, "Fear Prompts Self-Defense as Crime Comes to College," *New York Times*, September 7, 1994, sec. A, p. 1.
[48] Sandi Turner and Nancy Zecella, "Campus Areas Act as Magnet for Crime," *New York Times*, August 24, 1995, Editorial Desk, sec. A, p. 22.
[49] Carter and Bath, "The Evolution and Components of the *Jeanne Clery Act*," p. 35.

has been almost impossible"[50] because postsecondary institutions are not "coming clean" with their crime statistics. Victims also appeared in media stories about violent and unsafe campuses. In 1997 Christy Brzonkala claimed to have been repeatedly raped by two student athletes during her first two weeks on campus at Virginia Tech and that institutional officials did nothing in response to her complaint; she ultimately sued Virginia Tech for her victimization.[51] Finally, Congressman William Goodling (R-PA) told the *Washington Times* in a letter to the editor that many students arrive at college "naïve about the dangers" posed by unsafe and violent college campuses.[52]

In each of these quotations, credentialed experts and legitimate victims repeated the SOC framework by declaring that college campuses were unsafe and violent, that college or university administrators did not care about the security of their students, and that steps had to be taken to force postsecondary institutions to cooperate so that student and parental awareness about the dangers faced on college campuses was raised. Once awareness was raised, lives could potentially be saved, because students (and their parents) would know the risks they faced.

SOC activists and media also helped institutionalize the claims surrounding the problem of violent and unsafe college campuses by continuing to typify disparate incidents of campus violence as routine, serious, and the result of college or university administrators failing to take necessary preventive steps. Reporters used compelling descriptive terms in presenting claims about unsafe and violent campuses, as shown in the following storylines:

- "Open the books on campus crime" (inferring that existing law enforcement records or logs had not been "opened" to the public)[53]

---

[50] Marlys Harris, "For Too Many Students Today, the College Experience May Include Crime, Bigotry, and Political Controversy in the Classroom" (1991), retrieved November 1, 2008, http://money.cnn.com/magazines/moneymag/moneymag_archive/1991/09/10/86827/ index.html.

[51] Debbie Goldberg, "Crime on Campus: How Safe Are Students?" *Washington Post*, April 6, 1997, Education Review Section, p. RO1.

[52] Bill Goodling, "Editorial Was Irresponsible and Flat Wrong," *Washington Times*, September 14, 1991, Commentary, Editorial, Letters Section, p. D2.

[53] Editorial, "Open the Books on Campus Crime," *USA Today*, November 13, 1989, p. 10A. See also Kevin Teasley, "Open Books Won't Stop Campus Crime," *USA Today*, November 13, 1989, p. 10A.

- "Crime on campus: how safe are students?" (inferring there is a legitimate question about just how safe are college students while on campus)[54]
- "The campus crime wave" (inferring that crime on campus has increased to the point it has now peaked into a "wave" of violence)[55]
- "Guns of academe: officer's plea to bear arms stirs anger at 2 colleges" (inferring the situation on campus had become so bad that security officers felt the need to be armed)[56]
- "Violence increases on nation's college campuses" (a straightforward claim that campus violence had increased)[57]

Thus, SOC strategically used electronic and print media to help frame the problem such that journalists' reports about campus violence echoed SOC's claims, including claims that crime statistics were not available to the public or to the parents of current or prospective students.

Constructing an Ideology

In chronicling SOC's activities during the 1980s and 1990s, one finds SOC representatives were always careful to emphasize that they were concerned about *college student* victimization, rather than about the victimization of *young adults* who happened to be attending college. This difference is subtle but important. By emphasizing their concern was for *students*, the Clerys and SOC planted an image in the public's mind – that of innocent young people attending college to learn what was necessary to join the world of work and experience the joys that should define their "college years." Violent victimization was not supposed to be on the agenda, yet, because of institutional apathy (if not outright negligence), students were being put at high risk for experiencing violent victimization. As Connie Clery described the situation

---

[54] Goldberg, "Crime on Campus."

[55] Anne Matthews, "The Campus Crime Wave," *New York Times*, March 7, 1993, sec. 6, p. 38.

[56] Norimitsu Onishi, "Guns of Academe: Officers' Plea to Bear Arms Stirs Anger at 2 Colleges," *New York Times*, April 30, 1995, sec. 13NJ, p. 6.

[57] Rick Kerr, "Violence Increases on Nations' College Campuses," NPR, *Morning Edition*, October 24, 1996.

in a 1997 interview with CBS News, "It's been 10 years [since the death of my daughter]. Do you think I'm not tired of it? But we lost our daughter. There is nothing worse in the world than to lose a child. *And I don't want anyone else being victimized, having their lives ruined, if I can help it."*[58] In their interviews, press releases and press conferences, and in testimony before various state legislative and congressional committees, the Clerys and their SOC representatives carefully constructed an ideology that framed the issue of unsafe, violent campuses in very specific terms: innocent student victims were effectively being "led to slaughter" because "evil" postsecondary institutional administrators callously disregarded what they knew was happening, vis-à-vis campus violence. Institutional callousness toward students, in turn, directly contributed to large numbers of those students each year being murdered or injured in violent on-campus victimizations.

SOC thus framed the problem not as increases in interpersonal violence among students or of random violence that was suddenly affecting college students or that urban violence had swept onto campus. Although these themes were occasionally interwoven into interviews with SOC representatives or in legislative testimony, the consistent message from SOC was this: the new evil offenders in all this violence were *not* the actual perpetrators but were instead college or university administrators who seemingly cared more about their schools' marketing image than about the safety of their students.

Figure 1 depicts the cycle of unsafe and violent campuses according to SOC's claims. College campuses are unsafe and violent places because of uncaring institutions and a lack of regulatory oversight by government agencies (e.g., the U.S. Department of Education) or through legislative mandates. After students are murdered, raped, or assaulted on campus, institutional coverups and other activities ensue to prevent information about these violent acts from reaching the public. These events in turn lead to still more violent and unsafe campuses, with the cycle then repeating itself at institutions of higher learning across the United States.

SOC argued that, by "raising public awareness" about unsafe and violent college campuses, students and their parents would then take the

[58] Braver, "Campus Crime" (emphasis added).

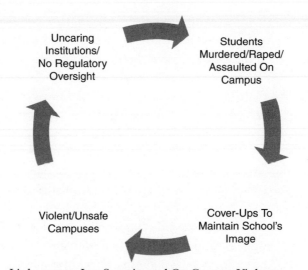

Figure 1. Links among Lax Security and On-Campus Violence.

necessary steps and *demand* crime information from colleges and universities. They would also pressure the federal government to demand accountability from college or university administrators. Regulations forcing these administrators to publicize their crime statistics and security policies would reduce the level of apathy by administrators to the plight of students and their safety, which would reduce efforts to cover up the problem and would ultimately result in reductions to the incidence of on-campus violence. Pressing for government intervention into how colleges and universities were addressing the problem of unsafe and violent college campuses was a key legacy of the Clerys and SOC.[59]

Influencing Public Policy

One of the goals of activists who construct new social problems is to facilitate change in how institutions – whether the legal system, educational institutions, or government agencies – respond to the problem and its victims.[60] Often activists recommend large-scale policy responses aimed at alleviating the problem. SOC and the Clerys,

---

[59] Chapter 7 examines SOC's legacy in the social construction of campus crime as a new social problem.

[60] Best, *Random Violence*, pp. 121–122.

for example, were instrumental in getting no less than six federal laws passed that directly changed how postsecondary institutions addressed the problem of unsafe and violent campuses and how schools assisted the needs of the victims of campus violence.

The **Student Right-to-Know and Campus Security Act of 1990.** Almost from the day of its founding, SOC began pressuring state and federal lawmakers to pass new legislation that would force postsecondary institutions to release their campus crime statistics. By the late 1980s, SOC and the Clerys had successfully pressured at least four states, beginning with their home state of Pennsylvania,[61] into passing campus crime laws that generally required colleges and universities to annually make their crime statistics available to the public.

Once their efforts bore fruit at state levels of government, SOC then directed considerable lobbying efforts toward Congress, pressing for *federal* legislation that addressed the problem of unsafe and violent campuses and institutional reluctance to collect and publish campus crime statistics. Indeed, Connie Clery once said, "I knew I wouldn't live long enough to get legislation passed in every state, so I decided to start working for a federal law."[62] Their efforts included multiple appearances on Capitol Hill where they, along with Frank Carrington, testified before Congressional committees or subcommittees. Before these committees, they spoke passionately about how violent and unsafe college campuses were and about campus administrators' lack of concern over student safety and security.[63]

Finally, in 1990 the Clerys' and SOC's efforts were rewarded when Congress passed and President George H. W. Bush signed into law the

---

[61] *College and University Security Information Act* (24 P.S. §§ 2502–1–2502–5). These statutes are not without critics. See Bonnie S. Fisher, Jennifer Hartman, Francis T. Cullen, and Michael Turner, "Making Campuses Safer for Students: The *Clery Act* as Symbolic Legal Reform," *Stetson Law Review* 31 (1, 2002): 61–91. See also Magnus Seng, "The *Crime Awareness and Campus Security Act*: Some Observations, Critical Comments, and Suggestions," pp. 38–42 in Bonnie S. Fisher and John J. Sloan III (Eds.), *Campus Crime: Legal, Social, and Policy Perspectives* (Springfield, IL: Charles C. Thomas, 1995); and John J. Sloan and Jessica M. Shoemaker, "State-Level Campus Crime Initiatives: Symbolic Politics or Substantive Policy?" pp. 102–121 in Fisher and Sloan, *Campus Crime*, 2nd ed. (2007).

[62] Carter and Bath, "The Evolution and Components of the *Jeanne Clery Act*," p. 29.

[63] Retrieved October 20, 2008, http://www.securityoncampus.org/congress/0314 1990.html.

Student Right-To-Know and Campus Security Act.[64] Title II of the *Campus Security Act* required that all postsecondary institutions eligible to participate in federal financial aid programs under Title IV of the *Higher Education Act of 1965* had to make available to the public an annual report that included not only statistics on reported crimes occurring at the school but a description of the each institution's security policies.

Beginning September 1, 1991, all Title IV–eligible institutions would compile crime statistics and security policies, which would then be published annually in the form of a campus security report. The initial reports were supposed to be issued on September 1, 1992 and each year thereafter. This annual security report, available to all current and prospective students and employees, was required to include descriptions of a variety of institutional policies relating to the reporting of crimes and other emergencies on campus, access to campus facilities, campus law enforcement authority, and crime prevention programs. The report also had to include statistical counts of reported on-campus murders, forcible rapes, robberies, aggravated assaults, burglaries, and automobile thefts for the preceding three years. Institutions were also required to include in the report statistical counts on the number of arrests for on-campus liquor law violations, drug abuse violations, and weapons possessions. The report would also certify that the institution had an established campus security policy. Failure to comply with the reporting requirements could result in civil penalties of $27,500 per infraction imposed by the U.S. Department of Education and possible loss of eligibility to receive federal financial aid funds should the violations be serious enough. As one researcher noted,

> [The legislation's] primary objective was to require postsecondary educational institutions...to report crime statistics and security procedures to the [U.S.] Department of Education. Such reports were to receive widespread distribution to the campus community and

---

[64] *Student Right-to-Know and Campus Security Act of 1990*, 20 USC 1092. In 1998, Congress amended the law to change its title to the *Jeanne Clery Disclosure of Campus Security Policy and Campus Crimes Statistics Act of 1998* in memory of Ms. Clery and to pay homage to the Clerys for their public interest work on behalf of college students and their families.

to prospective students and employees. The Act was heralded as a significant step toward addressing the problem of crime on our nation's college campuses.[65]

The assumption by SOC and Congress was that by *requiring* postsecondary institutions to gather and disseminate crime and security information, awareness of campus crime and security among students' and employees' – current and prospective – would be enhanced. Students and employees would then take appropriate steps to help reduce their risk of becoming victims while on campus. SOC and Congress also assumed that the sanctions that could be imposed, beyond those associated with negative publicity for noncompliance, would help to ensure institutional compliance.

Expanding the **Campus Security Act.** Efforts by SOC and the Clerys did not stop with passage of the original *Campus Security Act* in 1990.[66] During the next ten years, the Clerys and SOC were able to greatly expand federal law relating to unsafe and violent campuses and campus security:[67]

- SOC helped procure clarification in 1992 that campus police and security records about crimes involving student perpetrators should *not* be shielded as "confidential student educational records" protected under the *Federal Educational Right to Privacy Act* – the so-called Buckley Amendment – to the *Higher Education Act of 1965*.
- SOC was influential in convincing Congress to pass a 1992 amendment to the *Campus Security Act* called the *Campus Sexual Assault Victims' Bill of Rights* requiring colleges and universities to implement policies that guaranteed certain basic rights for all sexual

---

[65] Seng, "The *Crime Awareness and Campus Security Act*," p. 38.
[66] Carter and Bath, "The Evolution and Components of the *Jeanne Clery Act*." See also a history of the *Clery Act* at the Security On Campus, Inc., Web site. Retrieved September 8, 2008, http://www.securityoncampus.org/congress/cleryhistory.html.
[67] In total, SOC was either peripherally or directly involved with helping pass nearly a dozen bills relating to campus crime statistics, campus security policies, campus crime victims' rights, and related issues that were introduced in nearly every Congress between the 101st in 1990 and the 110th in 2008. A complete list of these bills, their sponsors, and related documents is available at the Security On Campus, Inc., Web site. Retrieved October 20, 2008, http://www.securityoncampus.org/congress/index.html.

assault survivors and expanded the scope of statistics that had to be
reported by colleges to include forcible (such as rape) and nonforc-
ible (such as incest) sex offenses.[68]

- SOC also helped obtain a 1998 amendment to the *Campus Security
  Act* clarifying that the Buckley Amendment does not prohibit public dissemination of the results of disciplinary action taken by a college or university against a student accused of a crime.

- In 1998 Congress amended the legislation and renamed the
  Campus Security Act as the *Jeanne Clery Disclosure of Campus Security
  Policy and Campus Crimes Statistics Act of 1998* (the *Clery Act*). The
  Clery Act expanded the original crime reporting requirements of
  the *Campus Security Act* to include identification of geographic areas
  where reported crimes occurred on campus (including residence
  halls), in certain noncampus buildings, and in public places; additional offenses; and the requirement that campus policy or security
  create daily crime logs and make them available on demand.[69]

- In 2000 an amendment called the *Campus Sex Crimes Prevention Act*
  was added to the *Clery Act* that required postsecondary institutions
  to collect and disclose information about the number of convicted
  sex offenders who are enrolled, employed by, or volunteering at the
  college or university.

SOC's efforts continued into the first decade of the new century as
well. For example, in 2005 SOC helped persuade Congress to desig-
nate the month of September as "National Campus Safety Awareness
Month." SOC would play an active role in this event, as it was responsible for facilitating the development of "display banners, promotional

---

[68] Frank Carrington apparently played a key role in this legislation. On a flight to
Washington, DC, Carrington was reading an early draft of the bill he had completed and which he was going to share with the Pennsylvania delegation to the
House of Representatives for introduction during that session of Congress. Sitting
next to him on the plane was Rep. Jim Ramstad (R-MN), who asked Carrington
what he was reading. When Carrington told him and shared the document with
him, Ramstad became interested in the bill and ultimately worked with Carrington
and Representative Susan Molinari (R-NY) to get the legislation passed. See Carter
and Bath, "The Evolution and Components of the *Jeanne Clery Act*," pp. 35–36.

[69] In 1999 U.S. Department of Education compliance regulations adjusted the reporting deadline to October 1 of each year beginning with the reports due in 2000.
The intent behind the change was to allow institutions the time to finalize their fall
enrollment figures. Personal communication with S. Daniel Carter, Security On
Campus, Inc., April 25, 2010.

posters, and materials throughout the campuses."[70] SOC also created a "Campus Security Awareness Month" Web site that provided interested consumers with easily accessible information on such topics as sexual assault prevention, alcohol abuse, hate crimes, and hazing.[71] In 2006 SOC received a grant from the U.S. Department of Justice to offer comprehensive *Clery Act* training for representatives of postsecondary institutions desiring to learn more about the *Clery Act*'s reporting requirements and its provisions for victims' rights.[72] Finally, in 2008, SOC successfully lobbied for legislation that amended the "timely warning" requirements of the *Clery Act* to now require that colleges and universities provide "timely warnings" to the campus community via electronic communication, such as email, or a prerecorded telephone message that would be sent within 30 minutes of a "critical incident" occurring on campus that was deemed by campus officials to pose a significant threat to campus safety or security.[73]

All of these activities highlight and underscore the influence SOC and the Clerys had on legislative responses to the new problem of unsafe and violent college campuses. After repeatedly and successfully lobbying state legislatures, SOC and the Clerys pressed Congress to respond with federal legislation to force postsecondary institutions to do something about violent and unsafe campuses. Those efforts resulted in passage of landmark federal legislation directed at forcing colleges and universities to make public the extent and nature of violence and other crimes on their campuses. Continuing efforts by SOC

---

[70] Jonathan Kassa, "Security on Campus: Our Mission Is Safer Campuses for Students," pp. 191–194 in Michelle Paludi (Ed.), *Understanding and Preventing Campus Violence* (Westport, CT: Praeger, 2008). Noteworthy was a 2008 Resolution passed by the House of Representatives (H.R. 1288) supporting the goals of National Campus Safety Awareness Month, which specifically mentioned SOC's role in promoting safety awareness programming at colleges and universities nationwide: "Whereas each September since 2005, *SOC has partnered with colleges and universities across the United States to offer National Campus Safety Awareness Month educational programming* on sexual assault, alcohol and other drug abuse, hazing, stalking, and other critical campus safety issues..." (emphasis added). Retrieved October 20, 2008, http://www.campusafetymonth.org.

[71] Kassa, "Security on Campus," p. 191. See http://www.campusafetymonth.org for information on Campus Safety Month, retrieved September 22, 2008.

[72] http://www.securityoncampus.org, retrieved November 1, 2008.

[73] Security On Campus, Inc. press release, April 23, 2008. Available at http://www.securityoncampus.org/reporters/releases/0423_2008.html. Retrieved September 25, 2008.

ultimately resulted in additional legislation that included other areas, such as victims' rights, the presence of sex offenders on campus, and timely warnings for on-campus emergencies. SOC also partnered with the U.S. Department of Justice to train college and university administrators in complying with federal legislation. Finally, SOC created consumer-friendly and easily accessible information about violent and unsafe campuses at their Web site, which also included links to additional information.

Since the late 1980s, Security On Campus, Inc., played a pivotal role in constructing the new social problem of campus crime by engaging in a variety of activities outlined by the theoretical framework discussed in Chapter 2. The group – particularly its cofounders Connie and Howard Clery, along with its chief legal counsel, Frank Carrington – used the tragic rape and murder of the Clery's daughter in her dormitory room at Lehigh University in 1986 as the launching point to bring to the public's attention the new problem of unsafe and violent college campuses and to argue that college or university administrators cared more about the image of their schools than about the safety of their students.

Over the course of its long crusade, SOC has succeeded in naming the problem and taking ownership of it. As grieving parents, the Clerys could certainly claim ownership of the problem of campus violence. That their daughter had been a victim gave them credibility, which became enhanced when other parents, victims, and campus law enforcement professionals joined "the cause." The Clerys and representatives of SOC spent at least a decade making significant claims about the problem of unsafe and violent college campuses, while continually expanding and elaborating the problem's domain. Their claims were then carried by numerous electronic and print media outlets, which communicated to the public an emotionally charged perspective that helped legitimize and ultimately institutionalize the problem. SOC wove its claims into an ideology about the problem, which was fed to the mass media. As a result, that ideology became *the* way not only to frame discussion about the problem but to address the need to include compassion for student victims and disdain for college or university administrators.

Through its lobbying efforts, SOC was able to significantly influence policy makers, including Congress, to "do something" about the problem. SOC and the Clerys helped influence Congress to pass landmark legislation, the *Student Right-to-Know and Campus Security Act of 1990*, which, for the first time, required colleges and universities to publicly report their crime statistics and campus security policies. Subsequently, SOC was able to influence Congress to pass various amendments to the original legislation, which resulted not only in renaming the legislation to honor the memory of the Clerys' murdered daughter but in expanding the scope of the original legislation.

CONCLUSION

The claims made and the ideology constructed by SOC and the Clerys were interesting for several reasons. First, the tragic death of the Clery's daughter put a face on the violence and lack of security that SOC claimed was "the normal state of affairs" at American postsecondary institutions. That the Clerys often appeared in television interviews, attended professional conferences of campus law enforcement professionals, or spoke before congressional committees allowed *them* to also become the face of campus violence – that of the grieving parents, who knew all too well the devastating effects on the families of students who fell prey to unsafe and violent campuses.

Additionally, the claims made by SOC and the Clerys focused not on the actual perpetrators of the violence – the people who were murdering and raping college students – but on postsecondary institutional administrators, the "new villains" who not only were lax in their security efforts but also turned a blind eye toward the reality about how unsafe and violent their campuses were. This was something of an ironic turn because usually when new villains are associated with a new form of crime, they typically are the actual perpetrators of the behavior and not third parties whose omissions allowed the behavior to occur.

Further, in their claims SOC and the Clerys always focused on the problem of the victimization of college *students*, which is much different from saying the problem involved the victimization of *young adults*. By focusing on *students*, SOC created a particular image that, by default, cried out that the victims were innocent (after all, how could *students* be guilty of contributing to their own victimization?). Additionally, the claims that were made typically failed to include a context, such as a victimization rate per some unit of population, or

fell victim to statistical fallacies, such as suggesting that crime on campus followed particular temporal or spatial patterns on the basis of a
limited number of incidents. The claims did, however, effectively tie
together disparate events occurring, in some instances, thousands of
miles apart and making them seem the norm at colleges and universities. By claiming "big numbers" regarding victimizations on campus
(e.g., "a student murdered on campus every ten days") as the *norm*
but failing to include contextual details surrounding the incidents
described, SOC and the Clerys were able to successfully co-opt the
prospective targets of the problem: the millions of parents who,
each year, unknowingly were sending their children "to their doom"
because campus administrators cared more about the image of their
institutions than about the safety of their students.

Finally, SOC and the Clerys have evidenced a remarkable and long-
running influence on policy responses to campus crime, particularly
by Congress. SOC and the Clerys were able to influence nearly a dozen
bills considered by the House and Senate that addressed unsafe and
violent college campuses and eventually helped ensure passage of no
less than a half-dozen pieces of federal legislation, including the landmark *Student Right-to-Know and Campus Security Act of 1990*. They also
persuaded Congress to declare that September of each year would
be National Campus Security Awareness Month and received funding
to sponsor training for college or university administrators to help
ensure compliance with federal campus crime laws. Further, beginning with their home state of Pennsylvania, and then moving to other
states including Tennessee and California, they influenced state-level
legislative initiatives to address the problem.[74]

SOC's activities throughout the late 1980s and into the 1990s
show that its actions and strategies suitably fit the theoretical model
described in Chapter 2 on how new social problems come to be socially
constructed. Its momentum to keep campus crime in the public spotlight has continued to the present with no evidence of waning. SOC
will likely continue to be an active player in the social construction of
campus crime for some time to come.

---

[74] As of June 2007, some 30 states had passed "campus crime" legislation. See Sloan
and Shoemaker, "State-Level Campus Crime Initiatives."

CHAPTER FOUR

Constructing the Sexual Victimization
of College Women on Campus

Until the 1980s, most people assumed that college campuses were a safe environment for women. The little concern that existed for women's safety on campus was limited to stranger rapes, although these are relatively rare compared to women's victimization by men they know.[1]

Sadly, the sexual victimization of college women on campus is nothing new.[2] The stereotypical lecherous professor not only has been parodied in the arts but has become symbolic of how some members of the academy exploit their positions to garner sexual favors from students.[3] Beyond suffering sexual harassment from their professors, college women also experience various forms of sexual harassment from their peers as well.[4] Further, empirical evidence reveals that sexual assaults of college women by college men – including coercive fondling and

---

[1] Joanne Belknap and Edna Erez, "Violence against Women on College Campuses," pp. 188–109 in Bonnie S. Fisher and John J. Sloan III (Eds.), *Campus Crime: Legal, Social, and Policy Perspectives*, 2nd ed. (Springfield, IL: Charles C. Thomas, 2007).

[2] While this chapter focuses on the sexual victimization of college women as a component of the social construction of campus crime as a new social problem, college men also experience such victimization. Little scholarly or media attention has been paid to this issue, however. See Richard Tewksbury and Elizabeth Erhardt Mustaine, "Lifestyle Factors Associated with the Sexual Victimization of Men: A Routine Activity Theory Analysis," *Journal of Men's Studies* 9 (2001): 153–182.

[3] Billie Wright Dzeich and Linda Weiner, *The Lecherous Professor: Sexual Harassment on Campus*, 2nd ed. (Champaign: University of Illinois Press, 1990). But see also, Jane Gallup, *Anecdotal Theory* (Durham, NC: Duke University Press, 2002), for an interesting critique of the perspective used by Dzeich and Weiner.

[4] According to reports, "half of male students and almost one-third of female students admit that they sexually harassed someone in college, and about one-fifth of male students admit that they harassed someone often or occasionally." Susan Dyer, *Drawing the Line: Sexual Harassment on Campus* (Washington, DC: American Association of University Women, 2006), p. 4.

rape – also occur with some frequency on college campuses.[5] Only since the 1980s, however, has discourse about the sexual victimization of college women on campus changed, resulting not only in new orientations toward the issue but in policies aimed at both preventing it and responding to such behavior when it occurs.[6]

To understand how the construction of campus crime as a new social problem occurred during the late 1980s and into the 1990s, we now look at a second group of claimsmakers, campus feminists, outraged over what they saw as "epidemic levels" of sexual victimization experienced on campus by female students throughout their collegiate years.[7] Campus feminists claimed that young women enrolled at postsecondary institutions and hoping to obtain educational and economic equality were experiencing neither. Instead, they were being subjected not only to the physical and emotional horrors of being raped or sexually assaulted by dates and acquaintances (primarily college men) but also to the horror of having college or university administrators disbelieve, discredit, or attempt to silence them in an effort to preserve the public images of their colleges and universities. Just as Security On Campus, Inc., constructed the new problem of unsafe and violent college campuses by claiming that on-campus violence was rampant, that college or university administrators *knew* this but failed to take appropriate steps to address the problem, and that

---

5 Hester Lacey, "I Gave It a Name," *Independent* (London), October 31, 1993, Home News Page, p. 9. The story quotes Mary Koss, widely credited for creating the terms "date" and "acquaintance" rape, as saying "date rape has probably been around as far back as you want to trace human history. It was an insult that had no name."

6 Deborah Rhode, "Social Research and Social Change: Meeting the Challenge of Gender Inequality and Sexual Abuse," *Harvard Journal of Law & Gender* 30 (2007): 11–23; Sherry Young, "Getting to 'Yes': The Case against Banning Consensual Relationships in Higher Education," *American University Journal of Gender & the Law* 4 (1996): 269–304; and Carol Bohmer and Andrea Parrot, *Sexual Assault on Campus: The Problem and the Solution* (New York: Lexington Books, 1993).

7 Many of these women have been identified as members of the "second wave" of feminism and used college or university campuses as their base of operations during the 1980s and 1990s. For discussion of the "second wave" of feminism, see Michelle Fine, *Disruptive Voices: The Possibilities of Feminist Research* (Ann Arbor: University of Michigan Press, 1992); Becky Thompson, "Multiracial Feminism: Recasting the Chronology of Second Wave Feminism," *Feminist Studies* 28 (2002): 337–360; or Amanda Whelehan, *Modern Feminist Thought: From the Second Wave to "Post-Feminism"* (Edinburgh: Edinburgh University Press, 1995).

they also failed to adequately address the needs of victims, campus feminists, concerned with the sexual victimization of college women, likewise focused their attention on three fronts.

First, they helped to socially construct a new type of rape – what is now known as date and acquaintance rape – which involved offenders known to their victims and which, according to claimsmakers, was *routinely* occurring in campus dormitories or at campus social settings, such as fraternity parties.[8] In essence, campus feminists were reconceptualizing rape as involving not only strangers but people known to one another, a notion that *dramatically* challenged existing ideas about who perpetrated rape. Campus feminists claimed that most people believed a rape could be perpetrated *only* by a stranger, who typically either attacked the victim in a secluded public place or broke into the victim's residence and forced her to have sexual intercourse with him.[9] This group of claimsmakers sought to turn that notion on its head by claiming that rape involving dates and social acquaintances not only existed on college campuses but had reached epidemic levels, and *they had the data to prove it*. Second, they also claimed public "misconceptions" about rape were widespread, labeled them as "rape myths," tied them to the patriarchal organization of society more generally, and presented data showing that these beliefs were incorrect.[10] Third, campus feminists claimed that college or university administrators, again in the interests of protecting the institutions'

[8] While there are subtle differences between date and acquaintance rape, both involve forced or coerced sexual intercourse with the victim without her consent that is perpetrated by an offender known to her. In the case of date rape, the victimization usually occurs either during or at the end of the date, while in the latter instance, the rape typically occurs in a social setting, such as during a fraternity party.

[9] What is interesting here is that *legal* definitions of rape at the time did *not* mention the relationship between victim and offender as being of any importance. Most definitions of rape focused on the following elements: there was sexual intercourse with the victim by the offender, the intercourse was accomplished by the use or threatened use of force, and the victim did not give consent.

[10] For discussion of cultural rape myths, see, for example, Bettina Frese, Miguel Moya, and Jesus L. Megias, "Social Perception of Rape: How Rape Myth Acceptance Modulates the Influence of Situational Factors," *Journal of Interpersonal Violence* 19 (2004): 143–161; Christine M. Chapleau, Debra L. Oswald, and Brenda L. Russell, "How Ambivalent Sexism toward Women and Men Support Rape Myth Acceptance," *Sex Roles* 57 (2007): 131–136; and Susan Brownmiller, *Against Our Will: Men, Women, and Rape* (New York: Simon and Schuster, 1975).

public image, had failed their female students on three fronts. They had failed to acknowledge the scope of the date and acquaintance rape problem on their campuses, to take necessary steps to help prevent these assaults from occurring, and to appropriately respond to the needs of the victims of this new problem.[11] In particular, administrators were singled out for failing to "adequately" punish student perpetrators of these assaults, particularly when the alleged offenders were also student-athletes or members of campus fraternities.

In this chapter, we show how, during the late 1980s and through the 1990s, campus feminists came forward and engaged in a variety of activities that involved identifying and taking ownership of the problem of date and acquaintance rape occurring on American college and university campuses. To establish a new orientation, they claimed that rape was no longer solely perpetrated by strangers; rather, rape now included coerced sexual intercourse occurring between two people *known to one another*, notwithstanding long-held beliefs to the contrary. Further, though known to their victims, these men were *rapists* and should be punished – despite the fact that many were fellow students.

Campus feminists legitimized, institutionalized, and drew upon cultural resources to move the public to *demand* that policy makers – both legislators and those occupying postsecondary administrative positions – address the problem of date and acquaintance rape on college campuses. They also helped to shape the contours of those responses. Finally, through informal alliances with like-minded advocacy groups such as SOC, campus feminists brought to the public's attention the plight that college women faced as the victims of date and acquaintance rapes occurring on campus. Just as SOC had done, feminists demanded that college administrators undertake better efforts to prevent and respond to campus-based date and acquaintance rape victimizations, even if it meant that victims had to sue postsecondary institutions and ask the courts to force school administrators to do so.

---

[11] In Chapter 5, we discuss how some date and acquaintance rape victims sued post-secondary institutions for negligence relating to their victimization, and a few collected significant damage awards from the schools. This group of victims also made a significant contribution to the social construction of campus crime.

The combined efforts of this second group of claimsmakers not only resulted in federal legislation being passed that focused on the on-campus sexual victimization of college women but changed how postsecondary institutions responded to the problem. Through their actions, campus feminists were thus able to construct a new problem – date and acquaintance rape of college women – and to shape policy responses to it. Their contributions, along with those of SOC, ultimately contributed to the social construction of campus crime as a new social problem.

THE SOCIAL CONSTRUCTION OF CAMPUS DATE AND ACQUAINTANCE RAPE

For decades, feminist scholars have generally argued that the sexual victimization of women, including rape, sexual harassment, and intimate partner violence, was a by-product of society's being organized along patriarchal lines.[12] As a result, various forms of "violence against women" were widespread and touched the lives of *almost every woman* in some way, whether at school (sexual harassment, rape, other forms of sexual assault),[13] in the workplace (sexual harassment), in social settings (rape, other forms of sexual assault), or at home with intimates (intimate partner violence, marital rape, other forms of sexual assault).[14]

Feminist activists argued that one subpopulation facing a particularly high risk of experiencing sexual victimization, especially rape, was college women.[15] Their reasoning focused on opportunity: college

[12] Examples include Diana E. H. Russell, *Sexual Exploitation: Rape, Child Sexual Abuse, and Workplace Harassment* (New York: New York University Press, 1984); Pauline Bart and Eileen Moran (Eds.), *Violence against Women: The Bloody Footprints* (Thousand Oaks, CA: Sage, 1993).

[13] For our purposes, *sexual assault* is a general category of behavior that includes nonconsensual, coerced sexual intercourse or other penetration of oral or anal cavities; nonconsensual sexual contact, such as fondling of the genitals or breasts; or noncoercive sexual behavior, such as men exposing themselves to women.

[14] Marie Leidig, "The Continuum of Violence against Women: Psychological and Physical Consequences," *Journal of American College Health* 40 (1992): 149–155.

[15] Bonnie S. Fisher, Leah E. Daigle, and Francis T. Cullen, *Unsafe in the Ivory Tower: The Sexual Victimization of College Women* (Thousand Oaks, CA: Sage Publications, 2010).

women had close daily interaction with men (fellow students and faculty members), and these interactions occurred in a range of unsupervised settings on campus, including in faculty offices; in dormitory rooms; and at fraternity parties, a mainstay of the college years. In many of these routine settings, for example, at fraternity parties, alcohol and recreational drugs were both frequently available and abused by partygoers. Feminists made repeated claims that these substances, especially alcohol, when combined with a "party culture" permeating college campuses, increased the risk for college women of experiencing various forms of sexual victimization.[16] The problem campus feminists faced was there was little, if any, empirical support for their claims. As a result, they were largely rhetorical and were fairly ineffective in capturing the attention of either policy makers or the public.[17]

Naming the Problem

In the mid-1980s, two reports emerged about levels of sexual victimization experienced by college women while on campus that ultimately provided campus feminists with the empirical evidence they sought: a 1985 study of rape victimization among college women, funded by *Ms.* magazine; and a report that same year by the Project on the Status and Education of Women on gang rapes occurring on college campuses.

The Ms. Campus Project on Sexual Assault. Funded by a grant from the National Center for the Prevention and Control of Rape, the Ms. Foundation undertook a study of more than 7,000 students at

---

[16] For example, Bonnie S. Fisher, John J. Sloan, Francis T. Cullen, and Chungman Lu, "Crime in the Ivory Tower: The Level and Sources of Student Victimization," *Criminology* 36 (1998): 671–710.

[17] "Ten years ago [in the late 1970s], there was no convincing evidence that acquaintance rape existed, although counselors suspected it." Deidre Carmody, "Increasing Rapes on Campus Spur Colleges to Fight Back," *New York Times*, January 1, 1989, sec. I, National Desk, p. 1. An exception here was the path-breaking empirical work of Diana E. H. Russell who, in the late 1970s, examined the prevalence of rape among a sample of 930 adult women living in San Francisco and "discovered" marital rape. Russell's study not only generated empirical estimates of the scope and nature of rape victimization suffered by sample members but was among the first to use a set of "behaviorally specific questions" relating to rape as part of the interview. See Diana E. H. Russell, "The Prevalence and Incidence of Forcible Rape and Attempted Rape of Females," *Victimology: An International Journal* 7 (1982): 81–93.

35 American colleges and universities to uncover "patterns of sexual aggression at America's institutions of higher learning."[18] The study was under the direction of Mary Koss, a psychology professor at Kent State University, who had previously studied the sexual assault experiences of college women.[19] In October 1985 *Ms.* published a story containing preliminary results of the study.[20] The story reported that Koss had found that *one in four college women had been the victims of a rape or an attempted rape and almost 90 percent of the victims knew their attacker.* The study also reportedly found that 75 percent of the *victims* of rape involving attackers known to them did *not* identify their experience as a rape; that 1 in 8 college women had, using prevailing legal standards, been the victims of rape; and that 1 in 12 college men in the study admitted *they* had engaged in behavior that fit prevailing legal definitions of rape, yet virtually none identified themselves as "rapists."[21] The one-in-four figure quickly and routinely began appearing in media reports about rape on college campuses[22] and became a crucial rallying point for campus feminists, who had argued for years that a large proportion of college women were routinely being sexually victimized on campus.[23]

[18] Ellen Sweet, "Date Rape: The Story of an Epidemic and Those Who Deny It," *Ms. Magazine,* October 1985, pp. 56–61.

[19] In the mid-1980s, Koss developed the "Sexual Experiences Survey" (SES) as a new instrument to study rape and sexual aggression. The survey consisted of a set of behaviorally specific questions relating to a range of sexual experiences, what Koss described as a "continuum of sexual victimization," including "hidden" incidents that, while meeting then current legal definitions of rape, had not been reported to police. Koss argued that using behaviorally specific questions rather than a single item, as had been the norm, allowed interviewers to probe respondents about the types of experiences the respondent had encountered and thus helped broaden the scope of the inquiry. See Mary Koss, "Detecting the Scope of Rape: A Review of Prevalence Research Methods," *Journal of Interpersonal Violence* 8 (1993): 198–222. The original version of the survey – it was subsequently revised – and discussion of it is found in Mary Koss and Christine Gidycz, "The Sexual Experiences Survey: Reliability and Validity," *Journal of Consulting and Clinical Psychology* 53 (1985): 442–443.

[20] Sweet, "Date Rape."

[21] Ibid., p. 58.

[22] We found mention of the one-in-four figure in *at least* 100 different sources retrieved during searches of Lexis-Nexis databases for the period 1986–2000. Space limitations prohibit citing all those sources.

[23] As one can imagine, the one-in-four figure created a great deal of controversy. In particular, criticisms arose of the behavioral definitions and measures used in the studies, which ultimately affected how many rapes were being counted by the

The Project on the Status and Education of Women. In December 1985 the Project on the Status and Education of Women released a report stating that gang rapes on college campuses across the United States were "common." In the report, some 50 instances of gang rape were documented and evidence presented that such incidents were a "large part of the fabric of college life."[24] The *Washington Post* published a story highlighting results of this report, including a description of one of the incidents the study had documented:

> A 17 year-old college freshman was invited to a fraternity party by her girlfriend. She went and had more to drink than she had planned. There was nothing non-alcoholic served at the party; it was hot and crowded. She saw people going upstairs and assumed it was less crowded there. Three men asked her go up with them and she went. They took her into a bedroom and raped her.[25]

The story went on to report that "no one knows how often it [gang rape] occurs" but that the report's authors believed there was "much more of it [occurring] than anyone realized."[26] Finally, the story chronicled how victims were often "blamed" for what happened to them, including having authorities question them about their sex lives and alcohol-using behavior. Similar stories about gang rapes "routinely" occurring on college campuses also appeared in various media stories reporting on the larger issue of rape on college campuses.

researchers. Neil Gilbert was among the first to criticize the original Koss Sexual Experiences Survey and estimates of how many college women were experiencing sexual victimization that were based on its use. For examples of Gilbert's critiques, see Neil Gilbert, "The Phantom Epidemic of Sexual Assault," *Public Interest* 103 (1992): 54–65, and Neil Gilbert, "Miscounting Social Ills," *Society* 31 (1994): 18–27. See also "Debate Rages over Definition of Rape and Date Rape," NPR, *Morning Edition*, September 1, 1993. Gilbert's critiques helped change how rape and sexual aggression were measured in subsequent victimization surveys. For analysis and discussion of the advances that have occurred in measuring the sexual victimization of college women over the past 15 years, see Fisher, Daigle, and Cullen, *Unsafe in the Ivory Tower.*

[24] Julie Ehrhar and Bernice Sandler, *Campus Gang Rape: Party Games?* (Washington, DC: Association of American Colleges, 1985).

[25] Judy Mann, "Campus Gang-Rape Report," *Washington Post*, December 20, 1985, Metro Section, p. B-3. For a more recent discussion of gang rapes on college campuses, see Peggy Sanday, *Fraternity Gang Rape*, 2nd ed. (New York: New York University Press, 2007).

[26] Mann, "Campus Gang-Rape Report."

Making Claims about Campus Date and Acquaintance Rape

Campus feminists quickly used the results from Koss's study as "proof" that sexual violence perpetrated against college women by college men was of epidemic proportions, yet largely hidden from view.[27] The reason the problem was hidden from either campus authorities or local law enforcement officials was because the offenders were people *known* to the victims. Whether because of the proliferation of rape myths or for other reasons, victims either did not *perceive* they had been raped or, when they *did* report what had happened to authorities, failed to establish the validity of their claims to postsecondary or law enforcement officials. This response by authorities resulted in the "revictimization" of these women by the very institutions they believed would help and support them. In short, campus feminists claimed the prevailing wisdom was that a man known to a woman – casually or through a long-term relationship – *could not rape her*. As a result, behavior that otherwise fit common legal definitions of rape, because it had occurred on dates or at campus parties and involved persons known to victims, could not be "real" rape.

Thus began the process of claims making by campus feminists: that one in four college women had been raped by either a date or an acquaintance, and victims (offenders, too) often did not believe that what had happened was "real" rape. According to these claimsmakers, conventional thinking about rape was too narrow because "real" rape was perceived as being limited to forced sex with offenders who were strangers to the victims. For example, in 1990 testimony before the Senate Judiciary Committee's Hearings on Violence against Women, Robin Warshaw described the "prevailing rape myth" in American society:

> For too long, rapes between men and women who know one another have been a hidden phenomenon, *largely because these rapes do not fit our society's idea of what rape really is.* ... The myth imagines rape as the act of a crazed stranger ... who jumps out at his victim on a darkened street, holds a gun to her head, and then rapes her. While rapes fitting that profile do occur, most rapes happen very differently.[28]

---

[27] However, see Gilbert, "The Phantom Epidemic of Sexual Assault," and "Miscounting Social Ills."

[28] Robin Warshaw. Quote from U.S. Congress. Hearing of the Senate Judiciary Committee, "Legislation to Reduce the Growing Problem of Violent Crime

Warshaw further suggested that "the acceptance of acquaintance rape is deeply rooted in our in system of social beliefs about rape and assumptions about sex roles."[29] Susan Estrich echoed this sentiment in her book *Real Rape*: "Many women continue to believe that a man can force you to have sex against your will and this it isn't rape *as long as they know you and don't beat you half to death in the process*."[30] Some members of Congress voiced their agreement with this point. For example, Senator Joseph Biden (D-DE) was quoted by the *Washington Times* as saying, "[It is] a myth that 'real rape' happens only when a man jumps out of the bushes and attacks an unsuspecting victim. In fact, rape by someone the victim knows is 'real rape.'"[31]

Campus feminists claimed that because of prevailing cultural beliefs about rape – rape myths – which both men *and* women had accepted, women forced to have sexual intercourse against their will with men while on dates or in social settings such as parties often did not *perceive* they had *actually been rape victims* because the offender was known to them. Feminists claimed these beliefs were ultimately grounded in a larger rape culture that characterized American society more generally, where rape and other forms of sexual violence against women were supported by prevalent attitudes and social norms.[32] In turn, these attitudes and norms condoned, normalized, and even *encouraged* sexual violence against women in a variety of settings, including on college campuses.[33]

These activists also claimed examples of behaviors typifying this rape culture were legion, including victim blaming in rape cases and the sexual objectification of women in advertising, popular films, and

against Women" (August 29, 1990). Transcript from *Federal Document Clearing House Congressional Testimony*. Available on LexisNexis® Congressional; accessed September 17, 2008 (emphasis added). See also Robin Warshaw, *I Never Called It Rape* (New York: Harper and Row Publishers, [1988] 1994).

29 Warshaw, *I Never Called it Rape*, p. 34.

30 See Susan Estrich, *Real Rape* (Cambridge, MA: Harvard University Press, 1988), p. 4 (emphasis added).

31 Commentary, "Is 'Date Rape' a Fraud?" *Washington Times*, September 5, 1990, sec. G, p. 2.

32 See, for example, Emilie Buchwald, Pamela Fletcher, and Martha Roth (Eds.), *Transforming a Rape Culture*, 2nd ed. (Minneapolis: Milkweed Editions, 2005); Brownmiller, *Against Our Will*.

33 Retrieved October 30, 2008, http://en.wikipedia.org/wiki/Rape_culture.

on television.[34] The Project on the Status and Education of Women report went so far as to suggest the larger rape culture not only had found a home on college and university campuses but was epitomized by the goings-on at fraternities and by the behavior of some student-athletes.[35] Social psychologist Chris O'Sullivan, in a letter to the editor of the *New York Times* described these fraternity activities:

> Such groups of men on campus...have set up the sexual humiliation of women as a positive value, rewarding it with approval. In many fraternities, these values are expressed in a variety of practices, from having ugly-date contests...to arrangements for observing sexual encounters, including peepholes in bedrooms and videotaping setups.[36]

O'Sullivan further complained in the letter that a story the *Times* had run about campus date and acquaintance rape that emphasized "better security" as the primary solution to the problem "promoted an image of [rape] as involving an 'uncouth stranger breaking into a student's room or assaulting her as she walks to her dorm.'"[37] O'Sullivan and campus feminists were thus making the point that "security as the solution" completely ignored the *real* solution to the problem, which was college or university administrators taking appropriate steps to address the campus rape culture.

Within the walls of the ivory tower, male students were quickly becoming identified as likely offenders, and stories chronicling their involvement in campus rapes became national news. For example, at Brown University in 1990 more than 30 male students were identified *by name* as "date rapists" in graffiti that were repeatedly scrawled on the walls of the women's restroom at the university library.[38] In 1993 a

[34] Ibid.
[35] Ben Macintyre, "American Universities Send Fraternities to the Doghouse," *Times* (London), August 30, 1994.
[36] See Chris O'Sullivan, "Campus Rape Is Usually Fraternity-Related," *New York Times*, December 5, 1990, sec. A, p. 26; and Anthony Flint, "Lawsuits New Weapon against Campus Rape," *Boston Globe*, September 25, 1989, National/Foreign, p. 1.
[37] Chris O'Sullivan, "Stop Blaming Victims in Campus Rape," *New York Times*, January 23, 1989, sec. A, p. 24.
[38] William Celis, "Date Rape and a List at Brown," *New York Times*, November 18, 1990, sec. I, p. 26; "Group of Females List Alleged Rapists' Names on Campus Restroom Walls," *CBS Evening News with Dan Rather*, December 13, 1990; Catherine Foster,

group of nine female undergraduate art students at the University of Maryland randomly selected the names of 50 male students from the University's campus directory and created posters that included the men's names and a caption that read "Potential Rapists." The group then hung dozens of the posters at various locations around the campus, including inside the student union.[39]

Other feminists suggested that real rape included not only situations involving coerced sex with someone known to the victim but also sexually explicit or tinged street remarks – the "verbal sexual coercion" of women.[40] Still other feminists insisted that even in situations where victim consent was given, if the victim was under the influence of drugs or alcohol, her consent was negated.[41] Finally, some campus feminists went so far as to suggest there was no distinction between normal sex and criminal rape, or that a woman's consent to have sex, because of inherent power differences between the sexes, was simply not possible.[42]

Campus feminists, including students and faculty members, thus took an existing problem – rape and the conventional beliefs surrounding it – and expanded and elaborated upon its domain and began making significant claims about its scope, magnitude, and seriousness. "Real rape" no longer would include only forced sexual intercourse perpetrated by strangers against victims but forced sexual intercourse between dates or acquaintances and *their* victims.

"Problem of Rape on Campus Tackled Anew by Activists," *Christian Science Monitor,* December 26, 1990, p. A-7; William Celis, "Agony on Campus: What Is Rape?" *New York Times,* January 2, 1991, sec. A, p. 1.

[39] Janet Naylor, "Potential Rapists Flyer Stirs University of Maryland Flap: Feminists Posted Names at Random," *Washington Times,* May 7, 1993, sec. A, p. 1.

[40] Sarah Crichton, Debra Rosenburg, Stanley Holmes, Martha Brant, Donna Foote, and Nina Biddle, "Sexual Correctness: Has It Gone Too Far?" *Newsweek,* October 25, 1993, pp. 52–57.

[41] For example, according to Boise State University's student code of conduct, consent for sexual relations cannot be given by someone who is intoxicated. Gabe Murphy, "Got Rape?" (2008), retrieved October 30, 2008, http://media.www.artiberonline.com/media/storage/paper890/news/2008/04/14/Opinion/Got-Rape-3321948.shtml. For additional discussion of collegiate codes of conduct, particularly in the area of sexual assault, see Students Active for Ending Rape, *Title IX and Sexual Assault,* retrieved October 30, 2008, http://www.safercampus.org/documents/titleIX_national7.pdf.

[42] Katie Roiphe, "Date Rape's Other Victim," *New York Times,* June 13, 1993, sec. 6, p. 26.

Identifying New Victims and Villains

In expanding the domain of real rape and making claims about it, feminists identified new victims and villains associated with the date rapes they argued were "routinely" occurring on college campuses. The obvious new victims were college women coerced into having sexual intercourse with their dates or acquaintances to the point where a crisis was occurring. Beyond using the Koss data, feminists also presented alarming statistics showing that rates of rape were *much higher* for college women than for women of comparable ages in the general population. For example, *Newsweek* reported in a 1993 story that women in the age category of 16 to 19 years were at the highest risk for rape victimization, followed by those ages 20 to 24 – both categories obviously encompassing a large percentage of college-age women.[43] *The Boston Globe* reported in a 1993 story that fully "one-half of female college students in Massachusetts were afraid of becoming victims of date rape."[44]

Campus feminists also identified new villains involved with date and acquaintance rape and focused on two primary candidates. First, college men were identified as a new breed of perpetrators, particularly members of college fraternities and student-athletes.[45] This theme was especially strong during the "date rape drug" scare of the late 1990s, when the illegal substances Rohypnol ("roofies") and GHB (gamma hydroxybutyrate), which produce coma-like effects on users including memory loss, were alleged to be dumped routinely and clandestinely into the drinks of college women attending on-campus parties. Women who consumed these tainted drinks were then raped by fellow students attending the parties.[46] While there was little systematic

---

[43] Crichton et al., "Sexual Correctness: Has It Gone Too Far?"

[44] Alice Dembner, "Massachusetts Students Upbeat amid Sobering Problems," *Boston Globe*, September 12, 1993, National/Foreign, p. 1.

[45] Celis, "Agony on Campus: What Is Rape?"; Gerald Eskenazi, "The Wrong Kind of Headlines," *New York Times*, February 27, 1989, sec. C, p. 8. See also David Holmstromm, "Do Aggressive Sports Produce Violent Men?" *Christian Science Monitor*, October 16, 1995, Features, p. 1; Ellen Dabbs, "Intentional Fouls: Athletes and Violence against Women," *Columbia Journal of Law and Social Problems* 31 (1998): 167–190.

[46] Michael Klein, "As Spring Break Begins, Alarm Goes Out on 'Date Rape' Pill," *Philadelphia Inquirer*, March 10, 1996, p. AO2; Marie McCullough, "Rape-Drug Fears Come to Penn State," *Philadelphia Inquirer*, October 13, 1996, p. AO1; Anita

evidence to support these contentions, anecdotal evidence nonetheless percolated in the news media and helped fuel stories highlighting the fears of college women about their safety. In some instances, postsecondary institutions even warned college women before spring break to be careful about having these substances dumped into their drinks while vacationing at well-known spring break locations such as Ft. Lauderdale.[47]

A second set of new villains that campus feminists identified as associated with the problem of campus date and acquaintance rape included college or university administrators. Feminists claimed administrators had failed to acknowledge that on-campus date and acquaintance rapes were problems at their schools. As a result, they failed not only to take proactive measures to prevent date and acquaintance rapes from occurring but to respond properly to the needs of student victims. For example, in the late 1980s campus feminists accused college or university administrators as suffering from a "fiefdom syndrome," and one campus official was quoted by the *Boston Globe* as saying "no one wants to be known as the college where people get raped."[48] In the early 1990s, an episode of CNN's *Larry King Live* featured several campus date rape victims, all of whom claimed their respective schools' administrators knew about the problem of date rape but either covered it up or felt it wasn't "that big of an issue" and took no steps to address it.[49] A caller to the show also made some interesting claims:

> Caller #3 [Concord, New Hampshire]: In the early 1980s, I was president of a women's dormitory, and we had several rapes on campus. When myself [*sic*] and other dorm presidents tried to go to the girls to tell them about what was going on...we were told [by senior-level administrators] we were "not allowed to say anything."[50]

The Associated Press, in a story covering the proceedings of the Seventh Annual Conference on Campus Violence held at Towson State University in Baltimore in 1994, quoted several university officials as

---

Manning, "Drugged and Defenseless, Date Rape Pills Rob Victims and Prosecutors of the Ability to Fight Back," *USA Today*, October 29, 1996, p. 1D; Floyd Phelps, "Ravages of Rohypnol," *Security Management* 40 (1996): 14.

[47] Klein, "As Spring Break Begins, Alarm Goes Out on 'Date Rape' Pill."
[48] Flint, "Lawsuits New Weapon against Campus Crime," p. 1.
[49] CNN, "Are Your Kids Safe on Campus?" *Larry King Live*, December 3, 1993.
[50] Ibid.

saying "college administrators are afraid of bad publicity [arising from date rapes on their campuses] because they're afraid of losing students"; administrators "want potential tuition-payers to think their campus is safe and wonderful"; campus rape "is a little like a family secret: there's shame attached."[51] Women students at the State University of New York at New Paltz campus encountered resistance from the central campus administration when they attempted to change the school's student code of conduct to delineate more fully what constituted "consent" by the parties involved in sexual trysts.[52] Finally, the former editor in chief of the *Harvard Crimson* complained in a letter to the editor of the *New York Times* that "if students never hear an administrator condemn an incident of date rape on campus, are they [students] safe to assume that date rape is not an important problem there?"[53] Campus activists then used these accounts to claim that at the same time campus administrators were welcoming women to their campuses, they were turning a blind eye both to the extent of date and acquaintance rapes on their campuses and to the plight of victims.

Concerning college or university administrators' failure to take action to prevent date rape, both campus feminists and SOC made similar allegations during the late 1980s and through the 1990s that campus administrators were not doing enough. For example, a 1998 article in the monthly newsletter *Campus Safety Watch* alleged that deans and student affairs personnel were obscuring "their inherent institutional responsibility to ensure a safe campus environment."[54] Attorney Philip Burling, writing in a legal compendium on postsecondary liability for campus victimizations, suggested that "*higher education itself was complicit*" in not taking necessary steps to try and prevent date and acquaintance rapes from occurring on college campuses.[55]

[51] Eun-Kyung Kim, "Many College Officials Reluctant to Discuss Campus Crime," Associated Press, Domestic News, February 5, 1992.
[52] Evelyn Nieves, "Trying to End a Sad Ritual of College Life," *New York Times*, March 17, 1996, sec. I, p. 33.
[53] Andrew Wright, "End the Inequities of Campus Justice," *New York Times*, May 14, 1996, sec. A, p. 22.
[54] Howard Clery and Connie Clery, "Campus Crime a Growing Scandal – Campus Administrators Asleep at the Switch," *Campus Watch* 4 (1998): 6 (emphasis added).
[55] Phillip Burling, *Crime on Campus: Analyzing and Managing the Increasing Risk of Institutional Liability*, 2nd ed. (Washington, DC: National Association of College and University Attorneys, 2004), p. 3 (emphasis added).

Finally, campus feminists also argued that college or university administrators had failed in their dealings with campus rape victims. Too often, administrators either ignored victims altogether or actively worked to convince them to pursue internal disciplinary proceedings against student perpetrators rather than filing criminal charges. For example, in a 1989 *New York Times* story on campus date rape, college women who had been the victims of date or acquaintance rape at several schools were quoted as saying they were "reluctant" to report what had happened to them to campus authorities because "colleges often show more concern about the offender's rights than about the victim's rights."[56] A 1991 *USA Today* story detailed how Carleton College allegedly treated one campus date rape victim enrolled at the school:

> Carleton College student Kristene Maxie expected the school to protect her. After she was raped, she expected it to punish her attacker. But Maxie, one of four students charging in a lawsuit that the school didn't provide a safe environment and inadequately disciplined her attackers, says that Carleton "let her assailant get away with rape."[57]

Similar allegations were raised by student victims at a number of schools around the nation,[58] while Frank Carrington, chief legal counsel at SOC, was quoted in a 1991 *USA Today* story as saying: "I've talked to hundreds of campus rape victims and *almost without exception*, they're saying the stonewalling and brutal treatment they get from college officials is worse than the original crime. It demeans the crime [victim] to say this [incident], in effect, isn't a crime."[59]

Domain Elaboration and Diffusion

Once the activists had named the problem, made claims about it, and identified new victims and villains, they also further elaborated on the

---

[56] Deirdre Carmody, "Increasing Rapes on Campus Spur Colleges to Fight Back," *New York Times*, January 1, 1989, sec. I, p. 1.

[57] Judy Keen, "Colleges 'Degrade' Rape Victims," *USA Today*, June 11, 1991, p. 1A. But see also Joseph Healey, "Courts Can't Handle Every Campus Rape," *USA Today*, News, June 12, 1991, p. 10A.

[58] Daniel Carter and Catherine Bath, "The Evolution and Components of the *Jeanne Clery Act*: Implications for Higher Education," pp. 27–44 in Bonnie S. Fisher, and John J. Sloan III (Eds.), *Campus Crime: Legal, Social, and Policy Perspectives*, 2nd ed. (Springfield, IL: Charles Thomas, 2007).

[59] Keen, "Colleges 'Degrade' Rape Victims," p. 1A (emphasis added).

domain of the new problem of campus date and acquaintance rape. Domain elaboration involves activists identifying "new aspects of the problem" that "offer a fresh angle from which to view the problem – additional implications that demand attention."[60] Doing this "allows the activists to make the problem relevant to and enlist support from additional audiences such as physicians, teachers, school nurses, and the like."[61] Included in domain elaboration are geographic diffusion and temporal diffusion – the former showing that the problem had crossed geographic boundaries and the latter showing that the problem, while long existing, had not been addressed by previous generations for various reasons but that society could now do something about it.

Similar to strategies that SOC used, campus feminists offered new aspects of the problem and a fresh angle from which to view it. By couching the problem of on-campus date and acquaintance rape in larger arguments about the nature of rape in society, campus feminists linked sexual violence against college women as the by-product of a larger system of patriarchy, around which, they argued, American society was organized. Until existing power inequalities between the sexes were abolished, gender inequality would continue to express itself in sexual violence perpetrated against women, including college women.[62] Campus feminists used the existence of an alleged campus rape culture or alleged attitudes of entitlement among college men regarding sex with college women to show how male college students' attitudes and behaviors exemplified patriarchy on college campuses. Feminists thus not only communicated to the public the message about the "dangers of patriarchy" but also linked those dangers to the existence of a campus rape culture and the seeming "wave" of on-campus sexual assaults involving college women that was occurring during the late 1980s and 1990s.[63]

---

[60] Joel Best, *Random Violence: How We Talk about New Crimes and New Victims* (Berkeley: University of California Press, 1999), p. 169.

[61] Ibid.

[62] Susan Faludi, *Backlash: The Undeclared War on American Women* (New York: Doubleday, 1991).

[63] Catherine MacKinnon, *A Feminist Theory of the State* (Cambridge, MA: Harvard University Press, 1989); Andrea Dworkin, *Life and Death* (New York: Free Press, 2002); Andrea Dworkin, *Intercourse* (New York: Basic Books, [1986] 2006); Diana E. H. Russell, *Dangerous Relationships: Pornography, Misogyny, and Rape* (Thousand Oaks, CA: Sage Publications, 1998).

Such linkages were explicitly made by feminists in interviews with various national media outlets. For example, Laura X, director of the National Clearinghouse on Marital and Date Rape, told the Associated Press in 1989: "What happens is that a guy pays for dinner, the movies, and he thinks you get what you get in a marriage. They see it as a mini, quasi-marriage.... I don't think we're getting rid of date rape until we get rid of that concept."[64] Peggy Reeves Sanday in a 1992 interview on the syndicated talk show *Geraldo* also made damning claims linking patriarchy with campus date and acquaintance rape when she said that college men were "learning about sex from one another" and were "enacting a male defined fantasy."[65] Some newspaper op-ed columns *written by men* even echoed these concerns. Bill Stevens, who was then a local prosecutor in Florida, wrote about the problem in a 1989 op-ed column for the *St. Petersburg Times:*

> There's the key: teaching men that when women say no to sex, they mean it – and that to continue to force the action is rape. A popular notion among some men is that saying "no" is part of a game. If the man doesn't "take charge," the woman will think he's a wimp. That's a dangerous, and incorrect, assumption, often fostered by... porno magazines. In the real world, successful relationships, whether sexual or otherwise, depend on sensitivity and tenderness.[66]

Campus feminists also used stories of a date and acquaintance rape occurring on one college campus to link that particular incident to those occurring on other campuses, thus making it seem that date and acquaintance rape victimization of college women was a "national epidemic."[67] The following quotes from various news stories on campus date and acquaintance rape are illustrative:

---

[64] John Roll, "Many Rape Victims Blame Themselves, Fail to Report Attacks," Associated Press Domestic News, January 12, 1989.

[65] CNN, "Discussion of Campus Rapes Involving Student Athletes," *Geraldo*, January 17, 1992.

[66] Bill Stevens, "The Burden Is on Men, Society, to End Date Rape," *St. Petersburg Times*, June 4, 1989, Hernando Times column, p. 2.

[67] Feminists were not the only people making this claim. In a 1991 *USA Today* story, Congressman Jim Ramstad (R-MN) said "it's estimated that a college student is raped *every 21 hours*" (emphasis added). Mr. Ramstad did not indicate the source for this claim. See Keen, "Colleges 'Degrade' Rape Victims."

- "Acquaintance rape *happens all the time* and college freshmen have to realize that it can happen to them."[68]
- "Sexual assaults on campuses have reached *epidemic proportions.*"[69]
- "University counselors and students say they believe that acquaintance rape *occurs far more than is reported* or than studies show."[70]
- "*College women*...especially first-year students, *are particularly vulnerable* to 'date rape.'"[71]
- "When they can speak anonymously, nearly 10% of *college men admit to sexual acts that meet the legal definition of rape* or attempted rape. More than half of those assaults occurred on college campuses and most involved women they already knew."[72]

This group of claimsmakers also pointed out that date and acquaintance rape had "long existed" but had not been addressed previously, largely because conventional beliefs about the crime had been "too narrow."[73] According to a *Newsweek* story in 1991, Mary Koss was quoted as saying "There was a time...when a fair number of people thought you *couldn't rape someone you knew.*"[74] As a result, when campus date or acquaintance rape victims came forward, either they were not believed or, if they were believed and they pursued criminal charges, they faced very uncertain outcomes as juries generally were disinclined to hold perpetrators responsible for date- or acquaintance-type sexual

---

[68] Laura Sneade, "Date Rape: College's Dirty Secret" (1997), retrieved October 31, 2008, http://oncampus.richmond.edu/academics/journalism/magazine/4-97/features/articles/f-daterape.html (emphasis added).

[69] Benjamin F. Clery (President, Security On Campus, Inc.) "Testimony on Campus Crime and *The Accuracy in Campus Crime Reporting Act of 1997* (HR715) before the House Education and Workforce Committee Hearing" (July 17, 1997) (emphasis added). Transcript from *Federal Document Clearing House Congressional Testimony.* Available from LexisNexis® Congressional; accessed September 18, 2008.

[70] Celis, "Agony on Campus: What Is Rape?" (emphasis added).

[71] Cheryl Laird, "Young Women 'Easy Targets' for Date Rape," *Houston Chronicle*, August 30, 1993, Women's News, p. C1 (emphasis added).

[72] Alice Dembner, "Efforts by Universities to Curb Date Rape Falling Short," *Boston Globe*, May 18, 1997, p. A1 (emphasis added).

[73] Eric Reitan, "Date Rape and Seduction: Towards a Defense of Pineau's Definition of Date Rape," paper presented at the 65th annual meetings of the Southwestern Philosophical Society, Memphis, Tennessee, November 14–16, 2003. See also Russell, *Sexual Exploitation;* Faludi, *Backlash.*

[74] Eloise Salholz, Michael Mason, Todd Barrett, May Talbot, Patricia Kind, and Emily Yoffe, "Women on Trial," *Newsweek*, December 16, 1993, p. 22 (emphasis added).

assaults. For example, while not distinguishing date and acquaintance rapes involving college women from those involving women more generally, the National Violence Against Women Survey nonetheless found that

> cases involving intimates were less likely than those involving non-intimates to be prosecuted (32.1 and 44.4 percent, respectively). Once they were referred for prosecution, rapists who were intimates were significantly less likely than rapists who were non-intimates to be convicted of a crime (36.4 and 61.9 percent, respectively). These findings indicate that it is more difficult to successfully prosecute rape cases that involve intimates than those that involve non-intimates.[75]

Similar results were found by Fisher and her colleagues in their national-level study of college women's sexual victimization experiences: these women were reluctant to move forward with prosecutions in date or acquaintance rape cases: "Another common answer was that they lacked proof that the incident happened. About one-fourth of the rape victims feared a negative reaction from the police: either they would be treated hostilely...or the police would not think the incident was serious enough."[76] At this point, campus feminists and their allies had successfully used the strategies that Best argued are crucial for constructing a new social problem. They had taken an existing problem – rape – and claimed that popular conceptions of the crime did not include coerced sexual intercourse perpetrated by dates or acquaintances of victims. They then named the new problem – date and acquaintance rape – and made a series of claims about its occurrence on college campuses, the most important being that one in four college women had been raped by someone known to them, usually a fellow student. They also expanded and elaborated on the domain of date and acquaintance rape by pointing to connections among three powerful forces: patriarchal arrangements that characterized American society more generally; societal rape myths; and

---

[75] Patricia Tjaden and Nancy Thoennes, *The Extent, Nature, and Consequences of Rape Victimization: Findings from the National Violence against Women Survey* (Washington, DC: United States Department of Justice, 2006), p. 36.

[76] Bonnie S. Fisher, Francis T. Cullen, and Michael G. Turner, *The Sexual Victimization of College Women* (Washington, D.C.: United States Department of Justice, Bureau of Justice Statistics, 2000).

a rape culture existing on college campuses. Campus feminists also named new victims and villains – naive college women, in particular those who were in their first year of college, and male perpetrators (also students) and postsecondary institutional administrators. Finally, feminists also claimed ownership of the problem of campus date and acquaintance rape, established a particular orientation about it, and then helped legitimize and institutionalize the problem.

Claiming Ownership of Date and Acquaintance Rape

According to Best, in taking ownership of the new social problem, claimsmakers become *the* authorities on the problem. Then, by giving interviews to the media, having their opinions solicited by policy makers, and defining a particular orientation toward the problem, that orientation or frame becomes the "authoritative way" to understand the new problem.[77] This was especially true of campus date and acquaintance rape.

Recall that the Clerys and SOC were able to assume, largely unchallenged, ownership of the problem of unsafe and violent college campuses because of the murder of the Clery's daughter at Lehigh University in 1986. Because college *women* were the new victims of acquaintance or date rape, campus feminists and their supporters – almost all of whom were women – quickly assumed a kind of logical ownership of the problem. Then, using Koss's results combined with anecdotal evidence, they became "legitimate authorities" on the problem. Finally, their rhetoric concerning the source of the problem – the campus rape culture and its ties to the larger patriarchy with its imbedded power inequalities between men and women – helped establish a particular orientation for how the problem of on-campus date and acquaintance rape should be viewed and understood.

One could argue the backdrop of the larger feminist movement occurring in the United States during the 1970s and 1980s was the basis by which campus feminists claimed ownership of the date and acquaintance rape problem. During that period, feminists more generally were demanding that women's reproductive rights be protected and the scope of economic inequality between men and

---

[77] Best, *Random Violence*, pp. 173–174.

women be lessened. It appears that once it was "discovered," feminists then added date and acquaintance rape to their growing list of grievances. An additional part of the backdrop was the fact feminists had been pushing for changes in procedural, evidentiary, and substantive components of rape laws for years – so-called rape law reforms – many of which were directly related to how the criminal justice system responded to claims of date and acquaintance rape. Of particular interest to feminists was pushing the states to implement "rape shield laws," which precluded defense counsel in rape cases from probing the victim about her past history of sexual experiences. Feminists also focused on abolishing rape corroboration requirements, which placed a burden on the victim to prove she had resisted her attacker by presenting evidence of additional physical injuries, such as bruises or black eyes, beyond those typically associated with penetration.[78]

Journalists' accounts seemed to agree with this assessment concerning the larger background that was in place at the time. For example, a 1990 *Christian Science Monitor* story suggested:

> Twenty years after the last cycle of activism opened doors into the workplace for women and gave them reproductive choices, a new breed of feminism is emerging on [college] campuses. Last year, the National Organization for Women (NOW) had a march for women's equality that drew at least 200,000 students from 400 college campuses.... This kind of activism is occurring at a time when many colleges and universities are dealing with the issue of so-called date, or acquaintance, rape.[79]

USA Today, in a 1993 story, echoed those sentiments:

> The new emphasis [on date rape] on campus also reflects a change in the relationship between the sexes, experts say, as a generation weaned on the tenets of women's liberation runs into what they see

---

[78] For discussion of the rape law reform movement, see David Bryden, "Redefining Rape," *Buffalo Criminal Law Review* 3 (2000): 317–360; David Bryden and Sonja Lengnick, "Rape in the Criminal Justice System," *Journal of Criminal Law and Criminology* 87 (1997): 1194–1238; and Julie Horney and Cassia Spohn, *Impact of Rape Reform Legislation in Six Major Urban Jurisdictions in the United States: 1970–1985* (1989), retrieved November 24, 2008, http://dx.doi.org/10.3886/ICPSR06923.

[79] Catherine Foster, "Problem of Rape on Campus Tackled Anew by Activists," *Christian Science Monitor*, December 26, 1990, The U.S., p. 7.

as sexism and growing violence toward women.... They write the names of men they say are dangerous dates on bathroom walls. They march to chants of "take back the night," and hold angry meetings with deans.[80]

Finally, a 1993 *Newsweek* magazine story suggested that "feminist politics have now homed in 'like missiles' on the twin issues of [college] date rape and sexual harassment."[81]

Regardless of the actual impetus for their actions, by the early 1990s campus feminists had successfully claimed ownership of the problem of date and acquaintance rapes occurring on college campuses. It was they who first began to speak publicly about the problem by appearing on television talk shows and discussing its extent and effects. They shared their stories with reporters and offered consoling messages to victims. They consistently emphasized that nonconsensual coerced sexual intercourse occurring between partners known to each other was real rape, despite social conventions to the contrary. They loudly trumpeted the perceived causes of campus date and acquaintance rape as grounded in an omnipresent rape culture that had taken hold on college campuses and which was epitomized by fraternities. Further, it was unusual *not* to see Koss's one-in-four figure used in news stories about campus date and acquaintance rape among college women. Inclusion of that figure drove home the point that, literally, *millions* of college women were at risk for experiencing devastating sexual victimization during their four or five years as undergraduate students. Campus feminists also organized activities to "raise awareness" about campus date and acquaintance rape, such as Take Back the Night rallies, and put college or university administrators, who they argued had done nothing to acknowledge, prevent, or address the problem, in the limelight and hold them accountable for their "deliberate" failures. All of these strategies and activities ultimately resulted in a particular orientation about on-campus date and acquaintance rape being created and then presented to policy makers and the public.

[80] Anita Manning, "Gender Wars on Campus," *USA Today*, September 2, 1993, News, p. 1A.
[81] Crichton et al., "Sexual Correctness: Has It Gone Too Far?"

Establishing an Orientation

Campus feminists had the important task of creating a particular way of thinking about campus date and acquaintance rape that represented their world view and which could be routinely disseminated via print and electronic media outlets. Having media present this orientation, combined with the attention gained from topical stories arising on a campus-by-campus basis, would pique not only the public's interest but the interest of policy makers and members of various federal agencies (e.g., the U.S. Department of Justice; the U.S. Department of Education). These agencies would then seek activists' "authoritative" opinions about the problem of campus date and acquaintance rape for the purpose of assisting policy makers in crafting responses to the problem. From the perspective of campus feminists, appropriate responses would, among other things, have to hold the new villains of campus date and acquaintance rape – both perpetrators and college administrators – accountable for their actions.

The orientation that campus feminists presented revolved around the three key points mentioned earlier: campus date and acquaintance rape was real rape, contrary to conventional thinking; the problem had reached epidemic proportions on college campuses; and college or university administrators had failed to acknowledge the problem, take necessary steps to prevent it, or adequately respond to its victims.[82] In stories published in major newspapers, during interviews with various media representatives or on national talk shows, and in congressional testimony, campus activists often presented these three points. As a result, when a story about campus date or acquaintance rape was carried by electronic or print media sources, the story would nearly always point out the "problem" with conventional views on rape; would present startling statistics about the extent of the problem, usually the Koss one-in-four figure; and would provide examples,

---

[82] During the 1990s, Koss and colleagues' work began appearing more frequently in scientific journals, resulting in their work gaining even more scientific credibility not only among social scientists but among women's studies faculty members as well (most of whom were also ardent feminists). Members of the latter group were in an excellent position, on a campus-by-campus basis, to organize students and help hold college or university administrators accountable for failing to address the "epidemic" of campus date rape.

based on victim accounts, of how college or university administrators had failed to do anything to address the escalating problem or to aid victims. For example, the following excerpts from a story that appeared in the *Washington Post* in 1992 contain all of these elements and illustrate the orientation that campus feminists were creating in media coverage of campus date or acquaintance rape:

> Last year, freshman Katie Koestner drew national attention to the 299 year-old College of William and Mary when she publicly claimed she had been raped by a fellow student.... [That] college administrators found [it] to be a sexual assault, not a rape, is still topic A [on campus]. As Koestner has taken her story to national talk shows and most recently sold her account to Home Box Office for a "docudrama," the [campus] debate has become increasingly personal.... College and law enforcement officials are grappling with the murky issue of date rape which often comes down to one person's word against another.... In recent years, more women at schools across the country have been speaking out about date rape. Students at Brown and Northwestern universities have even posted the names of alleged rapists on bathroom walls.... Koestner has also come under fire...for bringing bad publicity to the school.[83]

Along with this new orientation, campus feminists presented possible solutions. Some of these included having colleges and universities develop freshman orientation programs that would educate and raise awareness about the dangers of date and acquaintance rape on campus. Other suggestions included either incorporating specific descriptions of the unacceptable behavior into existing codes of student conduct or creating new codes altogether. Still others suggested that providing appropriate institutional sanctions for those engaging in the behavior would be a wise choice by school administrators. Finally, some feminists proposed that schools design programs that were aimed at changing college men's attitudes about rape. Journalistic accounts of these suggestions are illustrative:

- In 1989 the *New York Times* reported that college officials, concerned over an apparent steady increase in campus rapes, were

---

[83] Brooke A. Masters, "Alleged Date Rape is College's Topic A," *Washington Post*, April 27, 1992, p. B1.

strengthening security and reinforcing freshman orientation with programs on how to avert rape.[84]

- A 1990 *Washington Times* story reported that Lyn McCoy, a community educator and activist, recommended that the University of Maryland adopt mandatory educational sessions for freshman on the subject of date rape; that rape counseling be made available to students during freshman orientation; and that an annual sexual assault awareness program be developed by the university.[85]

- A 1991 story in the *New York Times* reported that, to protect their reputations and shield themselves from lawsuits [by victims], growing numbers of colleges and universities were confronting the problem [of date and acquaintance rape] through campus education programs, easier ways for women to report rapes, the formation of men-only discussion groups, and better legal counseling on campus.[86]

- A 1993 story in the *New York Times* reported that on-campus educational programs designed to prevent date and acquaintance rape on campus, and grievance procedures involving on-campus cases were proliferating.[87]

Institutionalizing the Problem and Devising Responses

As Best points out, some issues (such as "wilding"), after a brief moment in the public limelight, quickly disappear.[88] Others, however, become institutionalized and part of the fabric of social life. As a new problem moves toward becoming institutionalized, various processes are activated. Legislative hearings will be convened, and new laws passed seeking solutions for the new problem. The legal system and its agencies (e.g., police departments and prosecutors' offices) change how they respond to the new problem and its victims. For example, the police may begin keeping track of reported incidents or devise new methods to help prevent the problem. Researchers begin studying the problem and present their findings and policy suggestions. Ultimately, the

---

[84] Carmody, "Increasing Rapes on Campus Spur Colleges to Fight Back."

[85] Carleton Bryant, "UMd Women Hold Rally. University Has Rape Problem, They Say," *Washington Times*, April 19, 1990, p. B2.

[86] Celis, "Agony on Campus: What Is Rape?"

[87] Jane Gross, "Combating Rape on Campus in a Class on Sexual Assault," *New York Times*, September 25, 1993, sec. I, p. 1.

[88] Best, *Random Violence*, pp. 29–31, 166–167.

momentum of interest in the problem is increased, while at the same time, the initial claims may continue being supported.[89]

Campus feminists, using a variety of tactics, successfully institution-alized the new problem of date and acquaintance rape on college campuses. As a result, during the 1990s a new orientation developed in the ivory tower about campus date and acquaintance rape and became part of its social fabric. That orientation also became more ingrained among members of the general public. Through their alli-ances with SOC and other groups, campus feminists helped influ-ence the passage of federal legislation mandating that postsecondary institutions compile and disseminate statistics on the number of rapes occurring on their campuses, including statistics for date and acquaintance rape, and develop and follow specific procedures when responding to these victims. Finally, an explosion of research on cam-pus date and acquaintance rape occurred, with results of these studies feeding back into continuing claims being made by campus feminists about the scope and magnitude of the problem and its short- and long-term psychological and physical consequences for victims.

Campus feminists used specific strategies to advance their desire to change how college campuses responded to the problem of cam-pus date and acquaintance rape. Claimsmakers were thus proposing changes in how postsecondary institutions would *behave* when one of these incidents occurred. For example, schools could incorporate efforts to "raise awareness" about campus date rape into freshman orientation programs. Institutions could also address the problem via revised codes of student conduct, the most radical of which was proba-bly the Code of Student Conduct at Antioch College, in Yellow Springs, Ohio. The code mandated that consent from the woman had to occur "at each stage as sexual contact advanced toward intercourse."[90] Thus, as Best suggested, institutions – in this case, postsecondary institutions – changed the way they were responding to the new problem that cam-pus feminists had helped construct. Through new education and prevention programs that schools implemented, through enhanced codes of student conduct drafted and implemented, or through the

[89] Ibid., p. 48.
[90] Gross, "Combating Rape on Campus in a Class on Sexual Assault."

sanctioning of fraternities for inappropriate behavior, the problem of collegiate date and acquaintance rape became institutionalized.[91]

Beyond voluntary changes schools were apparently undertaking, change was also being imposed on them from the outside through legislation. For example, the *Campus Security Act* and its subsequent amendments, particularly the *Campus Sexual Assault Victims' Bill of Rights* passed by Congress and signed into law by President George H. W. Bush in 1992, created a new set of mandates for postsecondary institutions in terms of how they would respond to campus crime (generally) and campus date and acquaintance rape (in particular).

Recall that the *Campus Security Act* required postsecondary institutions to annually compile and make available to the public statistics on the number of rapes that were reported to campus authorities, as well as developing and making publicly available a campus security plan. The *Campus Sexual Assault Victims' Bill of Rights* amendment further enhanced the *Security Act*'s requirements by mandating that postsecondary institutions "develop and make available, policy statements dealing with on-campus sexual assaults."[92] The amendment also required that postsecondary institutions afford certain rights to both sexual assault victims and alleged perpetrators, including:

- Accused and accuser must have the opportunity to have others present at campus disciplinary hearings.
- The institution shall inform both parties of the outcome of campus disciplinary proceedings.
- The institution shall notify survivors of available counseling services.
- The institution shall notify survivors of options for changing academic and living arrangements.[93]

[91] For commentary on the Antioch Code of Student Conduct, see the following: Ellen Goodman, "The Struggle on College Campuses to Create Standards of Sexual Equality," *Boston Globe*, September 19, 1993, Op-Ed, p. 75, and Gross, "Combating Rape on Campus in a Class on Sexual Assault," who reported that the Antioch policy "was born in the fall of 1990, after several sexual assaults on campus, when a group of students calling themselves the 'Womyn of Antioch' protested the lack of campus policies regarding date rape and threatened 'radical, physical action' if their demands were not met." For a description of how colleges and universities were dealing with the role of fraternities in campus acquaintance and date rapes, see Bruce Macyntire, "American Universities Send Fraternities to the 'Doghouse,'" *Times* (London), August 30, 1994, Overseas News, p. 4.
[92] Carter and Bath, "The Evolution and Components of the *Jeanne Clery Act*," p. 35.
[93] Ibid.

In theory, this legislation – when combined with new orientation programs for incoming students, new codes of student conduct, and other on-campus initiatives – would *finally* address the claims of campus feminists. First, college or university administrators were being forced by the legislation to acknowledge there was a problem and devise solutions to it. Second, the new villains – college men and college or university administrators – could no longer "cover up" the problem, discredit sexual assault victims out of hand, steer victims away from pursuing criminal prosecution of offenders, or claim that victims "had consented" to the behavior. Revised and stricter codes of student conduct were supposed to address the "but she consented" issue, while legislation forced changes in how postsecondary institutions responded to campus rape victims, regardless of whether a stranger, a date, or an acquaintance was involved as the alleged perpetrator. Finally, the issue of preventing campus date and acquaintance rape was also addressed via amendments to the *Campus Security Act*'s requirements that postsecondary institutions make public the policies they had adopted concerning how on-campus date and acquaintance rape cases would be handled by schools' student disciplinary "courts."

CONCLUSION

By socially constructing date and acquaintance rape as a "new" problem on college and university campuses in the United States during the late 1980s and 1990s, campus feminists and their allies – students and faculty members – contributed to the social construction of campus crime as a new social problem. They used the strategies and engaged in many of the activities suggested by the constructionist framework concerning how new social problems are created. Ultimately, this group of activists was successful in institutionalizing campus date and acquaintance rape into the social fabric of not only American colleges and universities but society more generally.

Following a pattern comparable to what SOC did in constructing the new problem of "unsafe and violent college campuses," campus feminists named the problem, claimed ownership, expanded and elaborated on its domain, made significant claims about its scope and nature, created a new orientation about the problem, identified new victims and villains, and helped institutionalize it. They also helped to shape policy responses to the problem, whether those responses came from inside postsecondary institutions or from elected officials who passed campus-focused legislation. At each step, campus feminists made use of mass-media outlets to assist in their efforts to move collegiate date and acquaintance rape from the periphery to the center of public and postsecondary institutional discourse about campus crime. They were able to convince the public that a new, heinous threat existed that placed millions of unsuspecting women in danger – women who had gone to college seeking to develop the skills needed to join an increasingly competitive work force.

Feminists also linked date and acquaintance rape to existing patriarchal arrangements in society more generally, which helped create an orientation about the problem. Citing relevant social science research along with anecdotal accounts from various sources, campus feminists then presented evidence of how the larger patriarchy was expressing itself on college campuses via a rape culture, into which college men were being indoctrinated and which was embodied in college fraternities. Campus feminists also presented evidence showing that college men admitted the behavior in which they were engaging – date and acquaintance rape – was wrong but did not characterize it as real rape. Campus feminists and their allies also presented arguments concerning why the problem of on-campus date and acquaintance rape had not previously been addressed – blaming social conventions about what constituted real rape – and pointed out that those conventions were also to blame for why proper responses to the problem were not occurring. Through informal linkages with other groups such as SOC and via publicity generated at the national level, campus feminists helped shape policy solutions to the new problem of campus date and acquaintance rape, including federal legislation mandating that college or university administrators take the problem more seriously, develop programs and policies to prevent and respond to it, and no longer dismiss, out of hand, victims' claims.

CHAPTER FIVE

Constructing Postsecondary Institutional Liability for Campus Crime

On the one hand, we have a very tight regulatory environment and horrific liability exposures today. On the other hand, we have security folks, accustomed to compartmentalized jobs, who now find themselves on the front lines. Anything that happens on campus – from date rape, to murder, to IT encroachments – lands at their feet.[1]

Call it what you will, as long as you make it a priority on your campus.[2]

American colleges and universities have evolved into such complex organizations that it is not unusual for them to resemble small cities.[3] To illustrate, college campuses occupy physical space, in some cases several square miles, and often possess lines of demarcation (e.g., gates and fences or green space) that separate them from adjacent spaces. Colleges and universities provide housing to hundreds – perhaps even thousands – of young people in dormitories and on-campus apartments, and many of them are living away from their families for the first time. Thousands of people may be drawn to postsecondary institutions as visitors and because of the employment opportunities they offer. Colleges and universities are also home to many entertainment options, including cultural events such as concerts or musical

---

[1] See Michael Fickes, "More Security Technology on Campus" (2004), retrieved November 19, 2008, http://www2.peterli.com/cpm/resources/articles/archive.php?article_id=682.

[2] Julie Sturgis, "Security Versus Safety" (1999), retrieved November 19, 2008, http://www2.peterli.com/cpm/resources/articles/archivephp?article_id=138.

[3] College or university campuses possess many of the same features that sociologists have long argued are asociated with larger residential communities. See, for example, John J. Sloan and Nina Mansour, "Communities and Crime: The Case of College Campuses," paper presented at the annual meetings of the Academy of Criminal Justice Sciences, Pittsburgh, November 15, 1992.

performances; artistic readings and lectures; and seasonal athletic competitions, which sometimes occur before 100,000 or more people gathered in large stadiums. College and university campuses commonly offer physical fitness facilities and may provide dental, optical, mental health, and medical services to countless students, visitors, and patients. Indeed, in some instances a college campus may house a major medical center, which could include one or more hospitals, numerous clinics, and even high-level research laboratories devoted to solving the problems of emerging diseases.[4]

As colleges and universities grew in size and mission, their daily operations became increasingly more complex. This growth resulted in their safety and security needs also becoming more pressing and more complicated.[5] As is the case with their city counterparts, colleges and universities have to provide a range of safety and security measures for students, staff, and visitors to help prevent and respond to not only criminal events but those events involving natural or man-made disasters, such as toxic spills and fires.

THE SCOPE OF CAMPUS SECURITY

As the scope and complexity of operations at American colleges and universities became ever more sophisticated, particularly over the past few decades, protecting the physical security of the campus community could no longer be entrusted to a few paraprofessionals

---

[4] At the University of Alabama at Birmingham, for example, the medical center operation comprises four hospitals, including a Veterans Administration hospital, dozens of clinics and centers delivering a variety of health-related services, and more than a dozen health-services-related laboratories engaging in research for the government that is occasionally designated as "classified." The campus itself now encompasses some 88 square city blocks adjacent to downtown Birmingham.

[5] For a recent and extensive analysis of the security issues which confront postsecondary institutions, see Jerlando Jackson and Melvin Terrill (Eds.), *Creating and Maintaining Safe College Campuses: A Sourcebook for Evaluating and Enhancing College Safety Programs* (Sterling, VA: Stylus, 2007). See also testimony by Steven Healy, president of the International Association of Campus Law Enforcement Administrators (IACLEA) before the United State House of Representatives Committee on Education and Labor, Hearings on Making College Campuses Safer, 110th Cong., 1st sess., May 15, 2007. Healy stressed that a "one size fits all" approach to campus security would result in failure to adequately secure any one campus. Retrieved December 6, 2008, http://www.access.gpo.gov/congress/house/house06ch110.html.

leisurely "patrolling" the campus to ensure that everything was in order – no break-ins occurring, no fires in buildings left to burn, no facilities being flooded from broken water pipes.[6] "Campus security" now encompasses myriad activities designed to address specific issues. Among the more popular are controlling access to on-campus buildings; protecting institutional infrastructure from internal and external threats; ensuring that local area computer networks and sensitive databases containing student, employee, and hospital patient records are not breached; and enforcing state and local laws and ensuring that public order is maintained.[7]

Colleges and universities are taking other steps to decrease opportunities for crime to occur on campus, and these steps are widely diffused. For example, many college campuses now provide services know as "campus escort" or "campus taxi cabs" for students and employees that provide free rides around campus, particularly at night.[8] Colleges and universities have also widely adopted and installed emergency "blue light telephones" that are strategically placed on walkways and in parking facilities on campus. Resembling old-style pay phones, when activated by pushing a button, they ring directly to a central dispatcher, who then alerts campus security or police that the caller requires assistance.[9] Physical security professionals – often certified by

[6] Along those lines, Kenneth Peak has argued that campus police officers employed by today's colleges and universities actually wear "three hats" – those of law enforcer, security guard, and "door-shaker." See Kenneth Peak, "The Professionalization of Campus Law Enforcement: Comparing Campus and Municipal Law Enforcement Agencies," pp. 228–245 in Bonnie S. Fisher and John J. Sloan III (Eds.), *Campus Crime: Legal, Social, and Policy Perspectives* (Springfield, IL: Charles C. Thomas, 1995).

[7] Bonnie S. Fisher and John J. Sloan, "Campus Crime Policy: Legal, Social and Security Contexts," pp. 3–17 in Bonnie S. Fisher and John J. Sloan III (Eds.), *Campus Crime: Legal, Social, and Policy Perspectives*, 2nd ed. (Springfield, IL: Charles C. Thomas, 2007). See also Samuel G. McQuade, 2007. "High Tech Abuse and Crime on College and University Campuses: Evolving Forms of Victimization, Offending, and Their Interplay in Higher Education," in Fisher and Sloan, *Campus Crime*, 2nd ed. (2007), pp. 304–325.

[8] For an interesting analysis of the use of campus escort services at the University of California at Davis, see Sari Kaiwen Li, "Use of Campus Escort Service," UC Davis Student Affairs Research and Information Report #369 (Davis University of California at Davis, 2006), retrieved November 19, 2009, http://www.sariweb.ucdavis.edu/downloads/369.2006 %20Escort%20Service%20Quick%20Survey.pdf.

[9] For discussion of blue-light emergency phones on college campuses, see Laurén Abdel-Razzaq, "Blue Light: WSUPD's Little Known Phone System," *South End*,

such national-level professional organizations as the American Society
of Industrial Security (ASIS) – and campus police officers, whose training is at least comparable to that received by municipal police officers
and county sheriff's deputies, have become a more visible presence
on college campuses and have assumed ever greater responsibilities
for ensuring campus safety and security.[10] Postsecondary institutions
have also adopted other safety features such as design-build standards
for campus buildings intended to eliminate convoluted hallways or
environmental design (CPTED) for campus lighting, landscaping,
and parking lot or deck design to help prevent crime.[11]

As the security needs of modern colleges and universities have
grown ever more complex, technology has increasingly come to fore
as the primary means to address those needs. For example, encoded
"key cards" are routinely issued to college students to access their dormitories or to employees to access buildings in which their offices
or laboratories are located. Surveillance via closed-circuit television
(CCTV) is also used on many college campuses to monitor parking

December 9, 2008, retrieved December 4, 2009, http://www.thesouthendnews.
com/news/blue-light-wsupd-s-little-known-emergency-phone-system-1.1097072,
and Hobart and William Smith College, "Blue Light Emergency Phones" (n.d.),
retrieved November 19, 2009, http://www.hws.edu/studentlift/campsafety_blue_
light.aspx.

[10] "ASIS...is the preeminent international organization for security professionals.
Founded in 1955, ASIS is dedicated to increasing the effectiveness and productivity
of security professionals by developing educational programs and materials that
address broad security interests, such as the ASIS Annual Seminar and Exhibits,
as well as specific security topics." Retrieved November 20, 2009, http://www.
asisonline.org/about/history/index.xml. For analysis and discussion of the evolution
of modern campus police agencies, see John J. Sloan, "The Modern Campus Police:
An Analysis of Their Evolution, Structure, and Function," *American Journal of Police*
11 (1992): 85–104. For comparison of the characteristics of campus police agencies
and their municipal counterparts, see Max Bromley and Brian Reaves, "Comparing
Campus and Municipal Police: The Human Resources Dimension," *Policing: An
International Journal of Police Strategies and Management* 21 (1998): 534–546.

[11] CPTED develops strategies to address how the natural and built environments
interact to create opportunities for criminal victimization. For discussion, see
Matthew Robinson, "The Theoretical Development of Crime Prevention through
Environmental Design (CPTED)," *Advances in Criminological Theory* 8 (1999): 427–
462; National Crime Prevention Council, *Designing Safer Communities: Crime
Prevention through Environmental Design* (Washington, DC: National Crime
Prevention Council, 1997); and Diane Zahm, *Using Crime Prevention through
Environmental Design in Problem Solving* (Washington, DC: U.S. Department of
Justice, 2007), retrieved November 19, 2009, http://www.cops.usdoj.gov/files/ric/
publications/e0807391.pdf.

decks and lots, as well as open green spaces. Campus police and security forces have also begun using crime mapping technology to analyze calls for service and criminal victimization patterns and as a tool for making better use of personnel.[12] Sophisticated information technology systems are used at many colleges and universities to deter intrusions into key components of campus computational infrastructures, such as local area networks.[13]

With passage of the *Campus Security Act* in 1990 and subsequent amendments to it, federal law now *requires* postsecondary institutions to provide to the U.S. Department of Education and the public a description of schools' campus security policies and operations in an annual security report. Among other pieces of information, the report is to include a description of the power and authority of the campus security or police department and jurisdictional boundaries; instructions concerning how and to whom campus crime should be reported by victims or witnesses; and the mechanisms that institutions will use to provide "timely warnings" to the campus community in the event an emergency threatens the health or safety of employees and students.[14]

All this security takes resources. As a result, American colleges and universities are devoting significant portions of their operating budgets to that end. For example, the *Philadelphia Business Journal* recently reported that Philadelphia's "big six" universities – the University of Pennsylvania, Villanova University, Drexel University, St. Joseph's University, Temple University, and La Salle University – were annually spending between $13 million and $21 million on campus security, including costs associated with staffing fairly large

[12] For an illustration of the use of crime mapping on a college campus, see Matthew B. Robinson and Sunghoon Roh, "Crime on Campus: Spatial Aspects of Crime at a Regional Comprehensive University," pp. 231–255 in Fisher and Sloan, *Campus Crime*, 2nd ed. (2007); and George F. Rengert, Mark T. Mattson, and Kristen D. Henderson, *Campus Security: Situational Crime Prevention in High-Density Environments* (Monsey, NY: Willow Tree Press, 2001).

[13] See, for example, Samuel G. McQuade, *Understanding and Managing Cybercrime* (Boston: Pearson Education, 2006).

[14] Security On Campus, Inc., "College Campuses Will Now Get Immediate Emergency Warnings under New Higher Education Law Signed by President George W. Bush" (2008), retrieved December 9, 2008, http://www.securityoncampus.org/reporters/releases/081520 08.html.

and sophisticated police and physical security departments at the schools.[15] *USA Today* reported that in recent years a school such as Missouri State University, which enrolls some 20,000 students, was spending about $2.3 million annually on campus security and that its annual security costs were rising at a rate of about 5 to 6 percent per year.[16] Security experts estimate that the "average" postsecondary institution in the United States spends between $1 million and $2 million annually on its campus police department, with additional costs accruing for other aspects of security, particularly those relating to information technology security.[17]

To help with rising security costs, college and university administrators have begun taking advantage of grants available from the U.S. Department of Homeland Security or the U.S. Department of Justice's Office of Community-Oriented Policing Services.[18] Some schools have even taken to lobbying Congress directly to provide higher education with more funding for campus security,[19] while some security experts have called on colleges and universities to lobby not only Congress but also the U.S. Department of Education for funding that would be earmarked for use in postsecondary campus security operations.[20] In short, securing today's college and university campuses involves significant expenditures, large staffs, and increasing reliance on sophisticated technology.

---

[15] Peter Key, "For the City's Big Six Colleges, Security Is No Small Matter," *Philadelphia Business Journal*, January 4, 2008, retrieved November 19, 2008, http://wwww.bizjournals.com/philadelphia/stories/2008/01/07/story13.html.

[16] Pamela Brogan, "Fed Funding for Campus Security Debated," *USA Today*, March 7, 2008, retrieved November 19, 2008, http://www.usa today.com/news/washington/2008–03–07/campus-safety_N.html.

[17] Fickes, "More Security Technology on Campus."

[18] For example, the Office of Community Oriented Policing Services with the U.S. Department of Justice sponsored the "Secure Our Schools" program, which provided up to $16 million in competitive grants to campus police agencies during fiscal year 2009 "to provide funding to law enforcement agencies to assist with the development of school safety resources and provide improved security at schools and on school grounds." Retrieved December 4, 2009, http://www.cops.usdoj.gov/Default.asp?Item=2126.

[19] Fickes, "More Security Technology on Campus."

[20] Stephanie Silk, "School Security from A–Z," *Access Control and Security Systems*, January 1, 2007, pp. 22–23.

SHINING A LIGHT ON CAMPUS SECURITY

With this backdrop in mind, during the late 1980s and through the 1990s another group of claimsmakers came forward and furthered the social construction of campus crime as a new social problem. This group consisted largely of college students (and their families) who had experienced criminal victimizations while on campus and who presented a damning claim: security at most postsecondary institutions in the United States was lax at best and nonexistent at worst. As a result, college students were being subjected to horrific victimizations at the hands of not only other students but also predators not affiliated with the college or university who gained easy access to campus facilities where they perpetrated serious crimes including murder, rape, armed robbery, and assault.

Student victims and their families publicly proclaimed in mass-media outlets that postsecondary institutions *routinely* failed to make campus security a priority. As a result, students were being assaulted, raped, and murdered in their dorm rooms, as they walked about the campus, as they parked their cars in its lots and decks, or while they attended campus social events. Victims and their families further claimed that college and university administrators routinely covered up these security failures, while simultaneously ignoring the plight of victims who were harmed because of lapses in campus security.

Interestingly, these claims were similar to those made by both SOC and campus feminists. By making similar claims, student victims ultimately forged informal alliances with SOC, campus feminists, and "victims' rights" groups. Demands from these alliances ultimately resulted in congressional action to address the "problem of lax security" at postsecondary institutions and the plight of campus crime victims. However, whereas SOC and campus feminists targeted elected policy makers in their lobbying efforts, student victims and their families chose a different route: suing postsecondary institutions and petitioning the courts for redress. By filing lawsuits against postsecondary institutions, students and their families sought to recover from colleges and universities not only compensatory damages but punitive damages as well. Thus, victims sought to punish offending schools for their "negligence," while simultaneously sending a message to other schools that similar behavior would not go unpunished.[21]

In coming forward and making their claims, student victims and their families followed a now familiar path: they named and took ownership of the problem, expanded and elaborated upon the problem's domain, helped legitimize and institutionalize the problem, and shaped policy responses to it. In this chapter, we describe and analyze student victims of campus crime and their families as claims-makers and the strategies they used to construct lax postsecondary institutional security as a new problem in the ivory tower. Specifically, we describe the claims they made about campus security and about the responses of postsecondary institutions to their victimization. In doing so, we examine in particular electronic and print media's focus on how some of these victims brought their claims into court and sought to recover damages they alleged were caused by lax security on college campuses. Finally, we discuss how these victims' claims helped institutionalize and shape both court-related and legislative responses to the new problem of lax security on American college and university campuses.

CONSTRUCTING POSTSECONDARY INSTITUTIONAL LIABILITY

To understand how student crime victims who sued their schools over lax security contributed to the construction of campus crime as a social problem, one must first examine the claims they made and then understand how these claims helped catapult this group of claims-makers to the forefront of the wave of attention being paid to campus crime in the late 1980s and 1990s. Recall that Connie and Howard Clery founded SOC using an out-of-court settlement received from Lehigh University after they sued, claiming that lax campus security had caused their daughter's brutal rape and murder. Recall too, that campus feminists made claims about the role that lax security played

---

[21] Phillip Burling, *Crime on Campus: Analyzing and Managing the Increasing Risk of Institutional Liability*, 2nd ed. (Washington, DC: National Association of College and University Attorneys, 2004).

in contributing to collegiate date rape victimizations. There was a cacophony of voices shouting to the media that college and university administrators were routinely failing to implement reasonable security measures to address foreseeable criminal victimizations occurring on their campuses. As a direct result of this "negligence," college students were being murdered, raped, and assaulted.

Establishing Claims of Lax Campus Security

Until the latter part of the 1980s, American jurisprudence lacked any instance of an appellate court affirming a lower court judgment against a college or university for damages arising from on-campus criminal victimizations.[22] However, as postsecondary institutional liability expert Michael Clay Smith observed: "Times [have] changed. As campus crime has grown rife, and recognition of it has become widespread, a deluge of damage actions by campus crime victims has begun to roll down across the country. Precedents have [now] been established by appellate courts in at least five states."[23] Smith argues that by 1990, partly as a result of lawsuits filed during the 1980s, college and university administrators had systematically begun taking steps to upgrade campus security operations including going to ever greater lengths to warn students about crimes occurring on campus.[24]

Beginning in the late 1980s and continuing through the mid-1990s, print and electronic news outlets began carrying stories about student victims of campus crime and their claims that security at American colleges and universities was lax at best and nonexistent at worst. Journalists were particularly tuned in to and fascinated with student victims who actually filed civil lawsuits against their schools claiming the school was responsible for their victimization. For example, in 1989 the *Boston Globe* carried a story with the headline: "Lawsuits new weapon against campus rape." What was interesting about this particular story was not that it reported on the rape at Colgate University of a sophomore student by her acquaintances at a fraternity party or

---

[22] Michael C. Smith, "Institutional Liability Resulting from Campus Crime: An Analysis of Theories of Recovery," *Education Law Reporter* 55 (1989): 361–368.
[23] Ibid., p. 361.
[24] Michael C. Smith, "Vexatious Victims of Campus Crime: Student Lawsuits as Impetus for Risk Management," *Journal of Security Administration* 15 (1992): 5–17.

her coming forward to pursue criminal prosecution of the offenders. What was interesting to the *Globe* was her claim that the university had "failed to provide a safe environment" for her and fellow Colgate students, and because of that failure, her victimization had occurred. What also interested the *Globe* was the fact she was suing Colgate for $5 million over her victimization. In its story, the *Globe* reported that compared to issues such as cultural diversity or shrinking levels of state support that colleges and universities were facing at the time, postsecondary institutional liability for criminal victimizations was becoming "the far more pressing issue." To drive home that point, the story mentioned that multimillion dollar jury awards to, and large settlements occurring with, campus crime victims were becoming common as "the extent of college responsibility [for criminal victimizations] [was] tested."[25]

That civil liability for campus victimizations had become a "far more pressing issue" for postsecondary institutions was a theme that repeatedly appeared in stories on campus crime during the late 1980s and through the 1990s, appearing in major print and electronic media sources, as the following excerpts illustrate:

- "Liability challenges are emerging as a major weapon in the continuing war against rape on college campuses."[26]
- "Liability is by far the more pressing issue for colleges."[27]
- "What is new: Students – and juries – holding schools liable for... crimes."[28]
- "University officials are bracing for a flurry of liability suits."[29]

A 1989 interview by *USA Today* with Michael Clay Smith, chief legal counsel at the University of Southern Mississippi, provided further insight into the pressing issue for postsecondary institutions. When asked if there is any institutional liability "for failure to warn students about [campus] crime," Smith responded:

---

[25] Anthony Flint, "Lawsuits New Weapon against Campus Rape," *Boston Globe*, September 25, 1989, National/Foreign, p. 1.
[26] Ibid.
[27] Ibid.
[28] Haya El Nassar, "The Liability of Campus Crime: Increasingly Schools Held Accountable," *USA Today*, June 4, 1992, News, p. 3A.
[29] Ibid.

If they fail to warn when they should warn, and if they fail to provide adequate protection. Courts have held universities... liable in large damage suits by students injured in crime. In each of these cases, the college knew of the problem but failed to disclose the hazard and failed to provide adequate security.[30]

What is interesting is that the *USA Today* reporter, by interviewing the chief legal counsel for the University of Southern Mississippi, had procured an *expert's* opinion on the issue of institutional liability arising either from victims' claims of lax security or from failure to warn students about crime-related dangers on campus. In stories about students suing schools over their victimization, reporters' soliciting of legal experts' opinions or the opinions of security experts became very common. Additionally, mass-media stories began linking claims by victims of campus crime with those made by SOC and campus feminists about unsafe and violent campuses or collegiate date and acquaintance rape. In effect, journalists' accounts were asking a simple yet unanswered question: if college campuses were safe, why were so many schools being sued for millions of dollars by student crime victims and their families?

What was also interesting in these stories was that a subtle shift occurred in whom the media identified as the perpetrators of on-campus victimizations. Instead of claiming that fellow students were the perpetrators (per the claims of SOC and campus feminists), stories appearing in print and electronic media sources about student victims suing their schools increasingly suggested that *outsiders* were the perpetrators. Stories of student lawsuits arising from on-campus victimizations frequently mentioned that the individuals involved as suspected perpetrators were "intruders," "outsiders," or "not affiliated" with the school where the victim was enrolled and where the victimization had taken place. Thus, not only were college campuses unsafe and violent places because of *student* perpetrators, but victims were now coming forward and claiming to the media that their rape or assault or robbery victimization had been the work of individuals *not even associated* with the school – "predators" who were taking advantage

---

[30] Pat Ordovensky, "Crime on Campus: Colleges Are Taking Crime More Seriously," *USA Today,* June 6, 1989, News, p. 15A.

of lax to nonexistent campus security to make their way onto campus and target unsuspecting students as their victims.

Naming the Problem and Claiming Its Ownership

As the 1990s began and more stories about students suing colleges and universities over lax security appeared in mainstream media outlets, a common theme in the stories was that victims claimed colleges and universities had some type of a "legal duty" to *prevent* them from being victimized.[31] Student victims were thus raising a specific legal claim and expressing that claim to the press.

On examining these stories, victims' legal claims tended to arrange themselves along the following lines. One set of claims was that an institution's legal duty flowed from a "unique" or "intrinsically special" relationship victims said existed between the postsecondary institution and its students. Victims claimed this relationship was similar to that of landowner-business invitee or to the more protective relationship existing between a landlord and a tenant. A second set of legal claims involved arguing that postsecondary institutions had a duty to protect students on the basis of *foreseeability*. That is, victims claimed that if victimizations similar to theirs had occurred recently on the campus, their victimization was foreseeable and the college or university should have taken steps to prevent the incident from reoccurring. Finally, still other victims grounded their claims against schools in existing common law theories of *negligence*,[32] arguing that the evidence in the case was such that it showed that the institution had breached its legal duty to the student and was therefore negligent because it had failed to address known risks to students' safety.

Turning to the courts to shape new policy relating to campus crime was a different course of action from that chosen by SOC and campus feminists, both of whom focused on getting elected policy makers to listen to their claims and then helped to shape laws that were ultimately enacted. While victims who sued their schools ultimately

---

[31] Burling, *Crime on Campus*, discusses various legal theories of duty that colleges owe students to protect them from criminal victimization. See also the following cases: *Whitlock v. University of Denver,* 744 P.2d 54 (Colo. 1987); *Mullins v. Pine Manor College,* 389 Mass. 47, 449 N.E.2d 331 (1983); *Knoll v. Board of Regents,* 258 Neb. 1 (1999); *Sharkey v. Board of Regents,* 260 Neb. 166 (2000).

[32] Burling, *Crime on Campus*, pp. 3–7.

did help shape *legislative* policy responses, they also helped shape postsecondary institutional response to campus crime by *litigating their claims* in court. Once courts began ruling in their favor, student crime victims had successfully changed the contours of the laws governing postsecondary institutional liability.

As accounts of student victims suing their schools flourished in newspapers and the major television networks, claims about lax security became an additional component in the ongoing social construction of campus crime as a new social problem. Mass media became ever more interested in victims' stories when some of them actually turned to the courts, litigated their claims, and were awarded *both* compensatory *and* punitive damages or reached large out-of-court settlements with the institutions involved.

To illustrate how victims named and claimed ownership of the problem, consider a 1990 *Christian Science Monitor* story about campus security that reported that, "spurred by incidents of violence, [campus] administrators and state legislatures are responding to *demands for greater safety* [on college campuses]."[33] A similar story appearing that same year in the *Washington Post* carried the headline "Lawsuits Increase as Campus Attacks Do." The *Post* story reported on the assault of a female student by a male intruder who had attacked her in a soundproof piano studio on the campus of George Washington University.[34] According to the story, after the victim reviewed the chain of events leading to her assault, she decided the university had "failed to protect her and other students" from such attacks and sued the university for $2 million. According to the victim, "GWU's security arrangements were 'wholly inadequate'" and the entire situation constituted "negligence and breach of warranty by GWU."[35]

---

[33] David Smith, "Campus Security Challenges Colleges," *Christian Science Monitor*, January 9, 1990, Ideas, University Life, p. 13 (emphasis added).

[34] Karen Swisher, "Lawsuits Increase as Campus Attacks Do – Colleges Scramble to Improve Security, Assistance to Victims," *Washington Post*, February 24, 1990, sec. I, p. A1.

[35] Ibid. Interestingly enough, a letter to the editor by the president of the Student Association at GWU claimed that campus security was *not* an issue and cited multiple examples of the steps GWU had taken to secure the campus: that GWU had installed "state of the art" security systems at the school's 13 residence halls; that the library and athletics center had "safe and stringent" rules of admittance; and that there were both a student-run and a campus police-sponsored "campus escort

In late September 1990, *USA Today* published a series of stories about crime and security issues at college campuses, and some of the stories highlighted crime victims' claims about security. These particular stories emphasized (according to victims) that lax security on college campuses "was routine," that schools were "failing to warn" students about crimes occurring on their campuses, and that institutional liability via civil judgments was being incurred "because of these failures." In one story, for example, experts including one institution's legal counsel, the general counsel for the International Association of Campus Law Enforcement Administrators, and the director of Campus Security at Princeton University were all quoted as agreeing that postsecondary institutions had a legal duty to warn students not only about known crime-related dangers on campus but also about known dangers *off* the campus as well.[36]

In another story in the *USA Today* series, security lapses at the University of Southern Colorado were chronicled in detail, including not only what the story described as "major deficiencies" in the campus security department but also apparent reprisals by the university against "whistleblowers" who dared come forward to complain to the media about ineffective or lax security arrangements at the school.[37] Frank Carrington, SOC's chief legal counsel, was quoted as saying "[the University of Southern Colorado] is the most egregious situation about which I know," while Arnold Trujillo, chief of the University of Colorado at Colorado Springs Police Department, was quoted as saying, "I wouldn't send *my* daughter there."[38]

Security experts were not the only individuals coming forward to express their opinions about alleged security lapses at postsecondary institutions. Legislators also became involved and expressed *their* concerns about campus security. For example, in a 1990 letter to the editor of the *New York Times*, State Senator E. Arthur Gray (D-39th District) wrote, "I believe that parents *have the right* to expect that their

service." John Norris, "A Safe Place to Learn," *Washington Post*, March 8, 1990, Editorial, Letters to the Editor, p. A26.

[36] Denise Kalette, "Colleges Confront Liability; Off-Campus Risk Warnings Urged," *USA Today*, September 14, 1990, News, p. 6A.

[37] Pat Ordovensky, "The Twin Fears of Campus Crime: Colo. Students Fear Crime, 'Punishment,'" *USA Today*, September 28, 1990, News, p. 1A.

[38] Ibid. (emphasis added).

children will live and study in a safe environment at college."[39] Senator Gray's letter went on to say that in an effort to hold universities more accountable, he was sponsoring legislation that would "require colleges to inform all applicants and employees of…security policies and procedures" and would require first-aid training for all personnel working in on-campus residence halls at all postsecondary institutions in the State of New York.[40]

A 1992 *USA Today* story, again reporting on liability issues arising from student victimizations occurring at postsecondary institutions, examined a lawsuit that arose at the University of Southern California.[41] According to the story, in 1988 a female USC student was assaulted and raped at gunpoint half a block from an off-campus dormitory where she was then living. She then sued the university over the victimization, and a jury found the university liable, awarding the student $1.62 million in damages. What was interesting about this story was that while the victimization had occurred in an area that was officially *off campus*, it was very close to one of the school's dormitories where the victim was living. According to the story, because the area in which the dormitory was located was "dangerous," the student claimed the university had a duty to warn students living there about the area's crime-related dangers. However, because USC failed to do so, the jury held it liable for the student's victimization and forced USC to compensate the student for damages she suffered.

Imbedded Themes. During the 1990s, news accounts of students and their families suing postsecondary schools for on-campus victimizations are interesting because they contained a common set of themes. First, the account would reveal the facts of the victimization – the usual who, what, where, and when – and would indicate whether the perpetrator

---

[39] The sentiment expressed by the senator that college students were "children" (rather than young adults over the age of majority) echoes sentiments routinely expressed by the Clerys and SOC through the 1990s and into today. Why parents would have the "right" to *anything* concerning their adult children attending college raises an interesting question: are postsecondary institutions, in addition to serving an educational function for students, also to serve as surrogate parents to them?

[40] E. Arthur Gray, "Students Need Better Security," *New York Times*, September 24, 1990, sec. 4, p. 20 (emphasis added).

[41] El Nassar, "The Liability of Campus Crime: Increasingly Schools Held Accountable."

was believed to be a student or an "outsider." Next, the story would report the student's or the student's family's claims over how the university had "failed to protect" or "failed to warn" students about crime-related dangers existing on or near the campus, while also failing to "follow-up" in a satisfactory manner with the student or the student's family after the victimization. Third, the story would then report how angry the student or the family was about the institution's lack of appropriate response, which then led to the lawsuit being filed that alleged the college or university "had a duty to protect" the student from harm. Fourth, the story would include quotes from experts, who, most of the time, were critical of the lack of security measures at the institution under scrutiny. Finally, the story would include the revelation that "many similar cases" had arisen at colleges or universities around the country and, as a result, "many schools" were being sued.[42] For example, in the 1990 *Washington Post* story on the incident at George Washington University described previously, the reporter presented a list of "six-figure settlements" that had been received by campus crime victims and the names of the schools involved in those settlements. While such templates used by media in the construction of social problems are not uncommon,[43] the templates relating to crime victims suing their schools were an especially important component in victims' naming and taking ownership of the new problem of lax security at postsecondary institutions.

Vague Definitions. As Best suggested, in naming the problem claimsmakers typically keep the definition of their newly identified problem as vague as possible.[44] Victims' claims about lax security and "failure to warn or to protect" provide good examples of this phenomenon. In reviewing media accounts – both electronic and print – of victims' claims about lax security on college campuses, the phrase "lax security" quickly became a catchall term used by

[42] Thus, the reader was left with no concrete information on whether postsecondary institutions were being sued at alarming rates or whether the rate of filing of lawsuits was increasing on an annual basis.

[43] Joel Best, *Random Violence: How We Talk about New Crimes and New Victims* (Berkeley: University of California Press, 1999).

[44] Ibid.

victims, their families, and reporters to refer to *any number* of security issues confronting modern colleges or universities. For example, lax security could involve a breakdown in access control to dormitory and classroom building entrances; not having enough lighting in common areas of the campus, such as parking lots and decks or walking paths; or inadequate levels of staffing for campus security or police departments. In short, in any given incident covered by the media, the story would indicate that "lax security on the part of the school" was the reason for the student's victimization *regardless of the circumstances surrounding it.*[45] In other words, whether the student was robbed at gunpoint while cutting across the school's intramural field, was assaulted in the stairwell of a parking garage, or was attacked while in the shower of her dormitory did not matter in terms of how the media framed the story for the public. All of these instances pointed out that lax security routinely existed on college and university campuses across the country.

Such stories, however, rarely reported that students sometimes propped open the doors to external entrances of dormitories or allowed access to strangers, thereby effectively defeating even the most sophisticated electronic or surveillance security strategies. In other words, in media reports on lax security occurring at postsecondary institutions, the role that *students* may have played in compromising campus security was *not* the issue. Instead, for reporters and student victims, blaming the *institution* for its lax security policies *was* the issue. As a result, the assault that occurred in the practice studio, the gunfight in the campus parking lot or at the outdoor concert on campus, the acquaintance rape in the dormitory – all these incidents could be blamed on lax institutional security, despite the fact the circumstances of the victimization itself and the nature of the alleged security lapses varied widely across the cases. Claims about lax security thus became a shorthand way for victims, their families, and reporters to describe *any* failure by *any* postsecondary institution at preventing *any* criminal

---

[45] Recall, for example, that Jeanne Ann Clery's death was attributed by her parents to her assailant gaining entrance to Ms. Clery's dormitory because one or more outside doors were propped open with pizza delivery boxes. State-of-the-art security systems installed on the outside doors of dormitories, no matter how good, are unlikely to prevent intruders, especially students, from gaining entrance to these buildings when doors are routinely propped open.

victimization – regardless of where the victimization occurred; whether the students involved potentially contributed to their own victimization; or the extent *other* students may have compromised security practices at the school, which then facilitated the victimization.[46]

Domain Expansion and Elaboration. In their claims, victims also expanded and elaborated upon the domain of the problem. According to victims, it just made sense that, because "everyone knew" college campuses and, in some instances, their surrounding neighborhoods were unsafe and violent places, lax security *had to be the* contributing factor in their particular victimization. If campus grounds were well-lit and foliage cut back and properly maintained, then rapes could not occur in large student parking lots. If universities were installing proper security systems to control access to dormitories or other campus buildings, then intruders – be they students or outsiders – could not freely enter and victimize those living, studying, or practicing there. If colleges *knew* areas near the campus were dangerous and warned students of that fact, students would take the necessary steps to not become victims as they walked home in the evening or to nearby retail establishments. Victims thus took existing claims about unsafe and violent campuses that SOC and its supporters were beginning to legitimize, along with claims made by campus feminists about sexual violence occurring on campus, and tacked them onto the issue of lax security on the part of postsecondary institutions as *the* reason campuses were unsafe and violent.

Additionally, by linking a victimization that occurred at College A, which resulted in a lawsuit over lax security, to instances of *other* postsecondary institutions, also being sued for comparable reasons, student victims could then show how lax security on college campuses had crossed *both* temporal *and* geographic boundaries. For example, after reporting on incidents that supposedly involved lax security occurring at the University of Southern Colorado, the media then linked those incidents to incidents involving similar allegations at

---

[46] In several stories reporting on how lax security contributed to on-campus victimizations, students were quoted as saying that, despite warnings from their college or university not to do so, students *routinely* engaged in behavior that compromised the security of dormitories and other campus buildings, such as propping open doors that otherwise were locked.

schools as geographically disparate as George Washington University, the University of Southern California, and the City University of New York campus in Brooklyn. Such links were created regardless of the fact the schools involved differed in such characteristics as size of student body, on- and off-campus living arrangements for students, proximity to high-crime areas near the campus, or number of on-campus residents. Media reports thus led the public to believe both lax security at postsecondary institutions and lawsuits arising over student victimizations because of it were widespread and occurring at every type of school – large or small, public or private, urban or rural – and large civil awards by juries or out-of-court settlements reached by victims with the institutions involved were common. The implication for public consumption was that victims and their families were successful most of the time in their legal claims against colleges and universities, which in turn, gave further credence to victims' claims concerning the widespread problem of lax security.[47]

Thus, during the late 1980s and 1990s, student victims of campus crime and families came forward and began making claims to the media that postsecondary institutions *routinely* failed to provide students with reasonable security measures and, in doing so, had failed to uphold their "legal duty" to "protect and warn" enrolled students about the "unsafe and violent" campuses on which their students resided. Through their claims, victims, their families, and their supporters successfully named and took ownership of the problem of lax security on college campuses. They also defined lax security loosely enough so as to encompass myriad situations ranging from improper lighting in a campus parking lot that facilitated an armed assault to allowing intruders into campus dormitories to rape or murder student residents. Victims, with the help of national media outlets, were able to claim that lax security at colleges and universities posed an imminent danger to students' safety and that litigation involving lax security was widespread. They did this by successfully linking a particular incident at one institution with an incident or incidents at *other* institutions.

---

[47] One has to wonder about the extent media reports of such lawsuits, coupled with the amount of damages awarded, encouraged attorneys around the nation to file lawsuits against colleges and universities alleging lax security.

Thus, the claimsmakers were able to turn individual *incidents* into *instances* of the problem, an important part of constructing a new social problem.[48] Finally, because the victims who came forward to sue their schools had suffered seriously traumatic victimizations, they had instant credibility with and sympathy from both journalists and the public. As a result, skeptics were unlikely to challenge either the legitimacy of the claimsmakers as actual "victims" or the legitimacy of what they were saying.[49]

Identifying New Victims and Villains

Identifying the new problem of lax security on postsecondary campuses leading to criminal victimizations also allowed activists to identify new victims and villains associated with the problem, in the same way that SOC and campus feminists had done successfully. Similar to claims made by those groups, media reports on crime victims and their families suing postsecondary institutions over lax security portrayed the student victims as innocents who had been subjected to violent assaults or even murder at the hands of others, at least some of whom were also students. These perpetrators, because of the school's lax security, had found their way into dormitories, classroom buildings, parking garages, or other facilities owned by the institution. Similar to successful claims made by SOC and campus feminists, student victims who sued their schools identified as the villains college and university administrators who failed to give enough attention to the security needs of their campuses. For example, the Associated Press articulated this concern in a story about the murder of a Yale student that occurred near the campus in 1991. In the story, the AP reported that "an editorial in the student newspaper echoed the complaint of many students when it said that the administration 'waits for problems to accumulate and then reacts, rather than acting earlier to protect.'"[50]

---

[48] Best, *Random Violence*, pp. 166–167.

[49] This is in line with the argument that Best makes when he suggested that, when new victims of a social problem are identified, they are portrayed in the media in such a way as to make it difficult for skeptics to question their claims without being vilified either by the press or by victims' supporters. Ibid., pp. 103–106.

[50] Larry Rosenthal, "Yale Slaying Brings Home Reality: College Campuses No Safe Havens," Associated Press, February 23, 1991, Domestic News.

While there were some similarities in the content of media reports about victims alleging lax security and suing their schools over it and reports containing the claims of SOC and campus feminists, there were some subtle differences between them. First, as previously described, student victims suing their schools over lax security largely claimed the perpetrators were "outsiders" who were able to victimize students on campus because the school's lax security facilitated the attacks in school buildings, on school grounds, or near the campus. For example, in the 1990 *Washington Post* story about lawsuits arising from campus victimizations described earlier, the story chronicled incidents that had occurred at Georgetown University, the Catholic University of America, Howard University, Pine Manor College (in Chester Hill, Massachusetts), and at the University of California at Santa Barbara and indicated that all the incidents involved outsiders who had perpetrated assaults, rapes, and robberies of student enrolled at those schools.[51] In effect, postsecondary institutions were now being damned by victims, not because schools had failed to address offenses perpetrated by offenders who were *known* to victims (as was the case with campus feminists arguing that colleges and universities were not adequately addressing campus-related date or acquaintance rape), but for failing to address offenses that were being perpetrated by *strangers* who were not affiliated in any way with the college or university.[52]

Second, print and electronic media stories showed that victims were "fighting back," not by seeking the involvement of elected policy makers to reguire college and universities to change their security arrangements but by suing postsecondary institutions in state and federal court.[53] When a student at one of the State University of

[51] Swisher, "Lawsuits Increase as Campus Attacks Do."

[52] In effect, the reports made it appear to the public that the ivory tower was "under attack" by "dangerous outsiders" bent on destroying its mission by violently victimizing students who had come there to engage in a "life of the mind." That institutional administrators were apparently contributing to the ultimate destruction of the ivory tower made the situation both more troubling and certainly more newsworthy.

[53] While true that the *Campus Security Act* contains a provision relating to campus security, to wit, all Title IV–eligible institutions are to provide to interested parties a description of institutional security policies, such as the power and jurisdiction of the campus security agency, Congress designed the *Campus Security Act* and its amendments to require postsecondary institutions to publicly report their *crime statistics* rather than mandate that schools take *specific steps* to make their campuses more safe or secure.

New York campuses was raped by an intruder who gained access to her room via an unlocked entrance to her dormitory, the student sued the school arguing that, as a landlord to its student tenants, it was legally obligated to protect them from harm that was foreseeable.[54] Because the institution knew about previous assaults that had occurred in the dormitory, yet had failed to warn students about them, the court held the school liable for the victimization.[55]

For the media, having college students or their families file lawsuits against colleges and universities over claims of lax security was *very* newsworthy: members of the ivory tower were, in effect, actively turning against it. Additionally, these stories could easily be tied to the growing number of claims by students and their families that the ivory tower, despite its name, was, in fact, a dark place plagued by violence and security lapses harmful to students' well-being. From the media's perspective, such lawsuits quickly became labeled as a "new weapon" in the fight against campus crime. As the lawyer in one such case told the *Boston Globe* "There are very few things that will move an institution to change their [security] policies – a lawsuit is one of them."[56] Similar sentiments were echoed in a 1991 story that appeared in the *Toronto Star* in which Jan Sherill, director of the Campus Violence Center at Towson State University in Maryland, was quoted as saying, "All you need is one really good liability case to force a changing of the [campus security] policy and how people react to it."[57]

Thus, student victims and their families successfully called attention to a new problem on college campuses – lax security – and identified innocent students as the new victims and negligent administrators as the evil villains involved. What was interesting in media portrayals of the victims was the fact they and their families were depicted as "fighting back" by suing the postsecondary institutions where the victimization occurred. The media also made it appear such lawsuits would be an effective weapon to address lax security at U.S. colleges and universities. Through such lawsuits, media reports implied that

---

[54] See *Miller v. State of New York*, 62 N.Y.2d 506, 467 N.E. 2d 493 (N.Y. 1984).
[55] Ibid.
[56] Flint, "Lawsuits New Weapon against Campus Rape."
[57] Lynne Ainsworth, "Seneca College Students Never Told They Might be in Danger of Being Attacked," *Toronto Star*, May 27, 1991, Life, p. B1.

college and university administrators were now on notice, and if they failed to address their schools' security needs, the institutions faced potential multimillion-dollar judgments, along with the negative press and the threat of reduced enrollment accompanying such judgments.

Interesting, too, is that victims involved in these lawsuits sought an avenue to have their claims addressed that differed from the avenue sought by other claimsmakers, including SOC or campus feminists. Instead of seeking intervention from state legislatures or the Congress to require postsecondary institutions to address the lax security they claimed facilitated student victimizations, victims sought to have the *courts* intervene and punish schools for their negligence. Additionally, by helping establish new legal precedent which resulted in creating a new standard of liability, other schools were put on notice of what *they* faced by failing to protect students from foreseeable victimizations.[58]

Establishing an Orientation

Best argued that when constructing a social problem, activists work to establish a particular way of thinking about or conceptualizing the problem and will use the media to disseminate that orientation. In doing so, the orientation becomes *the* way to understand the problem, and it is around that orientation media outlets will wrap a story and broadcast messages about it. Further, policy makers will often adopt that orientation and use it to define their responses to the problem.[59] In the case of student victims of campus crime and their families who sued schools over lax security, this group of claimsmakers also adopted an orientation that revolved around two key points. First, they argued that security on most college campuses was woefully inadequate, and as a result, prospective offenders – be they outsiders or other students – gained access to their targets: innocent college students who had no idea of the dangers they faced upon arriving on campus. Second, those who had been victimized were not going to accept criminal victimization as a routine part of life in the ivory tower. Instead, victims would fight back by suing the institutions, which, they claimed, had failed to protect them from harm despite schools' having a legal duty to do so.

---

[58] Burling, *Crime on Campus.*
[59] Best, *Random Violence*, pp. 173, 175.

Media reports typically painted a picture – often graphic – in which a student was innocently going about his or her business on or near campus, only to be attacked or otherwise harmed. The claims then followed: no, too few, or ill-trained security personnel were on patrol; inadequate surveillance devices were operating in parking lots or decks; maintenance had failed to trim overgrown foliage next to buildings, which provided harbor to attackers; strangers routinely gained access to dormitories. Thus, in no way did either the victims themselves or other students contribute to the victimization – it was solely the *institution's* fault. Because the victims were "innocent," no blame could be attached to their behavior. Rather, the blame fell exclusively on the institution. Having other activists, including SOC and campus feminists, make similar claims no doubt helped bolster the credibility of victims who sued their schools. Because *multiple* claimsmakers were now placing the blame for students' victimizations at the feet of the schools themselves – and national media outlets were routinely reporting these claims – individual victims who made claims that lax security at a particular college or university caused their victimization were more likely to be believed by the public, by lawyers, and by juries hearing these cases.

A key feature of this group's orientation was to present victims as being *brave* by coming forward and exposing the secret of lax security operating at postsecondary institutions. After experiencing the devastating effects of their victimization, they were still willing to potentially suffer the *additional* trauma of pursuing legal redress from their school. Thus, they were actually taking on the ivory tower by suing it. This David-versus-Goliath story contributed to media interest in reporting it. By portraying victims as brave survivors willing to pursue civil lawsuits to force postsecondary institutions to address lax security operations, the media effectively made them out as young heroes.

Institutionalizing the Problem and Shaping Policy Responses

Victims who came forward claiming that lax campus security caused their victimizations and who sued postsecondary institutions over this claim also helped to institutionalize the problem and shape policy responses to it. What is interesting is that, by pursuing their legal claims, victims sought help from a government institution but a different one from those approached by SOC and campus feminists – the courts rather than state legislatures and the Congress. Whereas SOC and campus feminists sought to change how postsecondary institutions addressed campus crime by convincing state legislatures and finally Congress to pass new laws such as the *Campus Security Act* and its subsequent amendments, victims who sued postsecondary institutions sought to change the law and the behavior of postsecondary institutions by asking the courts to create new standards of civil liability for postsecondary institutions.

In suing for damages, victims first sought to impose a financial cost on postsecondary institutions for failing to provide necessary security that would protect students from victimization. Multimillion-dollar lawsuits filed against colleges and universities over alleged lax security would instantly get the attention of not only college and university administrators and institutional boards of trustees but the public as well. It is one thing to have an irate parent or student show up in the dean of student's office complaining about lax security at the school. It is another situation entirely when the college or university is named as the defendant in a $10 million lawsuit over its campus security practices. In such a case, the institution is forced to expend fiscal resources in defending itself from the legal claims made by the plaintiff. Resources would be spent defending the school in the press against the claims. The school would also expend monetary resources if it reached an out-of-court settlement with the plaintiff. Should the plaintiff's claims prevail in court, juries would award damages to the victims, and again the institution would be punished financially. Thus, for the claimsmakers, colleges and universities would literally learn as a result of these lawsuits that they had "millions of reasons" to take their security policies and operations more seriously and change their behavior accordingly. Schools would also learn that lawsuits led to negative press, which could have detrimental effects on the schools' image and reputation, and institutions' behavior would again be changed and institutional wrongs corrected.

Second, by suing postsecondary institutions and making the legal claims they did, student victims, their families, and their attorneys apparently believed they could change the laws that defined the legal nature of the relationship between a postsecondary institution and its students. By arguing in the press and in court that a particular school was either negligent or had breached a contract with its students, victims believed their claims would result not only in favorable rulings by the courts in their individual cases but in the establishment of new legal precedent that would govern all subsequent cases. These new rules would thus force colleges and universities to change their behavior or risk being held liable for criminal victimizations that could be tied to lax security practices, especially if the victimizations were foreseeable.[60]

Finally, through informal alliances with SOC, campus feminists, and victims' rights groups, student victims and their families who claimed lax security was the normal state of affairs in the ivory tower convinced legislative policy makers to become involved in their plight. By getting legislators involved, student victims could convince legislators to pass new laws that focused on security as a subcomponent of larger concerns about campus crime and institutional responses to it. Thus, the *Campus Security Act* and its amendments made reference to campus security and implemented new requirements for schools involving such practices as the institution's provision of timely warnings to members of the campus community when an ongoing threat arose to the community's safety or security. Failing to take these steps could then result in civil fines levied against the school by the U.S. Department of Education or the loss of a school's Title IV eligibility as a recipient of federal financial aid.

Through their actions, student crime victims and their families who sued postsecondary institutions over lax security practices were showing how they were fighting to hold schools financially liable for failing to provide adequate security for students living on campus. Should they prevail, colleges and universities could then be forced to change their behavior when it came to securing the campus, or else pay a steep price – both a financial loss and a tarnishing of the school's image and reputation – for not doing so. At the same time, student crime victims and their families helped institutionalize lax campus security as a problem by convincing policy makers that it was an issue in need

---

[60] Michael C. Smith, "Institutional Liability Resulting from Campus Crime"; Burling, *Crime on Campus.*

of their attention. In so doing, victims helped to shape legislation that contained specific provisions relating to security on campus. As a result, student victims forced changes in postsecondary institutional behavior relating to how campuses were secured.

CONCLUSION

This chapter has described and analyzed how a third group of activists, student victims of campus crime and their families, came forward and made claims to the media that lax security on college campuses was routine and widespread and had caused students to suffer terrible criminal victimizations. By filing civil lawsuits in an effort not only to recover monetary damages but to force postsecondary institutions to change their security policies and practices, student victims helped construct lax campus security as a new problem that confronted millions of college students and ultimately contributed to the overall construction of campus crime as a new social problem.

Using various strategies, student victims and their families came forward to name and take ownership of the problem of lax security on college campuses. They successfully defined the problem in vague terms, making it a catchall phrase that encompassed a variety of issues ranging from improperly securing campus buildings to failing to warn students about past victimizations that had occurred on campus grounds. The group expanded and elaborated upon the domain of lax security, dovetailing it with claims being made by SOC and campus feminists about the unsafe and violent campuses that college students faced. With the assistance of the media, they successfully linked incidents occurring at one college with those occurring at others to create the impression that lax security was widespread and was contributing to the violence and lack of safety that was plaguing college campuses.

They also identified new victims and villains associated with the problem, using claims similar to those voiced by SOC and campus feminists – students were the innocent victims, and campus administrators the villains who failed to make protecting students from predators a priority. With the media's help framing the issue to the public, victims created a particular orientation about lax security – that it was widespread, that campus administrators knew it but did nothing, and that suing the schools was one way these brave survivors could punish institutional failure to address the issue.

Finally, student victims making claims about lax security on college campuses causing violent victimizations were able to institutionalize the problem and shape policy responses to it. For example, they pursued civil litigation in the courts and then, by joining with SOC and campus feminists, demanded that legislatures, including the Congress, do something to force colleges and universities to change how college campuses around the nation were secured. In choosing to litigate their claims, victims hoped to establish new legal precedent not only to have the courts award them significant monetary damages from individual schools but also to send a strong warning to other schools that they too risked significant economic loss and damage to their images and reputations if they continued to treat campus security in a flippant manner.

CHAPTER SIX

Constructing Binge Drinking
on College Campuses

Dude, dude! Wait just a minute here! UCONN should be the undisputed #1 party school in the country!!! On any night of the week (and I do mean any night), you can walk into 10 different wild parties at 10 different spots on or around campus. Don't forget, Spring Weekend at UCONN is the WILDEST partying on earth. If you've never been, let me give you an idea.... Thursday night is the first night where Carriage Housing Community packs in 20,000–25,000 people into the streets, the woods, and the houses. Friday night is next at Celeron Housing where the crowd has been increased to around 30,000–35,000 screaming drunken maniacs. Last but not least, Saturday finishes out the weekend in X Lot, a huge parking lot with hundreds of kegs feeding the needs of anywhere from 45,000–50,000 kids with enough alcohol in their systems to kill a team of Clydesdales![1]

Binge drinking remains higher education's "dirty little secret."[2]

The Ivory Tower image of America's college campuses is severely blurred by alcohol.[3]

For many students entering college, the first few months on campus provide them the opportunity to explore newfound personal

---

[1] Comment posted to the Web site PubClub.com about omitting the University of Connecticut from the site's *Top 10 Party Schools* list for academic year 2008–2009. Retrieved December 15, 2008. http://www.pubclub.com/collegefootball/index. htm. Perhaps the best-known and most widely cited source of such rankings is the annual list compiled by the Princeton Review in its *Guide to the 366 Best Colleges in America*, based on survey responses from more than 120,000 students concerning various aspects of life at the schools listed in the *Guide*. At least one other source that compiles such rankings is *Playboy* magazine, which over the years has published both other sources' "top ten" rankings, as well as compiling its own set of rankings, the most recent of which was published in 2006.

[2] Joseph R. Biden, *Excessive Drinking on America's College Campuses* (Washington, DC: Office of Senator Joseph R. Biden Jr., 2000).

[3] Claude Burgett, "Alcohol Abuse Plays Large Role in Crime," *USA Today*, December 5, 1990, News, p. 8A.

freedom. Choices that previously had been made *for* them by parents and school officials are now *theirs* to make. As a result, they are free to choose whether to attend class or skip and sleep in. They are also free to choose whether to study in the evening or, instead, play a video game, watch TV, or socialize with friends on various social networking Web sites such as *Facebook, MySpace,* or *Twitter.* They can choose to stay up as late as they wish and not have a parent tell them "it's time for bed" or sleep until noon without a parent telling them "it's time to get up." They can explore their own sexuality by dating or "hooking up" with peers.[4] Perhaps most important, students are free to experiment with alcohol or recreational drugs such as marijuana – both of which are readily available on today's college campuses.[5]

Drinking alcohol is both one of the earliest and most important choices new college students face as they transition into life on campus. According to some observers, both the proportion of students who drink and the amount of alcohol they consume is clear evidence that a core "party culture" – a set of beliefs and customs – exists at many postsecondary institutions.[6] In turn, exposure to the party culture quickly shapes students' attitudes toward, not to mention their behavior involving, the consumption of alcohol. For example, the collegiate party culture is alleged to approve of drinking not only *after* class in the evenings and on the weekends but *before* class as well.[7] The party culture also condones students' drinking alcohol before, during, and after sporting events, especially football and basketball

---

[4] "Hooking up," is an ambiguous term used by college students that describes a short-term physical relationship with a partner involving behavior ranging from kissing to sexual intercourse. The apparent key in hooking up is the "rule" prohibiting emotional involvement with the selected partner. For discussion of hooking up, see the following: Kathleen Bogle, *Hooking Up: Sex, Dating, and Relationships on Campus* (New York: New York University Press, 2008); and Tracy Lambert, Arnold Kahn, and Kevin Apple, "Pluralistic Ignorance and 'Hooking Up,'" *Journal of Sex Research* 40 (2003): 129–133.

[5] P. Clayton Rivers and Elsie Shore (Eds.), *Substance Abuse on Campus: A Handbook for College and University Personnel* (Westport, CT: Greenwood Press, 1997).

[6] Ryan Tate, Rich Zeoli, and Mary Sue Coleman, "The Right to Party," ABC News, *Nightline,* May 11, 1998; Elizabeth Vargas, Hugh Downs, and Barbara Walters, "A Sea of Alcohol," ABC News, 20/20, March 16, 1998.

[7] National Institute of Alcohol Abuse and Alcoholism Task Force on College Drinking, *A Call to Action: Changing the Culture of Drinking at U.S. Colleges* (Washington, DC: National Institutes of Health, 2002).

games, and is actively supported by multimillion-dollar marketing campaigns sponsored by the beer, wine, and distilled spirits industry.[8] In this party culture, drinking plays a pervasive role in routine on- and off-campus social gatherings by students.

"Boozing it up" is allegedly a socially accepted way for students to release the "pent-up stresses" associated with the sometimes fierce academic competition found at many big-name colleges and universities.[9] As part of the collegiate party culture, consuming alcohol may also be a key ritual in the annual pledge process occurring at many college fraternities and sororities each year, during which first-year students typically seek entry.[10] For student members of the party culture, drinking is a way for them to break down inhibitions that, for those who are shy or uncomfortable in social settings, can be useful for "breaking the ice" and making new friends. Ultimately, if the foregoing depiction of the campus party culture is correct, then drinking is the great unifier of the different. Drinking alcohol breaks down social barriers involving college students' race, economic status, ethnicity, or regional origins. All can be had or is possible with a few drinks. And, apparently, drink they do.

According to recent data compiled by the National Institute of Alcohol Abuse and Alcoholism (NIAAA), during 2007 about 60 percent of students enrolled at American colleges and universities self-reported they "regularly" drank alcohol.[11] About 5 percent of students self-reported they drank alcohol daily, and just over 40 percent of students reported they had consumed five or more drinks in a single sitting during the previous two-week period, behavior that public health researchers and the U.S. surgeon general label as "binge

---

[8] Commission on Substance Abuse at Colleges and Universities, *Rethinking Rites of Passage: Substance Abuse on America's Campuses* (New York: National Center on Addiction and Substance Abuse at Columbia University, 1994), pp. 47–49.

[9] Leslie Thompson, "College Binge Drinking" (2009), retrieved June 19, 2009, http://www. collegebingedrinking.net/college-binge-drinking.html.

[10] See, for example, Thomas Workman, "Finding the Meanings of College Drinking: An Analysis of Fraternity Drinking Stories," *Health Communication* 13 (2001): 427–447. See also Elizabeth Vargas, John Stossel, and Cynthia McFadden, "Why Did Scott Die?" ABC News, *20/20,* August 1, 1999.

[11] National Institute of Alcohol Abuse and Alcoholism Task Force on College Drinking, *A Call to Action*, p. 17.

drinking."[12] Beyond statistical counts concerning the extent of drinking among college students, NIAAA data also reveal the potentially devastating negative consequences of alcohol abuse among college students. For example, NIAAA data indicate that 1,700 students between the ages of 18 and 24 annually die from alcohol-related unintentional injuries; that between 1998 and 2007 the number of students self-reporting they had driven under the influence of alcohol increased from 2.3 million to 2.8 million; that 696,000 students between the ages of 18 and 24 are annually the victims of alcohol-involved assaults perpetrated by other students; and that 97,000 students between the ages of 18 and 24 annually are the victims of alcohol-involved sexual assaults.[13]

While large numbers of colleges and universities have adopted policies or programs aimed at preventing and reducing drinking by college students, particularly those under the legal drinking age, some college and university presidents have grown frustrated with these efforts.[14] In August 2008, for example, more than 120 chancellors and presidents of U.S. colleges and universities signed a petition urging state legislatures to consider lowering the legal drinking age

---

[12] U.S. Department of Health and Human Services, *The Surgeon General's Call to Action to Prevent and Reduce Underage Drinking*, p. 19, U.S. Department of Health and Human Services, Office of the Surgeon General (2007), retrieved April 7, 2009, http://www.surgeon general.gov. The Harvard School of Public Health's College Alcohol Study series defined "binge drinking" as the consumption of five or more alcoholic beverages in a row at one sitting for men and four or more such beverages for women (the so-called 5/4 definition) on more than one occasion in a two-week period. See Henry Wechsler and Steven Austin, "Binge Drinking: The 5/4 Measure," *Journal of Studies on Alcohol* 59 (1998): 122–123. Various researchers have called this type of drinking "excessive," "heavy episodic," or "high risk." According to one researcher, "definitions of 'binge drinking' have ranged from vague to precise, but even the precise definitions are inconsistent. Because the researchers who study college alcohol use and abuse have failed to reach consensus on a definition for binge drinking, few results can be compared directly." See Todd Gomez, "College Undergraduate Binge Drinking: A Definitional Quandary, Yet Substantive Problem," pp. 121–144 in R. Chapman (Ed.), *When They Drink: Practitioner Views and Lessons Learned on Preventing High-Risk Collegiate Drinking* (Glassboro, NJ: New Jersey Higher Education Consortium, 2009), retrieved March 24, 2009, http://teacher-web.com/nc/psc/jtaylor/WhenThey DrinkBook.pdf.

[13] National Institute of Alcohol Abuse and Alcoholism, *What Colleges Need to Know Now: An Update on College Drinking Research* (Washington, DC: National Institutes of Health, 2007).

[14] See, for example, Henry Wechsler, Michael Seibring, I. C. Liu, and Madha Ahl, "Colleges Respond to Student Binge Drinking: Reducing Student Demand or Limiting Access," *Journal of American College Health* 52 (2004): 159–168.

from 21 to 18 years of age. That petition, sponsored by the Amethyst Initiative,[15] claimed the current legal drinking age not only had failed to curb underage college students from drinking but had promoted a campus culture that encouraged students to habitually abuse alcohol, a behavior that for many students characterizes their college years.[16]

Despite historical evidence that drinking on campus has always been a part of the landscape of college life, college students' alcohol consumption suddenly became a "new" problem during the 1980s and into the 1990s. What triggered this claim? Did the "discovery" of collegiate binge drinking as a new problem also tie into the construction of campus crime as a social problem? In this chapter, we examine those issues by describing how, during the 1990s and early 2000s, public health researchers and activists, including Mothers Against Drunk Driving (MADD) and Security on Campus, Inc. (SOC), discovered that a significant percentage of college students routinely abused alcohol in such a way as to constitute binge drinking and which, according to the claims, routinely resulted in serious – if not fatal – consequences. We show how public health claimsmakers systematically constructed collegiate binge drinking as yet *another* problem threatening the ivory tower. We also show how claims about collegiate binge-drinking behavior were tied to claims about unsafe and violent campuses and to claims about campus date and acquaintance rape which SOC and campus feminists, respectively, had already institutionalized.

In making and marketing their claims about collegiate binge drinking, public health researchers used mass media, both print and electronic, to broadcast several pertinent messages, including that a new and dangerous culture of drinking had taken American college

[15] The Amethyst Initiative was launched in July 2008 and is composed of chancellors and presidents of colleges and universities from across the United States who signed their names to a public statement saying that the problem of irresponsible drinking by young people continues despite the minimum legal drinking age being 21 years old, and that there is a culture of dangerous binge drinking on many campuses as a result. Retrieved December 15, 2008, http://www.amethystinitiative.org. The public interest group Mothers Against Drunk Driving (MADD) has taken major issue with the Amethyst Initiative and developed its own "Why 21?" program to "get the facts out about underage drinking" and keep the legal age for drinking at 21. Retrieved March 22, 2009, http://www.why21.org.

[16] Facts on File, *World News Digest*, "College Officials Urge Lower Drinking Age," September 25, 2008, Education News, p. 678-A2.

campuses hostage; a significant portion of the college student population, especially those under the legal drinking age, were binge drinkers; the negative consequences for students of their binge drinking
habits were significant and included poor academic performance,
unintentional injuries, criminal victimizations, and death; and postsecondary institutions were not effectively addressing the collegiate
binge drinking problem, thereby supporting its continuation. The
mass media picked up these themes and "spread the message" to
the public, especially to the parents of college students. As a result,
the new problem of collegiate binge drinking was brought to center
stage and became integral to the development of campus crime as a
new social problem.

Many of the same processes involved with socially constructing the
tripartite problems of "unsafe and violent campuses," "the sexual victimization of college women," and "lax security on college campuses"
as threats to the ivory tower were also involved in socially constructing
the problem of collegiate binge drinking. Public health researchers
named and then took ownership of the problem. They kept the definition of the problem vague (at least initially), while also elaborating and expanding on the domain of binge drinking, showing that it
had crossed geographic (i.e., on campuses throughout the country)
and temporal boundaries (i.e., across the months comprising a typical academic year). The researchers also identified new victims and
villains associated with the problem, legitimized the victims' claims,
and helped institutionalize this new problem. Finally, activists helped
shape policy responses to the problem, both by elected policy makers
and by college and university administrators.

COLLEGE STUDENTS' BINGE DRINKING

Alcohol use on college campuses has a very long tradition, including
as part of weekend "tailgating" parties before college football games,
as part of "mixers" occurring in Ivy League faculty clubs, and as part
of weekly "kegger" parties held in dormitories and fraternity houses.
"Happy hour" specials at bars located near college campuses, which
advertise discounted prices on beer and mixed drinks, also have a
long tradition. As Columbia University's Commission on Substance

Abuse at Colleges and Universities (CSACU) described on-campus drinking patterns, consuming "alcohol has long been a part of the college experience...accepted as a 'rite of passage.'"[17]

Despite widespread knowledge about and, one could argue, acceptance of the presence of alcohol on college campuses, during the 1990s electronic and print media outlets began trumpeting a message that large numbers of college students – including those under the legal drinking age – were participating in the "college experience" by seriously abusing alcohol. According to these stories, for many students alcohol abuse and binge drinking became symbolic of a newly acquired adult status, and, as a result, students were readily incorporating binge drinking into their college lifestyles.[18]

It was also during the 1990s that public attitudes toward college students' on-campus drinking behavior seemed to change as media reports emerged of what appeared to be the widespread binge-drinking-related deaths of, and serious injuries to, college students. According to news reports, far too many of these victims were under the legal drinking age at the time they died or suffered serious injury, and the incidents seemed to disproportionately occur during annual fall fraternity-pledging activities that included hazing of the pledges – a ritual that is seemingly common on many colleges and universities.[19] Some news accounts of incidents involving student deaths indicated that members of the fraternity to which the victim was pledging were

---

[17] Commission on Substance Abuse at Colleges and Universities, *Rethinking Rites of Passage*, p. 1. These "rites of passage" may include drinking games, such as when a student celebrating his or her 21st birthday attempts to consume 21 shots of liquor in one sitting. For discussion of college students' drinking games, see Lori Simons, Valerie Lantz, Stephanie Klichine, and Laura Ascolese, "Drinking Games, Binge Drinking, and Risky Sexual Behaviors among College Students," *Journal of Alcohol and Drug Education* 49 (2005), retrieved December 4, 2009, http://findarticles.com/p/articles/mi_g02545/is_3_49/ai_n29211874/.

[18] Workman, "Finding the Meanings of College Drinking."

[19] In many of the news stories about alcohol-related deaths involving fraternity pledges, hazing rituals were *explicitly* identified as the causal force. Use of such causal language contributed to the construction of fraternity hazing as a new problem that also threatened the integrity of the ivory tower. For a thorough discussion of hazing and fraternity life, see Hank Nuwer, *Wrongs of Passage: Fraternities, Sororities, Hazing, and Binge Drinking* (Bloomington: Indiana University Press, 2002); Hank Nuwer, *The Hazing Reader* (Bloomington: Indiana University Press, 2004); and Alan D. DeSantis, *Inside Greek U: Fraternities, Sororities, and the Pursuit of Pleasure, Power, and Prestige* (Lexington: University Press of Kentucky, 2007).

actually aware the pledge was in physical distress – unconscious or unconscious *and* vomiting – but members did nothing until it was too late. Further, some of the incidents resulted in lawsuits filed against the offending fraternity, the sponsoring college or university, or both, while others resulted in criminal charges filed against the students who were present but failed to take appropriate action in time to save the life of the pledge.[20] Still other incidents resulted in the national offices of the fraternities banning alcohol at all fraternity pledge activities.[21]

Changes in public attitudes toward college students' drinking were also influenced by several major reports issued by public health researchers during the 1990s that chronicled college students' alcohol consumption patterns, including the scope and magnitude of binge drinking among them.[22] These reports, particularly those coming from the Harvard School of Public Health's College Alcohol Studies (CAS) series,[23] both added fuel to the fire and contributed

[20] For example, Tom Krattenmaker, "Rutgers Fraternity Members Charged in Alcohol-Related Death of Pledge," January 10, 1989, Associated Press, Domestic News, BC Cycle.

[21] See, for example, discussion in Peter Lake, "Modern Liability Rules and Policies Regarding College Student Alcohol Injuries: Reducing High-Risk Alcohol Abuse through Norms of Shared Responsibility and Environmental Management," *Oklahoma Law Review* 53 (Winter 2000): 611–630. See also Michael Kuzmich, "*In Vino Mortuus*: Fraternal Hazing and Alcohol Related Deaths," *McGeorge Law Review* 31 (Summer 2000): 1087–1128.

[22] Philip Jenkins, *Decade of Nightmares: The End of the Sixties and the Making of 1980s America* (New York: Oxford Press, 2006), pp. 204–205, argues the 1980s were a period when substance abuse became the target of a national movement that was geared to protecting young people from its inherent dangers. Alcohol use was not immune from this targeting, Jenkins points out: "The 'anti-drunk movement' had an acute impact on the young, as it redefined the limits of adulthood." Jenkins points out that during the 1960s most states reduced their minimum drinking age below the familiar 21. However, between 1976 and 1983 a restrictive reaction arose across the United States, best illustrated by states scaling the legal drinking age back to 21, partly due to changes in conditions under which the states could receive federal highway funds. The federal government essentially told the states that if they wanted highway funds they had to raise the legal drinking age back to 21. In Jenkins's estimation, the anti–substance abuse movement adopted a "child protection rhetoric" that reversed formerly laissez faire social attitudes toward alcohol that had prevailed since the end of the Prohibition era.

[23] See Henry Wechsler and Toben Nelson, "What We Have Learned from the Harvard School of Public Health College Alcohol Study: Focusing Attention on College Student Alcohol Consumption and the Environmental Conditions That Promote It," *Journal of Studies on Alcohol and Drugs* 69 (2008): 481–490.

to the construction of college students' binge drinking as a serious new problem confronting the ivory tower. The reports also signaled the entry of public health authorities into the arena of college student drinking, and their expertise became very important not only in naming the problem but in helping claimsmakers influence discourse about, and the content of public policy toward, the issue.[24] Print and electronic media sources not only readily disseminated key results from these studies but also spread an implicit "control consumption" policy recommendation, along with criticism of college administrators for failing to do more to stem the tide of dangerous binge drinking sweeping their campuses.[25]

In combination, media coverage of students' drinking-related deaths and public health reports on students' binge-drinking behavior united to create a "rhetorical war on collegiate drinking," which represented a "significant change in [the] cultural framework about alcohol consumption [on college campuses], often labeled as 'neo-prohibitionist.'"[26] By first describing the extent and nature of alcohol abuse on college campuses and then naming that behavior as "binge drinking" and linking it to serious negative consequences, including death from alcohol poisoning, sexual victimization of female

[24] For an interesting discussion of public health models and the data on which they are often based, see Nancy Krieger, "The Making of Public Health Data: Paradigms, Politics, and Policy," *Journal of Public Health Policy* 13 (4, 1992): 412–427. Krieger argues (p. 413) that the form and content of public health data "embody underlying beliefs and values about what it is we need to know," and as a result, these data are not objective "facts" that are "collected." Rather, Krieger argues the collection and use of *any* data – whether compiled by public health researchers or other scientists – is influenced by underlying sets of ideological beliefs used to influence political discourse and public policy making. Thus, according to Krieger (p. 412), if public health researchers label infant mortality a problem of "minorities," and they present data focusing only on *racial* differences in rates of mortality, then data on infant mortality rates among poor mothers who are white are immediately removed from the discussion and analysis and, ultimately, from policy considerations.

[25] Implicitly, a call was going out to return to the days of colleges and universities serving *in loco parentis* – in place of the parents – and protect students from the dangers of alcohol. For discussion of the apparent return of *in loco parentis* to the ivory tower, see Randall Bowman, "Evolution of Responsibility: From *In Loco Parentis* to *Ad Meliora Vertamur*" (2007), retrieved October 15, 2009, http://www.accessmylibrary. com/coms2/summary_0286–32297466_ITM.

[26] Thomas A. Workman, "The Social Construction of Collegiate Binge Drinking as a Social Problem in America," paper presented at the 84th annual meetings of the National Communication Association, New York City, 1998, p. 4.

students, or unintentional injury, public health researchers helped to construct binge drinking as a new social problem among college students. Additionally, their work helped to legitimize SOC's and campus feminists' claims that alcohol was a *significant* causal mechanism in generating the violence they claimed characterized U.S. college campuses. Research by public health authorities also identified college administrators as being at least partly responsible for the claimed binge-drinking epidemic. In doing so, the researchers created additional pressure on college administrators to address apparent links between alcohol abuse among students and the violence that activists argued was plaguing college campuses.

Establishing the Claim and an Orientation
While reports of college student alcohol-related deaths are neither new nor novel in the history of higher education, during the late 1980s mainstream media coverage of such deaths apparently increased and began adopting a more critical orientation concerning the role of colleges and universities in these deaths. In January 1989, for example, the Associated Press released a story chronicling the death of 18-year-old fraternity pledge James Callahan at Rutgers University, who along with 13 other pledges at Lambda Chi Alpha participated in a drinking ritual that involved consuming "kamikazes," a potent mixed-drink consisting primarily of vodka. Callahan apparently drank until he dropped dead from alcohol poisoning after consuming 23 ounces of alcohol. Callahan's autopsy revealed that his blood alcohol content was .463, more than four times the legal limit. In response to this incident, fraternity members were charged with aggravated hazing under New Jersey state law. Also in response to the incident, the university's administration eventually closed the fraternity house and disbanded the campus chapter.[27]

Journalists' accounts of similar incidents became increasingly common during the 1990s. For example, two notable cases that received near saturation levels of coverage by major print and electronic media outlets involved the alcohol-related deaths of 20-year-old Benjamin Wynne at Louisiana State University (LSU) and 18-year-old Scott

---

[27] Krattenmaker, "Rutgers Fraternity Members Charged in Alcohol-Related Death of Pledge."

Kruger at the Massachusetts Institute of Technology (MIT) within two months of one another in 1997.[28] According to news accounts, Wynne died, and 12 other students were treated for alcohol poisoning by emergency medical personnel after a night of heavy drinking at a bar near the LSU fraternity where the members lived. An autopsy revealed that Wyne's blood alcohol content was .58, or nearly six times the legal limit. Kruger's death was also linked to fraternity activities. According to witness accounts, Kruger died after an evening of drinking at the Phi Gamma Delta fraternity house where he was living. His blood alcohol level was .41, or just over four times the legal limit. These two well-publicized incidents – combined with newspapers' eye-catching headlines such as "Sea of Booze Threatens to Engulf America's College Students,"[29] "College Taps Runneth Over,"[30] or "Tough Campus Test: Saying 'No' to Drink"[31] – painted a picture of college students apparently spending most of their free time consuming large quantities of alcohol and sometimes dying as a result.

News stories further advanced the notion that alcohol abuse among college students was both widespread and out of control:

- During academic year 1994, college students spent more on alcohol than on all other beverages and textbooks *combined.*[32]
- "Four *billion* bottles of beer consumed on college campuses tell their own story."[33]
- "Drinking starts on Thursday night and lasts through Sunday" (student at the University of Wisconsin at Madison referring to the drinking that goes on among students enrolled there).[34]

[28] See Bill Ritter and Charles Gibson, "Fraternity Drinking," *ABC Good Morning America*, October 1, 1997; Laura Rozen and Bob Edwards, "Alcohol Death at MIT," NPR, *Morning Edition*, September 1, 1997; Randall Pinkston, "Freshman at MIT Dies as a Result of Binge Drinking at Fraternity Party," *CBS Evening News with Dan Rather*, September 30, 1997.

[29] Christopher Connell, "A Sea of Booze Threatens to Engulf America's College Students," Associated Press, Washington Dateline, June 7, 1994.

[30] Editorial, *Fresno Bee*, June 11, 1994, p. B4.

[31] John Milne, "Tough Campus Test: Saying 'No' to Drink," *Boston Globe*, Metro/Region, April 2, 1995, p. 1.

[32] Linda Campbell, "Books Losing to Booze: Students' Heavy Drinking Is Proving a Worry to College Officials," *Plain Dealer*, June 17, 1996, p. 4E (emphasis added).

[33] Editorial, *San Francisco Chronicle*, August 30, 1995, p. A24 (emphasis added).

[34] Eldon Knoche, "Raise a Mug...or an Eyebrow at UW 'Party Rank,'" *Milwaukee Journal Sentinel*, August 20, 1997, p. 1.

- "Every academic year brings scores of stories of young men and women who drank until they died; or drank until they fell off a roof or out of a window; or until they passed out and choked to death on their own vomit."[35]
- "At Oklahoma State University...the student health center treats an average of 10 cases of severe alcohol poisoning a semester, up from six a decade ago."[36]
- "College students drink over 34 gallons of alcohol per person, per year. If this alcohol were placed in Olympic-sized swimming pools, the average would amount to every college student body in the U.S. consuming one entire pool per year."[37]
- "Eighty-seven [students] were arrested at the University of Connecticut when a spring celebration got out of hand."[38]

Thus, according to journalistic accounts, the message was clear and simple: alcohol abuse on college campuses was rampant; many students abusing alcohol were under the legal drinking age; students who abused alcohol were being seriously harmed, including suffering unintentional injuries or dying from alcohol poisoning; and college fraternities were routinely linked as either initiators for or enablers of this excessive drinking. These stories thus succeeded in bringing to the public's attention the serious negative consequences of students' alcohol abuse. This behavior and its negative consequences had now created yet *another* blemish on the ivory tower.

As stories of college students' alcohol abuse became more common in mainstream media sources, the new term also began appearing regularly – college students were not just abusing alcohol, they were "binge drinking" – and this behavior was being directly linked to the alcohol-related deaths of students. For example, in a September 1992 episode of CNN's talk show *Sonya Live*, the issue of binge drinking among college students was discussed:

[35] Jennifer Weiner, "Booze 101: A Course Colleges are Combating...Some Students Are Not Listening," *Philadelphia Inquirer,* August 31, 1997, Sunday Review, p. E01.
[36] William Celis, "Fatal Alcohol Abuse Persists on Campus, but Fewer Drink," *New York Times,* December 31, 1991, sec. A, National Desk, p. 1.
[37] William Wineke, "Study: Booze Spending Tops School Costs," *Wisconsin State Journal,* September 29, 1992, Metro Section, p. 1D.
[38] Jim Williams and Aaron Brown, "Drunken Riot Breaks Out at an Ohio University," *ABC World News Saturday,* May 9, 1998.

Maybe parents need to take a hard look at what their kids are doing on college campuses. A recent study revealed some of the most disturbing statistics I've seen. Forty-two percent of the students had engaged in *binge drinking* in a single two-week period. Fifty percent of the students became physically ill from alcohol or other drug use, while 28 percent have blackouts within the past year. What are we sending our kids to college for? To get a better education or to heighten their alcohol tolerance?[39]

As binge drinking increasingly became identified as the descriptive term for students' alcohol abuse, a new group of claimsmakers came forward: public health researchers. They argued that their studies showed binge drinking was widespread among a substantial portion of all college students. They also claimed that collegiate binge drinking was a source of serious psychological and physical harm not only to those who binge-drank but also to those who did not – what were dubbed "secondary effects" of the behavior. Public health researchers joined the ranks of other campus crime claimsmakers alongside SOC, campus feminists, and student victims and their families.

Naming the Problem and Taking Ownership
During the 1990s public health researchers released and widely disseminated several reports that first identified binge drinking as a "new and serious problem" on college campuses and made significant claims about its extent, nature, and apparent devastating negative consequences. Released by groups of highly regarded researchers, first at Southern Illinois University (the CORE Institute), then by the Commission on Substance Abuse at Colleges and Universities (CSACU) at Columbia University, and later in an ongoing series of reports by Harvard University's School of Public Health, these reports gained widespread acceptance by the media as "authoritative sources" on college students' alcohol-abusing behavior. While the CORE Institute and the CSACU reports received some notice from the media, Dr. Henry Wechsler and his team of researchers at Harvard's School of Public Health were primarily responsible for bringing the new problem of collegiate binge drinking to the public stage.[40]

---

[39] CNN, "Drug and Alcohol Abuse," *Sonya Live!*, September 18, 1992 (emphasis added).
[40] Workman, "The Social Construction of Collegiate Binge Drinking."

CORE Institute Surveys.   In 1986 the U.S. federal government passed
the *Safe and Drug-Free Schools and Community Act* (20 USC § 7101,
et seq.), which, along with subsequent amendments passed in 1989,
set aside federal funding directed at drug prevention initiatives in
higher education. In 1987 the U.S. Department of Education's Fund
for the Improvement of Postsecondary Education solicited proposals
for college-focused substance abuse prevention programs.[41] The
funded grantees then formed a committee to oversee and ultimately
develop an appropriate measurement instrument that could provide
participating schools with accurate information on the scope and
nature of substance abuse behavior engaged in by their students. This
committee developed what came to be known as the *CORE Alcohol and
Drug Survey* and began data collection at 105 participating schools
during the period 1989–1991.[42] In 1992 the CORE Institute released
its first CORE Report to college presidents that chronicled, primarily
in statistical terms, the extent and nature of alcohol use and abuse
among more than 56,000 students at participating two- and four-
year schools.[43] Additionally, the report presented trend analyses of
matched samples of students from 38 of the participating schools for
the period 1989–1991.

Selective results from the CORE Report almost immediately began
appearing in local and national mass-media outlets.[44] For example, the
Chicago Sun Times carried a story stating that the CORE Report found
"nearly 42 percent of college students admit to 'binge drinking' in
the two weeks prior to taking the survey... [and the survey] found a

[41] http://www.ed.gov/about/offices/list/ope/fipse/index.html, retrieved March 30,
2009.
[42] See Cheryl Presley and Philip Meilman, *Alcohol and Drugs on American College
Campuses: A Report to College Presidents* (Carbondale: Southern Illinois University,
1992), p. 3.
[43] Ibid., p. 4. Of the 96 schools that administered the CORE survey, only 78 of them
used random sampling techniques. The report included only data collected at
those schools.
[44] Several members of the U.S. House of Representatives had a press conference to
announce the release of the CORE Report on September 18, 1992. News Conference
with Representative Glenn Poshard (D-IL), Representative Herbert H. Bateman
(R-VA), Representative Bill Goodling (R-PA), Dr. Cheryl Presley, Southern Illinois
University, and Dr. Philip W. Meilman, College of William and Mary, "Re: Drug and
Alcohol Use on College Campuses," *Federal News Service*, September 18, 1992, Major
Leader Special Transcript.

strong connection between drinking and low grades." The story went on to highlight that the CORE Report found "binge drinking is frequently associated with sexual assault, residence hall damage, fights, and drunken driving," and "28% of surveyed students reported binge drinking more than once in the two weeks prior to taking the survey; 7% said they had binged more than five times; and that male students drank excessively more than female students."[45] The *Wisconsin State Journal* quoted the CORE Report claim that "alcohol is a factor in 90% of all campus rapes."[46] National news outlets such as the *New York Times* also carried excerpts from the CORE Report, noting that "students at small colleges drink more alcohol than their colleagues at larger schools" and "the study did not establish a causal link between drinking and low grades, but found a strong correlation."[47] Results of the study continued to routinely appear in news accounts about college students' alcohol abuse for the next 12 to 18 months. It was also the case that almost all of the stories focused on reporting the most serious negative consequences of students' binge drinking, especially serious injuries and deaths linked to alcohol poisoning from binge drinking.

Commission on Substance Abuse at Colleges and Universities. In 1992 the National Center on Addiction and Substance Abuse at Columbia University convened a blue-ribbon panel known as the Commission on Substance Abuse at Colleges and Universities (CSACU) to study the problem of collegiate substance abuse.[48] The panel consisted of, among others, current and past presidents of postsecondary institutions; college coaches, such as Joe Paterno from Pennsylvania State University; medical practitioners; and political figures (e.g., past and current U.S. senators), whose charge was to examine and then report on the substance-abusing behavior of college students. Using a variety of methods, including findings from focus groups, meta-analyses of published literature, and transcripts from government

---

[45] Roger Flaherty, "Drinking Still a College Sport; 42% Binge on Alcohol, National Survey Finds," *Chicago Sun-Times*, September 19, 1992, News, p. 5.

[46] Wineke, "Study: Booze Spending Tops School Costs."

[47] Associated Press, "Study Finds Students at Small Colleges Drink More," *New York Times*, September 20, 1992, sec. I, National Desk, p. 33.

[48] http://www.casacolumbia.org/templates/Home.aspx?articleid=287&zoneid=32, retrieved March 30, 2009.

hearings, CSACU issued its first report in 1994 that examined substance abuse – particularly alcohol abuse – among college students.

Similar to what happened with the CORE Report, journalists quickly began disseminating the CSACU Report's key findings. For example, the Associated Press released a story in June 1994 quoting the CSACU Report as having found that "51 percent of men and 37 percent of women had gone on binges [referring to drinking] at least twice in the past two weeks"; that "95% of violent crimes and 53% of injuries on campus are alcohol-related"; and that "60% of college women who acquire sexually transmitted diseases, including herpes and AIDS, were drunk at the time of infection." The AP story also quoted the CSACU Report as saying colleges "needed to take better steps to discourage binge drinking, including the banning of ads and promotions for alcohol found in campus newspapers."[49] The *Washington Post* carried a story in which it also quoted the CSACU Report as saying that the percentage of college women drinking alcohol "primarily to get drunk" had *tripled* since the mid-1970s and that the CSACU report had concluded that college student binge drinking was an "epidemic."[50] Among other outlets, the *Boston Globe*, the *Charleston Gazette* (West Virginia), *Philadelphia Inquirer*, and *Washington Times* all carried stories over the next year quoting the CSACU Report. These stories also included terms such as "epidemic" to describe the level of binge drinking among American college students and continued focusing on the most serious negative consequences for students of their drinking behavior.

Harvard School of Public Health's College Alcohol Study Series. Beginning in the mid-1990s and continuing into this decade, reports, monographs, and peer-reviewed articles that emerged from the Harvard School of Public Health's College Alcohol Study (CAS) series and its principle investigator, Dr. Henry Wechsler, became the most commonly cited authoritative source in mass-media coverage of college students' binge-drinking behavior.[51] According to the CAS Web site,

---

[49] Connell, "A Sea of Booze Threatens to Engulf America's College Students."

[50] Brooke Masters, "Women Drinking Like Men, College Alcohol Study Finds," *Washington Post*, June 8, 1994, sec. I, p. A1.

[51] According to its Web site, CAS researchers have published more than 80 peer-reviewed articles in public health, medical, social science, education, and economic journals. The Web site further claims the series of studies is the most widely cited

The Harvard School of Public Health College Alcohol Study (CAS) conducted 4 national surveys involving over 14,000 students at 120 four-year colleges in 40 states in 1993, 1997, 1999, and 2001. The schools and students selected for the study provided a nationally representative sample. In addition, CAS colleges with high levels of heavy alcohol use were re-surveyed in 2005.[52]

In December 1994 the *Washington Post* carried a story on collegiate drinking that excerpted results of the first CAS report, which had been published in the *Journal of the American Medical Association*.[53] The story quoted Dr. Wechsler as saying that "50 percent of male [college] students and 39 percent of female students are binge drinkers." The story went on to report CAS found "variation in binge drinking rates... [that] suggests that *colleges may create and unwittingly perpetuate their own drinking cultures* through selection, tradition, policy, and other strategies."[54] The story also included quotes from several students, including a Georgetown University student who said:

It's...the *culture of drinking*. It's less so for women and more so for men, to see the kind of stamina they have. There's a big thing to see if you can handle your liquor or drink somebody else under the table. That's encouraged at a party or just hanging out with friends.[55]

The same student was also quoted as saying "most students would *not* view drinking four or five drinks in one night as 'binge drinking.' Most

in the field of alcohol studies and has been featured in numerous radio (e.g., NPR), television (e.g., CNN, ESPN, ABC News, CBS News, NBC News, *Nightline*, and *Good Morning America*), newspaper (e.g., *Chronicle of Higher Education, New York Times, Washington Post, Los Angeles Times, Wall Street Journal, USA Today, Boston Globe, Boston Herald*), and magazine (e.g., *U.S. News and World Report* and *Sports Illustrated*) reports on college students' drinking behavior. The CAS has been supported by funding from the Robert Woods Johnson Foundation. Retrieved March 27, 2009. http://www.hsph.harvard.edu/cas/About/index.html.

52 Retrieved March 27, 2009, http://www.hsph.harvard.edu/cas/About/index.html.
53 Henry Wechsler, Alan Davenport, George Dowdall, Bruce Moeykens, and Stephen Castillo, "Health and Behavioral Consequences of Binge Drinking in College: A National Survey of Students at 140 Campuses," *Journal of the American Medical Association* 272 (1994): 1672–1677. Dr. Wechsler and his colleagues published many other articles in prestigious, peer-reviewed journals. An extensive bibliography of publications involving his group is available at the Harvard School of Public Health College Alcohol Studies Web site.
54 Christopher Daly, "Nearly Half of U.S. College Students Are Binge Drinkers, Study Finds," *Washington Post*, December 7, 1994, sec. I, p. A17 (emphasis added).
55 Ibid. (emphasis added).

would consider [binge drinking] as [consuming] 10 or 15 [drinks]."[56] The story implied that, at least from the perspective of college students, binge drinking – as defined by the CAS – was common and involved accruing a kind of "status" for students who could "handle their liquor."

Beyond national news outlets such as the *Washington Post*, regional news outlets also included CAS statistics in their stories about college student drinking:

- "One in five college students can be characterized as a frequent binge drinker."[57]
- "Nearly half of students on campuses are binge drinkers."[58]
- "Nationally, studies show that almost one-half of college students drink in binges."[59]
- "The Harvard study showed that 'binge drinkers' create problems for classmates who are not 'binge drinkers.'"[60]

Thus, both national and regional media outlets were trumpeting the problem of collegiate binge drinking – often citing the "50% of students binge drink" statistic – and implying that binge drinking was a normal part of the college campus culture. The reports also heavily emphasized the behavior's potentially grave negative consequences for participants (e.g., death from alcohol poisoning), as well as its impact on others (e.g., disrupting the lives of roommates who did not drink).

In 1997 CAS data again appeared in news reports on collegiate binge drinking and its negative consequences. For example, the *Boston Herald* ran a story on the death of a student from alcohol poisoning in which it quoted Dr. Wechsler as saying "every major university in the country will have some alcohol-fueled tragedy this year."[61] CAS

---

[56] Ibid.

[57] Karen Brady, "Researcher Returns to Western New York to Warn Colleges, Students on Binge Drinking," *Buffalo News*, December 15, 1994, Local, p. 10.

[58] Mike Matulis, "College Concerns: Nearly Half of Students on Campus Are Binge Drinkers," *State-Journal Register*, March 7, 1995, Local, p. 6.

[59] Jennifer Skordas, "Students Urged to Stay Sober on Break," *Salt Lake Tribune*, March 16, 1995, Utah, p. B1.

[60] Michael Slatin, "Campus Alcohol Use: Prevention Key Issue," *South Bend Tribune*, April 5, 1995, Local/Area, p. B4.

[61] Tom Cornell, "N.E. College Kids Are No Strangers to Binge Drinking," *Boston Herald*, August 28, 1997, News, p. 27. The article characterized Dr. Wechsler as "one of the nation's leading experts on binge drinking."

results from the 1997 study were also mentioned in stories on binge drinking and the serious consequences of the behavior that appeared in such newspapers as the *Columbus Dispatch,*[62] *Milwaukee Journal Sentinel,*[63] *Philadelphia Inquirer,*[64] *Atlanta Journal Constitution,*[65] and the *Boston Herald.*[66] Generally, the stories emphasized the "normality" of collegiate binge drinking by citing CAS statistics and continued emphasizing the negative consequences of binge-drinking behavior for both drinkers and those students who did not engage in the behavior.

Framing the Binge Drinking Problem
In focusing on binge drinking by college students as an example of an "unhealthy behavior," public health researchers gathered data from large samples of students across multiple campuses and presented findings that strongly reinforced the negative impact of the behavior. This fact lent credence to the scientific legitimacy of the research, which no doubt helped the claimsmakers as they pressed to bring to the public's attention the dangers of alcohol abuse. Further, the language used in electronic and print media stories in which the various reports on binge drinking were quoted, adopted a particular frame of reference that communications researchers suggest is common in public health research, which involves scrutinizing unhealthy behaviors and emphasizing the negative consequences of them.[67] Activists then used the language of the reports to illustrate to the public and policy makers not only that the behavior should be considered "deviant" but that criminalization might even be warranted in the "interest" of public welfare.[68]

[62] Doug Caruso, "Scientists Help Fight Drinking on Campus," *Columbus Dispatch,* February 27, 1997, News Local & National, p. 1C.

[63] Knoche, "Raise a Mug."

[64] Weiner, "Booze 101."

[65] Derrie Ferris Finger, "Campus Concern: Problem Drinking," *Atlanta Journal Constitution,* August 31, 1997, National News, p. 16A.

[66] Jack Sullivan, "Campus Alcohol Abuse Remains Problem," *Boston Globe,* September 30, 1997, News, p. 18.

[67] Ibid., p. 8. See also Joseph R. Gusfield, *Contested Meanings: The Construction of Alcohol Problems* (Madison: University of Wisconsin Press, 1996); and Brian S. Turner, *Medical Power and Social Knowledge* (London: Sage, 1995).

[68] Workman, "Social Construction of Collegiate Binge Drinking," p. 8. A good illustration of this process can be found in recent bans on the use of trans-fat in the preparation of restaurant foods in New York City, California, and Chicago. See Thomas Lueck and Kim Severson, "New York Bans Most Trans Fats in Restaurants," *New York*

Thus, with the assistance of journalistic accounts, activists took the results of the various public health studies on collegiate drinking and "created a belief that excessive drinking on the college campus [posed] a threat to the health and safety *of all college students*."[69] In effect, the language used by journalists in their stories as well as in the public health reports resulted in a framing of collegiate drinking that emphasized that binge drinking was characteristic of *all* collegiate drinking and that the behavior was seriously injuring and killing far too many of them.[70]

In disseminating results of the various reports on collegiate alcohol abuse, the term "binge" became a metaphor for "abuse," which implies a lack of moderation in one's appetites or control over them. Further, researchers developed a quantity-time ratio for the term – the "5/4 rule" (five drinks in one sitting for males, four drinks in one sitting for females on at least one occasion during a two-week period) – which CAS created and which was ultimately widely accepted by public health researchers and government agencies, including the NIAAA.[71] Creating the 5/4 rule allowed activists not only to *name* the problem but also to give it scientific credence. "Binging" could now be quantified through the 5/4 measure, and that measure was used to assess the extent and nature of the drinking problem across *students* (regardless of campus) and across college *campuses* (regardless of location).[72]

Media reports on the deaths of students from alcohol poisoning were thus combined with findings from scientific studies in such a way that the students who died (e.g., Scott Kruger, the MIT student who died from alcohol poisoning in 1997) became the face of binge drinking (in much the same way that Jeanne Ann Clery was the face of violent and unsafe college campuses). Mass-media reports also

Times, December 6, 2006, N.Y./Region, p. 8, retrieved December 4, 2009, http://www.nytimes.com/2006/12/06/nyregion/06fat.html?scp=3&sq=Banning%20of%20trans%20fats%20in%20restaurant%20food&st=cse.

[69] Workman, "The Social Construction of Collegiate Binge Drinking," p. 4 (emphasis added).

[70] Thomas Workman, "An Intertextual Analysis of the Collegiate Drinking Culture" (Ph.D. dissertation, Department of Communication Studies, University of Nebraska, Lincoln, 2001), pp. 243–244.

[71] Workman, "The Social Construction of Collegiate Binge Drinking," p. 11.

[72] See Workman, "An Intertextual Analysis of the Collegiate Drinking Culture," for a critique of the "5/4 rule."

sent a not-too-subtle message that *all* collegiate drinking not only was dangerous but *usually resulted in deadly consequences.*[73] By reducing the behavior to a "measure" (the 5/4 rule) or "case study" (e.g., the death of a student at a particular campus), the problem was given a "name" (binge drinking), and the public was provided with empirical evidence of its existence. Public health reports and the journalistic accounts that helped disseminate the results of various studies of collegiate alcohol abuse discussed binge drinking as if it were a thing to be "analyzed and conquered."[74] In turn, conquering binge drinking could be achieved only by immediately implementing new policies, such as banning alcohol from campus or from fraternity or sorority activities, providing alcohol education as part of new student orientation, or changing the norms of the campus drinking culture.

Expanding the Domain of the Problem

Activists' and journalistic accounts of collegiate binge drinking followed the now familiar pattern where a particular instance of the problem was presented in such a way as to imply the problem had crossed geographic and temporal boundaries. Similar to what happened with claims about violent and unsafe campuses, campus date rape, or lax security on college campuses, mass-media reports on collegiate binge drinking took individual instances of the behavior and proffered them as proof that binge-drinking behavior was a widespread and dangerous problem across *all* college campuses. For example, the following story that appeared in the *New York Times* in 1998 illustrates how binge drinking on campus had apparently the crossed geographic boundaries:

> The string of deaths followed the much publicized drinking deaths earlier this year at M.I.T. and Louisiana State University, and numerous less publicized deaths at Fordham University; Hartwick College in Oneonta, N.Y.; Clarkson University in Potsdam, N.Y.; St. Mary's University in Winona, Minn.; the University of Massachusetts at Amherst; Pennsylvania State University; and the State University College at Cortland, N.Y.[75]

[73] Ibid., pp. 12–13.
[74] Ibid., p. 13.
[75] Michael Winerip, "Binge Nights: The Emergency on Campus," *New York Times*, January 4, 1998, Education Life Supplement, sec. 4A, p. 29.

Thus, if a student binge-drank himself to death at a college in Washington State, another student fell from a window and was seriously injured at a school in Iowa, and a third student was involved in a drunk-driving fatality at a campus in Florida, this proved that binge drinking was everywhere and had thus crossed geographic boundaries. Further, journalists' accounts of collegiate binge drinking also showed the problem had crossed temporal boundaries by presenting stories of binge drinking incidents occurring after a home football game, before a home basketball game, and during spring break. Reports on the binge-drinking problem also zeroed in on fraternities as their locus. Because fraternities were characterized as such a large part of campus life, accounts from journalists and activists made the leap from reporting on a binge-drinking incident occurring at fraternity X at school Y, to inferring that *binge drinking was a routine occurrence at all fraternities on all American college campuses and pledges were needlessly dying as a result.*

In a story headlined "Campus Binge Drinking Persists" that appeared in both the *New York Times* and the *Houston Chronicle*, the reporter quoted the president of Virginia Polytechnic and State University (Virginia Tech) as saying "more students are drinking abusively [than in previous years]." The story then went on to say that "at Virginia Tech and Boston College, from Rutgers to Stanford, administrators are grappling with the problem." The story further characterized abusive collegiate drinking as having "intensified in recent years."[76] A *Boston Globe* story published in 1995 ran the headline "Tough Campus Test: Saying 'No' to Drink"; it stated that "partying" at the University of New Hampshire began on Thursday evenings and described students as "straggling back from bars, dorm rooms, or fraternity houses...heckling the residents of Englehardt Hall." The story went on to report that "drinking remains as inevitable a part of college life as required courses."[77] A 1996 story appearing in the *News and Observer* (Raleigh, NC) chronicled a fire at a fraternity house on the campus of the University of North Carolina at Chapel Hill in which five members of the house died, four of whom had been intoxicated. The story quoted the university chancellor as referring to collegiate

---

[76] Celis, "Fatal Alcohol Abuse Persists on Campus, but Fewer Drink."
[77] Milne, "Tough Campus Test."

binge drinking not only as a problem at UNC but as a "significant problem at virtually every campus in the country."[78] In short, media depictions showed that collegiate binge drinking was happening on every campus, was getting worse, had potentially lethal consequences associated with it, and had college administrators scrambling to take appropriate actions to make it go away.

Media reports on college binge drinking also routinely identified fraternities as being involved with students who were injured or died as a result of binge-drinking activities.[79] The stories also described binge drinking as a routine part of the fraternity pledge process. In several instances, media reports emphasized the involvement of fraternities in binge-drinking incidents:

- "I think underage...and out-of-control drinking by members of fraternities is the norm at many universities....What you have at a fraternity is a culture that focuses on alcohol consumption as a tangible measure of maturity" (quoting the acting president of the University of Iowa).[80]
- "Radford University has suspended two fraternities for violating campus drinking policies after a student from Manassas was found dead in her dormitory room the morning after she attended their keg parties...the two fraternities' disregard for campus rules have prompted calls for tougher enforcement."[81]
- "Too often, the fraternity experience of today is defined by alcohol" (quoting Robert B. Deloian, president of Phi Delta Theta's General Council).[82]

[78] Jane Stancill, "Panel to Battle Drinking at UNC," *News and Observer*, May 25, 1996, News, p. B3.

[79] To provide a sense of the presence of Greek organizations on college and university campuses in North America, consider that in 2009 the North American Interfraternity Conference – the largest organization of its type in North America – consisted of 73 member fraternities and sororities, representing 5,500 chapters on more than 800 campuses in the United States and Canada, and had approximately 350,000 undergraduate student members. Retrieved December 4, 2009, http://www.nicindy.org/about/.

[80] Associated Press, "Universities Battling Binge-Drinking Culture," *Telegraph Herald* (Dubuque, Iowa), October 2, 1995, News, p. A5.

[81] Eric Wee, "Death Leads to 2 Frats' Suspension," *Washington Post*, February 16, 1996, Metro, p. B3.

[82] "*Phi Delta Theta* International Fraternity to Ban Alcohol from All Chapter Residences," *Business Wire*, March 17, 1997.

- "But with recent studies suggesting that binge drinking...is most likely to occur among fraternity and sorority members, administrators are focusing new efforts on Greek row."[83]

Readers of these and similar stories were led to believe the college fraternity experience was *defined* by alcohol abuse and that fraternities *fostered a culture* in which drinking was not only accepted but encouraged "as a tangible measure of maturity." Such depictions had to terrify the parents of 18- and 19-year-old first-year college students who they knew were pledging fraternities. Their sons were apparently seeking admission into organizations that would indoctrinate them into a culture in which maturity was measured by how much alcohol one could consume in a single sitting. Even worse, in media coverage of such incidents, fraternity drinking was constantly linked to the deaths of pledges. Again, the serious negative consequences of binge drinking not only were being overemphasized but were now being tied to membership in various collegiate fraternal organizations.

Identifying New Victims of Binge Drinking

A familiar refrain in claimsmakers' messages about a new social problem is the identification of new victims and villains.[84] Recall that SOC identified "innocent and naïve students" as the new victims of, and postsecondary administrators as the new villains responsible for, violent and unsafe college campuses, and campus feminists identified college women as the new victims and campus administrators as the new villains responsible for campus date and acquaintance rape. Consistent with this process, public health advocates also identified new victims and villains involved with collegiate binge drinking.

In perusing media and public health reports on binge drinking during the 1990s, we found that the new victims of the problem appeared to consist of three groups of college students: underage drinkers who fell prey to a campus or fraternity culture that encouraged drinking; nondrinking students who experienced derision or ostracism for not

---

[83] Mary Beth Marklein, "Colleges Nudge Fraternities toward Restricting Alcohol," *USA Today*, October 22, 1997, Life, p. 5D.

[84] Much of this section was influenced by Workman, "An Intertextual Analysis of the Collegiate Drinking Culture."

going along with campus cultural norms that condoned excessive drinking or who had their class, study, or work schedules disrupted by friends or roommates who binge-drank; and crime victims, students dealing with the fallout of the bad behavior arising from their peers' binge drinking, including those who were victims of sexual assault, rape, and other criminal victimizations.

Underage Drinkers. Media stories on binge drinking appearing during the 1990s and into the 2000s tended to emphasize that many of the victims of binge drinking were under the legal drinking age and had fallen prey to the "culture of drinking," which media characterized as taking hold at college campuses. In fact, a major point made by media outlets and public health studies was that binge drinking disproportionately involved underage drinkers.

For example, a 1994 story on binge drinking by reporter David Baron that was carried on National Public Radio's *Morning Edition* described many college student binge drinkers as underage:

> *Baron:* Brian, a freshman at a Boston area college, is at a typical party in a crowded student apartment on a typical Saturday night. He's had a lot to drink.
>
> *Brian:* Five or six pints of Guinness and then two or three beers, so far. That's only –
>
> *Baron:* [interviewing] Are you expecting to have more?
>
> *Brian:* Yes, uh-huh. [a young woman laughs]
>
> *Baron:* Brian says he drinks heavily three or four nights a week, and so do his friends.
>
> *Brian:* I'm not drinking any more than anyone else, and not drinking much less though.[85]

In a 1997 interview with the *Washington Post*, the editor in chief of the Vanderbilt University campus newspaper said, referring to university efforts to address binge drinking on campus: "I don't think it's going to make much difference. Freshman who once drank in the dorms...now get fake IDs...and drive to the popular downtown [Nashville] bars 20 blocks away."[86] That same year, a story appearing

---

[85] David Baron, "Binge-Drinking College Students Impact Non-Drinkers," NPR, *Morning Edition*, December 7, 1994.

[86] Leef Smith and Jay Mathews, "In Va., a Sobering Lesson Doesn't Sink In," *Washington Post*, December 7, 1997, Metro, p. B1.

in the *St. Louis Post Dispatch* chronicled the deaths of several students from alcohol-related causes and *all* of them were under the legal drinking age.[87] Additionally, underage drinkers were now showing up in campus crime data mandated by the *Campus Security Act*. For example, in 1998 the *Chronicle of Higher Education* published a story with the headline "Alcohol Arrests on Campuses Jumped 10% in 1996." The story then reported that in 1996, more than 16,000 students had been arrested by campus police for underage possession of alcohol on campus or for being intoxicated in public on campus.[88] Thus, not only were public health surveys reporting that large numbers of college students were drinking and that many were underage, but *Campus Security Act*–mandated crime statistics were also showing that large numbers of underage students were drinking *and* the campus police were arresting them for doing so.

Nondrinkers of Alcohol. Media stories on binge drinking also chronicled the negative effects on nondrinkers of the culture of drinking on many college campuses. For example, in a 1994 *New York Times* story on college student drinking, the reporter quoted a group of women who were members of two sororities at the College of William and Mary as saying that "those who refuse to drink...are often left off of invitation lists for weekend parties or social outings."[89] Similarly, a 1994 story in the *Washington Post* quoted a Georgetown University senior, in describing the pressure to drink, as saying "in the meantime, you're not [drinking], you're sober, and you can get a lonely feeling from that."[90] Finally, a 1994 press release from Harvard cited the CAS report on how innocent nondrinkers were suffering because of binge-drinking peers. The press release described nondrinkers as experiencing insult and humiliation; as having serious arguments with peers who had been drinking; and as being pushed, hit, or assaulted. The students also had their property damaged, had to "babysit" a drunken classmate or roommate, had

---

[87] Scripps Howard News Service, "Surveys and Headlines Agree: Results of Campus Drinking Can Be Deadly," *St. Louis Post Dispatch*, December 28, 1997, Metro, p. C11.

[88] Kit Lively, "Alcohol Arrests on Campus Jumped 10% in 1996," *Chronicle of Higher Education*, May 8, 1998, Students, p. A48.

[89] Celis, "Fatal Alcohol Abuse Persists on Campus, but Fewer Drink."

[90] Daly, "Nearly Half of U.S. College Students Are Binge Drinkers, Study Finds."

their study or sleep time interrupted, and experienced unwanted sexual advances.[91]

In short, media reports made it appear that students who had not been "seduced" by the culture of drinking on college campuses were being informally sanctioned by those students who had accepted the norms of drinking culture. Binge drinkers disrupted the lives of non-drinkers, socially ostracized them, insulted and humiliated them, and even made unwelcome sexual advances toward them. These examples also illustrate how media sources and public health researchers not only had begun constructing direct effects of binge drinking on those engaging in the behavior but were now focusing on so-called secondary effects of the behavior on other students.[92] Interestingly, postsecondary institutions during the 1990s responded by creating on-campus dormitories that were "substance free" (i.e., no smoking, drinking, or drugs were allowed as a condition of living in them) as a potential safe haven for these students.[93]

Crime Victims. Media reports during the 1990s also focused on college students who suffered criminal victimization at the hands of fellow students under the influence of alcohol. In an editorial published by the *Christian Science Monitor* in 1992, U.S. surgeon general Antonia Novello said that "rape and sexual assault are also closely associated with alcohol misuse. Among college age students, *55 percent of perpetrators were under the influence of alcohol....*Administrators at one university found that *100 percent of sexual assault cases during a specific year were alcohol-related.*"[94] In a 1993 story on collegiate binge drinking, the *Boston Globe* reported that "alcohol is almost always involved in campus date rapes," citing as its source an alcohol and drug education

---

[91] Misia Landau, "Alcohol: The Spillover Hangover" (1994), retrieved April 8, 2009, http://focus.hms.harvard.edu/1994/Dec16_1994/Alcohol.html. See also Baron, "Binge-Drinking College Students Impact Non-Drinkers."

[92] See, for example, Henry Wechsler, Bryn Austin, and William DeJong, "Secondary Effects of Binge Drinking on College Campuses" (2000), retrieved April 11, 2009, http://permanent.access.gpo.gov/lps2771/effects.htm.

[93] See, for example, Carolyn Kleiner, "Schools Turn Off the Tap," *U.S. News & World Report*, August 30, 1999, p. 74; Claudia Kalb and John McCormick. "Bellying Up to the Bar," *Newsweek*, September 21, 1998, p. 89; and Jerry Adler and Debra Rosenberg, "The Endless Binge," *Newsweek*, December 19, 1994, p. 72.

[94] Antonia Novello, "Alcohol and Kids: It's Time for Candor," *Christian Science Monitor*, June 26, 1992, Opinion, p. 19 (emphasis added).

counselor at Northeastern University.[95] A 1995 story also appearing in the *Globe* presented even more startling information when it revealed that "seventy-five percent of offenders...in campus sexual assault cases had been drinking."[96] Finally, in prepared testimony before a Senate Judiciary Committee hearing on interstate alcohol sales via the Internet, Mothers Against Drunk Driving (MADD) board member Brendon Brogan said that "researchers estimate that two-thirds of rape and sexual assaults among teenagers and college students are perpetrated by people under the influence of alcohol."[97] Thus, many of the claims made by SOC and by campus feminists were being reinforced by media reports on the role of alcohol in facilitating on-campus sexual and other forms of violence. Assaults, verbal threats, property damage, and other victimizations were being *specifically linked* to collegiate binge drinking.

In summary, journalists' stories and public health reports on collegiate binge drinking successfully identified a set of victims touched by the problem: underage drinkers drawn into the culture of drinking; nondrinkers who had to deal with binge drinking's secondhand effects; and victims of various forms of physical or sexual violence and verbal threats. Thus, not only were the media identifying a new problem – collegiate binge drinking – but their stories helped to drive home the message that binge drinking was a deadly matter and parents had better be wary of what awaited their children heading off to college. Not only would their 18- and 19-year-old children be faced with the pressure to join a binge-drinking culture, the results of which could be catastrophic, but their children who chose *not* to indulge could *still* become the victims of those who binge-drank through sexual assaults, other forms of violence, or disrupted lifestyles, all of which could negatively impact on *their* education.

[95] Betsy Lehman, "The Lure of the Keg Can Be Hard to Resist," *Boston Globe*, September 20, 1993, Science & Technology, p. 39.

[96] Alice Dembner, "Campuses Try to Alter Pressure to Drink," *Boston Globe*, May 9, 1995, Metro/Region, p. 29.

[97] Brendon Brogan. Quote from U.S. Congress. Hearing of the Senate Judiciary Committee. "Alcohol Sales between States via Internet" (March 9, 1999). Transcript from *Federal Document Clearing House Congressional Testimony*. Available on LexisNexis® Congressional; accessed September 20, 2008.

Identifying New Villains Associated with Binge Drinking

Claimsmakers and media also identified new villains associated with the binge-drinking problem as consisting of three groups.[98] First, there were students who possessed "pro-drinking attitudes" and who bought into the norms of the campus drinking culture. The second group of villains included fraternities and, to a lesser extent, sororities, which condoned and enabled binge drinking as a normal part of Greek life on campus. Finally, postsecondary institutional presidents were also to blame, because they failed to recognize the problem while concurrently accepting advertising dollars from the alcohol spirits industry to help generate revenue for their institutions.

Students as the New Villains. Throughout the 1990s, journalists' accounts of collegiate drinking presented the public with the several messages. First, college students possessed pro-drinking attitudes in part because they perceived that drinking was a sign of adulthood and independence and because drinking helped them to fit in to a new environment – the college campus. Second, *all* student drinking was binge drinking. Third, *all* student binge drinking resulted in serious negative consequences not only for the drinkers (e.g., serious physical injury or death from alcohol poisoning) but for third parties, such as college women sexually assaulted at parties held in dormitories. Fourth, binge drinking resulted when students' pro-drinking attitudes were combined with easy access to alcohol via bars catering to college students, at fraternity parties, or at private parties held in students' dormitory rooms or apartments. Finally, this "morally unacceptable behavior" was worthy of appropriate intervention and correction.

There are multiple examples of how journalists during the 1990s portrayed students as having pro-drinking attitudes:

- According to "Charley," a student at the University of Alabama, "I didn't have my parents looking over my shoulder any more, and I got into a cycle where I would just go out and have a few beers at night, and that became an every-night occurrence, pretty much."[99]

---

[98] The analyses found in this section rely heavily on a model presented by Workman, "An Intertextual Analysis of the Collegiate Drinking Culture."

[99] "Drug and Alcohol Abuse," *Sonya Live!*, 1992.

- "It just makes it [drinking] more tempting [to students when college officials] put a clamp on it. They're going to want it. And as soon as they get to college, they're independent. They want to try those things that they weren't allowed to try when they were at home."[100]

- A female college student explained that she drank so much during her first year in school "because everyone else was – because I felt like I could fit in."[101]

- Students "were learning the wrong value right away; that is, they were learning that in order to be accepted...you've got to drink...[to be accepted into] a culture where drinking is an important part of acceptance."[102]

- "If you drink, you're popular. If you drink, people like you more because...people think it's cool to drink," according to a female student at Louisiana State University quoted in a story about the death of Benjamin Wynne.[103]

Further, electronic and print media sources suggested that *all* collegiate drinking was *binge* drinking. Television news shows, such as ABC's *20/20* or CBS's *48 Hours* would present viewers with video clips of students "throwing back" a mixed drink or a beer and of students intoxicated at parties, stumbling around campus, or passed out in parking lots. Such footage sent a clear message to the public that students either would not or could not drink responsibly.[104] Print media outlets also contributed to the perception that college students were irresponsible drinkers:

- "Kids feel they have to drink...it's really common for incoming freshmen to go out every weekend. That's what college is all about," claimed a 20-year-old finance major at the University of Wisconsin at Eau Claire.[105]

[100] CNN, "Panel Discusses College Binge Drinking," *CNN News*, June 7, 1994.
[101] Randall Pinkston, "New Survey Shows that More College Students Are Binge Drinkers," *CBS This Morning*, December 7, 1994.
[102] Adam Hochberg, "New Chancellor Leans on Greeks to Ban Booze," NPR, *All Things Considered*, August 30, 1996.
[103] Dean Reynolds and Elizabeth Vargas, "Binge Drinking on Campus," *ABC Good Morning America*, August 28, 1997.
[104] Workman, "An Intertextual Analysis of the Collegiate Drinking Culture," pp. 230–231.
[105] Celis, "Fatal Alcohol Abuse Persists on Campus, but Fewer Drink."

- According to a story on the death of Wayne Parsons from alcohol poisoning, "when Wayne went to a party with about 30 other people at a friend's apartment one night at the end of September, he gulped a large quantity of beer then, in 15 minutes, drank an oversized tumbler of about 32 ounces of tequila, friends told police."[106]
- "[Students] see drinking as a sign of adulthood.... When 60 percent of the campus isn't 21, they want to seem like they are," explained a 21-year-old junior at Northwestern University.[107]

Further, journalists and public health researchers routinely equated binge drinking with grave consequences, including poor grades, depression, criminal victimization, physical injury, and even death:

- "Students with 'D' and 'F' grade point averages consumed 11 drinks a week while students with an 'A' grades had an average of 3 drinks a week."[108]
- "It's sad, because a woman comes in and can't talk for 10 minutes because she's sobbing.... She says 'I woke up in bed and here was a young man, and I don't know how he got there or what happened. But we were both naked.'"[109]
- "This year, at least six deaths [of students] have been attributed to excessive drinking on college campuses...and deaths like the one at LSU [referring to the Benjamin Wynne case] are typically viewed by students as 'someone else's problem.'"[110]
- "On Nov. 10, University of Michigan sophomore Byung Soo Kim celebrated his 21st birthday by trying to drink 21 shots of whisky. He downed 20, then passed out, turned blue and stopped breathing. As Kim lay dying in a Michigan hospital...the next night, seven college students hopped into a Jeep 500 miles away on the campus of Colgate University. Moments later, the driver, a Colgate student who authorities say was dangerously intoxicated, veered off the road

---

[106] Ibid.
[107] Maribeth Vander Weele and Roger Flaherty, "Bottle Still a Big Player on Campuses: Student Drinking Hasn't Abated," *Chicago Sun Times*, September 20, 1992, Sunday News, p. 13.
[108] Ibid.
[109] Celis, "Fatal Alcohol Abuse Persists on Campus, but Fewer Drink."
[110] Matthew Mosk, "Universities Hard Pressed to Restrain Flow of Beer," *Record* (Bergen County, NJ), August 28, 1997, News, p. A1.

and struck a tree, killing four of the passengers. And by the time Monday classes began, five proud families who'd sent their children away to school were busy planning their funerals."[111]

- "At the very core of the college drinking problem is the matter of personal responsibility. Sooner or later students are going to have to take charge of their own lives and learn to say no to the people trying to kill them with friendship."[112]

As the preceding examples suggest, journalistic accounts of collegiate drinking implied that students were *choosing* to binge drink, with dire negative consequences the result. If this was the case, and they were not being seduced by the binge-drinking culture of college, were they really any different from *criminals* who rationally chose to violate the law?[113] By implying that students who binge-drank *chose* to do so, despite the fact many of them were underage (and therefore knew their behavior was illegal) and most knew that intoxication could seriously impair one's judgment, students could now be labeled as "deviants" and be held responsible for their behavior. Further, given the seriousness of the behavior and its apparent widespread nature, intervention into and correction of the behavior also seemed warranted.

Fraternities as the New Villains. During the 1990s and into this decade, fraternities were increasingly singled out as actively involved in, or indirectly associated with, the new problem of collegiate binge drinking and its dire consequences.[114] Ever since the film *Animal House* depicted fraternity life as largely one involving debauchery, constant drinking, and unchecked sexual escapades, journalistic depictions of fraternity life – particularly of "pledge week" activities – have presented fraternity members' alcohol abuse, including binge drinking, as the norm:

---

[111] Daniel McGinn, "Scouting a Dry Campus," *Newsweek*, November 27, 2000, pp. 83–85.

[112] Hank Nichols, "Students Alone at Fault in Binge Drinking," *Boston Globe*, October 12, 1997, New Hampshire Weekly, p. 2.

[113] See, for example, Alex Piquero and Stephen Tibbetts (Eds.), *Rational Choice and Criminal Behavior* (New York: Routledge, 2002).

[114] A search of the Lexis-Nexis News electronic database for the period 1989–2009 using the search terms "college fraternities and binge drinking" returned more than 1,000 source citations representing both electronic and print media outlets, not including *Time* magazine.

- "Statistics show that fraternity members have slightly below average grades. In light of that, in addition to their decaying houses, financial troubles, and continued reports of hazing, fighting, underage drinking, and sexism, Ms. Myers [president of Dennison University] says: 'you have to wonder what positives they are contributing.'"[115]
- "Members of college fraternities...drink far more heavily and a lot more often than do their non-Greek classmates, a national study by Harvard University researchers showed. Questioned about their drinking habits over the prior two weeks, the study found that 86 percent of fraternity house residents reported drinking at least five drinks in a row."[116]
- "'It was just assumed that we'd [fraternity members] drink whenever we could,'...says an insurance company computer analyst who spent four years in a popular jock-populated fraternity. 'I'd drink a beer in the morning, shots while I was studying, and at night we'd just drown in it. The next morning, we'd wake up all over the place, on the floor, on the stairs, all groggy and smelly and stupid, and it would all begin again. Funny thing is, I don't remember why the hell it was so important, what it was exactly that we were trying to get away from.'"[117]
- "The frequency of binge drinking by fraternity men...leads to an 'Animal House' style of living. It should cause great concern and immediate action at every institution hosting these groups," warned Dr. Henry Wechsler, CAS principle investigator.[118]

Such depictions helped to "frame" fraternity membership in such a way as to equate membership in fraternities with binge-drinking behavior by their members. In turn, fraternity binge drinking became associated with all sorts of grave consequences, including physical injury, alcohol poisoning, and death, especially among pledges who

---

[115] Sam Walker, "At Ohio's Dennison University, Fraternities Fight for Their Houses," *Christian Science Monitor*, February 6, 1995, Learning, p. 13.
[116] Staff, "Fraternities Out Drink Classmates," *Washington Post*, September 10, 1995, Around the Nation, p. A10.
[117] Patricia Smith, "A Frightening Campus Ritual," *Boston Globe*, September 11, 1995, Metro/Region, p. 15.
[118] William Honan, "Study Ties Binge Drinking to Fraternity House Life," *New York Times*, December 6, 1995, National Desk, Education Page, p. B16.

were under the legal drinking age. As a result, media depictions of fraternity life helped frame fraternity membership as morally unacceptable (i.e., deviant) behavior in need of correction.

Collegiate Administrators as the New Villains. Claimsmakers also set their sights on college and university administrators as villains for failing to act in light of the public health evidence concerning the extent of binge drinking on their campuses and the serious negative consequences accompanying the behavior. For example, a 1994 story in the *Boston Globe* about collegiate binge drinking suggested that college officials working to curb alcohol abuse believed that much of the drinking goes on out of sight and out of the college's control.[119] A 1992 editorial appearing in the *Columbus Dispatch* stated that "programs emphasizing abstinence [from drinking] are not working."[120]

Administrators themselves admitted to journalists that their efforts were hardly ringing successes. For example, Dr. Katherine Lyle, president of the University of Wisconsin system, told National Public Radio's *Morning Edition* that "our programs so far...have not been particularly effective in reducing drinking on the campuses."[121] Further, some journalists were reporting that "not everyone was on board" (referring to campus administrators) with policies or programs designed to reduce collegiate binge drinking. For example, the *Washington Times* story quoted the CSACU report as concluding that "[the administrators of] colleges and universities, the faculties, trustees...everybody has to get into this thing,"[122] inferring that not everyone on campus was involved and, should resistance to programs designed to reduce binge drinking be widespread, administrators were again to blame. Other stories seemed to indicate that administrators who implemented different programs on their campuses were trying to find a "magic bullet" but were instead finding failure. A 1991 *New York Times* story on binge drinking quoted one campus official as saying that such programs "are part of a

---

[119] Dembner, "Campuses Try to Alter Pressure to Drink."
[120] Earle Holland, "College Drinking May Show 'Just Say No' Doesn't Work," *Columbus Dispatch*, August 2, 1992, Editorial and Comment, Science, p. 7B.
[121] Baron, "Binge-Drinking College Students Impact Non-Drinkers."
[122] Maria Koklanaras, "Virginia College Boozers Don't Swig Up to U.S. Average," *Washington Times*, March 11, 1993, Metropolitan, p. B3.

'scattershot approach' undertaken in recent years by...universities" to try to control the problem.[123] Thus, administrators were apparently not "smart enough" to appropriately address a problem that was apparently going on right under their noses.

Other media reports suggested that administrators should adopt strategies to address binge drinking. For example, in a story on collegiate binge drinking, the *Philadelphia Inquirer* reported that "the [CASCU] panel recommended that colleges offer prevention and treatment programs, sponsor alcohol-free events and involve faculty, parents and alumni to fight alcohol abuse."[124] Other stories described schools that were either considering or had adopted a "zero tolerance" stance toward students (particularly, underage students) who binge-drank and were caught while intoxicated.[125] In such cases, suspension, followed by expulsion for repeat offenders, would occur. Thus, recommendations were being directed toward college administrators, inferring that they had not undertaken a reasonable course of action to prevent or control binge drinking. Finally, in what could best described as a "frontal attack" on administrators for failing to act to control collegiate binge drinking, an op-ed piece appearing in the *Washington Times* not only told administrators what they had *not* been doing but also what they *should* be doing: "Colleges could start by getting rid of co-ed dorms, giving young men and women a zone of privacy without the temptations of intimacy. Colleges could more rigorously maintain age restrictions against drinking, imposing strict sanctions by suspending or expelling chronic offenders."[126]

A second area of criticism leveled at college and university administrators involved ties between their schools and the beer, wine, and spirits industry. Claimsmakers argued that colleges and universities were making money in various ways from the spirits industry, including from advertisements appearing in student newspapers and from those found in football stadiums or basketball arenas. As a result,

[123] Celis, "Fatal Alcohol Abuse Persists on Campus, but Fewer Drink."
[124] Belinda Rios, "Drinking Binges Grow on Campuses and Envelop Women," *Philadelphia Inquirer*, June 18, 1994, National, p. A01.
[125] Kleiner, "Schools Turn Off the Tap"; McGinn, "Scouting a Dry Campus."
[126] Suzanne Fields, "An Equal Right to Dangerous Recklessness," *Washington Times*, June 9, 1994, Commentary/Op-Ed, p. A19.

administrators did not want to anger their benefactors by aggressively pursuing policies to reduce binge drinking that jeopardized revenue from the spirits industry. To illustrate, the *New York Times* quoted a first-year student at Southern Illinois University at Carbondale as saying "off-campus bars appealed to students with discount pitchers of beer. They've got all those specials at the bars on weekdays, so that's when everybody goes."[127] A 1994 *Boston Globe* story reported that "members [of a professional association of land-grant colleges] urged a ban on all alcohol-related advertising on campus."[128] Dr. Henry Wechsler was quoted in an exposé by the local newspaper in Eugene on drinking at the University of Oregon promoting a similar message:

> The alcohol industry exerts massive pressure on colleges and college sports, and universities do little to resist the pressure.... it has taken many millions of dollars in advertising at sports events and ongoing financial support of sports programs at many colleges over many decades to forge that link.... Providing [students] with these ads and cheap alcohol around the campus is like pouring oil on a fire.[129]

That same story reported that "it's not clear how much revenue the University of Oregon reaps from alcohol advertising."[130] A 1994 *Washington Post* story reported that:

> [Senator Edward] Kennedy criticized arrangements by which brewers sponsor athletics or other campus events aimed at promoting drinking. "It's a scandal and something ought to be done about it," he said. "These universities are themselves addicted to the very dollars that flow from the alcohol companies to the vaults of universities."[131]

In short, claimsmakers and their representatives were damning college administrators, particularly college and university presidents, for their ties to the spirits industry. According to the claimsmakers, such ties were the main reason that college officials were not taking the binge-drinking problem seriously enough.

---

[127] Associated Press, "44% of College Students Are Binge Drinkers, Poll Says," *New York Times*, December 7, 1994, Education Desk, p. B-12.
[128] Dembner, "Campuses Try to Alter Pressure to Drink."
[129] Tim Christie, "Study Links Sports, Advertising, Drinking," *Register-Guard* (Eugene, OR), December 11, 2002, News, p. 1.
[130] Ibid.
[131] Daly, "Nearly Half of U.S. College Students Are Binge Drinkers, Study Finds."

Claimsmakers thus presented an argument along these lines: alcohol advertising helped fuel the long-standing culture of drinking that had taken hold on most American college and university campuses. In turn, the culture had inspired students to abuse alcohol by engaging in binge drinking. In turn, binge drinking *always* led to serious negative consequences, such as death from alcohol poisoning or in a traffic accident. Equally troubling was the claimed occurrence of criminal victimizations, including sexual assault of college women or other physical violence that was linked to binge drinking. As a result, existing ties between the spirits industry and postsecondary institutions were morally unacceptable and needed dissolution. Only then could the chain of harmful forces acting on students be broken, and the binge-drinking scourge successfully controlled.

Institutionalizing the Problem and Creating Policy Responses

Public health claimsmakers – especially those involved with the CAS series – played a key role in institutionalizing collegiate binge drinking as a new problem threatening the ivory tower. Recall that when a new social problem becomes institutionalized, it becomes interwoven into the social fabric, and policy makers mobilize to address the problem, most often through legislative initiatives. Further, various social institutions, such as the legal system, change their behavior in response to the new problem.[132] For example, in the case of claims made about lax campus security leading to on-campus victimization, whereas courts during the 1960s and 1970s ruled that colleges and universities were not liable under existing civil law, during the 1980s and 1990s the courts reversed that position.

Collegiate binge drinking as a social problem became institutionalized during the 1990s and into the following decade as policy makers mobilized and formulated responses to address the problem. Without question, the contributions of public health researchers and media coverage of that research were critical to institutionalizing collegiate binge drinking as a new problem on college campuses. Scientific reports from the researchers granted legitimacy to claims from

[132] Joel Best, *Random Violence: How We Talk about New Crimes and New Victims* (Berkeley: University of California Press, 1999), p. 5.

grieving parents whose sons' or daughters' lives had been cut short by binge drinking. Various spokespeople, such as Harvard University's Dr. Henry Wechsler, became cultural authorities on the problem and on the claims surrounding it, as they came from highly respected and established institutions of higher learning.[133] Reports indicating that collegiate binge drinking had reached "epidemic proportions" struck a chord within the culture,[134] which had often expressed ambivalence about the issue of alcohol use and abuse.[135] If these reports helped to characterize the problem of binge drinking as a "fierce, fire-eating dragon" that was killing or gravely injuring 18- and 19-year-old students, then "the death of the dragon become[s] the only solution possible."[136]

As David Workman has suggested, media rhetoric on collegiate binge drinking implied that college officials' exerting *better control* over students' drinking behavior could be the answer to the problem.[137] If collegiate binge drinking was framed as lack of control on the part of students, while at the same time it was being "caused" by a culture of drinking that had taken over college campuses and was tacitly supported by the beer, wine, and spirits industry, then administrators needed to take steps to rein both in.

Words such as "regulation," "attack," "curb," "laws," and "ban" began appearing with increasing frequency in print and electronic media stories during the 1990s when the stories dealt with policies or programs aimed at "killing the dragon" of collegiate binge drinking.[138] For example, a 1991 story in the *Washington Post* described how some postsecondary institutions, such as Princeton University, were adopting new policies that completely banned alcohol on the campus:

> Princeton last month outlawed beer kegs at all university functions, singling them out as "a symbol of open access and excessive consumption." Other colleges have gone all the way and banned all alcohol

---

[133] Workman, "The Social Construction of Collegiate Binge Drinking as a Social Problem in America," pp. 5–6.
[134] Ibid., p. 9.
[135] See, for example, Gusfield, *Contested Meanings*.
[136] Workman, "The Social Construction of Collegiate Binge Drinking as a Social Problem in America," p. 15.
[137] Ibid., pp. 15–17.
[138] Ibid., p. 16.

at school functions. Some, such as Long Beach State in California, have established alcohol-free dormitories. Many college newspapers have stopped accepting beer advertising – long a mainstay of campus press revenue.[139]

A similar story appeared that same year in the *New York Times*, where the reporter emphasized that "a growing number of universities have ended serving alcohol on campus."[140] Fraternities also joined in the "ban the booze" movement when they began banning alcohol at their parties – sometimes under orders from national headquarters or other times under orders from the school where the fraternity was housed.[141] Other stories such as a 1992 editorial that appeared in the *Christian Science Monitor* spoke of the need for "better enforcement of underage drinking laws" and suggested that a "get tough" approach by college administrators would make a difference.[142] Even Congress became involved when Rep. Glenn Poshard (D-IL) called for hearings by the House Education and Labor Committee at a 1992 Washington, D.C., press conference announcing the release of the first CORE Report: "Because this issue is so important and the study is so relevant, we have asked our colleagues on the Education and Labor Committee, and they have agreed, to hold hearings on this [issue] next session."[143] Finally, as part of activities relating to NIAAA's National Alcohol Awareness Week, some schools began concerted efforts to address binge drinking: "This week's activities dovetail with National Alcohol Awareness Week and [West Chester University's] first concerted efforts to discourage binge drinking. 'The important thing we're trying to promote,' said senior volunteer Heather Yost, 'is to be

[139] Paul Taylor, 1991. "Underage Drinking Moves into Spotlight," *Washington Post*, October 29, 1991, sec. I, p. A3.

[140] Celis, "Fatal Alcohol Abuse Persists on Campus, but Fewer Drink."

[141] See, for example, "Fraternity Charter Is Taken Away in Fraternity Drinking Case," *New York Times*, March 3, 1991, sec. I, Metropolitan Desk, p. 51. The North American Interfraternity Council has actively worked to address alcohol abuse at college fraternities in both the United States and Canada by creating an Alcohol Summit Program. The council also actively works to dispel myths about fraternities and binge drinking. See "The Myths," retrieved December 4, 2009, http://www.nicindy.org.

[142] Editorial, "Drug War's New Front," *Christian Science Monitor*, February 10, 1992, p. 20.

[143] News conference with Representative Glenn Poshard, in "Re: Drug and Alcohol Use on College Campuses."

responsible.'"[144] All of these illustrations show that college and university administrators were considering a variety of options, ranging from prohibition to education, in an effort to reduce collegiate binge drinking. In line with Workman's observations, the rhetoric in journalists' accounts of student binge drinking revolved around schools developing better ways to regulate binging through awareness campaigns or, if needed, criminalizing the behavior through stepped-up law enforcement efforts. Regardless of the specifics, the goal seemed to be to press postsecondary institutions to better control the behavior of students who risked death or other serious consequences by binge drinking.

CONCLUSION

The construction of collegiate binge drinking as a new problem on American college and university campuses during the late 1980s through the 1990s followed a similar pattern to what we characterized for violent and unsafe campuses, date and acquaintance rape of college women, and lax campus security. In constructing the problem of collegiate binge drinking, claimsmakers came forward, named, and took ownership of the new problem. They described how binge drinking had crossed temporal and geographic boundaries, helped create a frame or an orientation for understanding the problem, named new victims and villains associated with binge drinking, legitimized binge drinking as a new problem, institutionalized collegiate binge drinking as a new problem, and helped influence policy responses designed to reduce the behavior.

In the case of collegiate binge drinking, the claimsmakers were public health researchers who played a central role in identifying the behavior as a new problem threatening the ivory tower. They conceptualized binge drinking and developed a quantitative measure of it, which provided estimates of its scope and magnitude to the public. Further, the claimsmakers described the serious negative consequences for students of binge drinking, including devastating

---

[144] Christopher Merrill, "WCU Homecoming Activities to Hit Upbeat Tempo after Week of Alcohol Awareness Programs," *Philadelphia Inquirer*, October 19, 2000, Neighbors Chester & Brandywine, p. B01.

physical injury or death. Additionally, they called on postsecondary administrators to develop policies to prevent and control binge
drinking on their campuses. Because the researchers were social scientists associated with major universities, such as Harvard's School of
Public Health, or were funded by federal agencies, such as the U.S.
Department of Education, their words lent credibility and scientific
authority to stories appearing in the media about college students'
drinking. Once electronic and print media picked up on reports
released by the researchers and began incorporating them into their
stories, there was little doubt that collegiate binge drinking was a new
monster preying on college students. Binge drinking was also linked
to a host of negative consequences ranging from rapes and violent
assaults occurring on campus, to poor attendance and academic performance by drinkers. Claimsmakers also pointed to the secondary
effects of the behavior, which negatively impacted on the class, study,
work, and leisure time of nondrinking roommates and friends.

Throughout the process of constructing collegiate binge drinking
as a new problem, the rhetoric of media reports sent not-so-subtle
messages to the American public, including:

- *All* college student drinking was binge drinking.
- *Nothing but* grave consequences, including death, occurred when
  students binge drank.
- Binge drinking had reached *epidemic proportions* on college campuses, particularly among students under the legal drinking age of
  21 years of age.
- *Fraternities* and their associated lifestyles, which emphasized binge
  drinking, were *killing our youth.*
- Postsecondary administrators were "in bed" with the spirits industry
  through advertising appearing in campus outlets, such as student
  newspapers or at campus stadiums.

Because a social scientific discipline such as public health had successfully identified, quantified, and characterized the new monster and
its destructive path, steps needed to be taken to kill it, or at least do a
better job of controlling it. Thus, prohibition of alcohol on campus
or other forms of control, including stepped-up enforcement by campus police of underage drinking laws, were possible solutions, along

with policies aimed at educating students on the dangers of binge drinking.

Public health researchers became the voice of the claimsmakers, as electronic and print media routinely incorporated their voices in stories about the devastating effects of alcohol abuse on college students. Because the social scientific evidence presented by Dr. Henry Wechsler and others was left largely unchallenged, these voices lent significant legitimacy to the claims being made. After all, these people were *scientists* who "knew their stuff" – or at least that was the assumption. Given a larger cultural ambivalence about alcohol use, when social scientists came forward with data showing that alcohol was killing and injuring a substantial portion of the college student population, a shift in public attitudes was likely facilitated. Suddenly there was stronger advocacy for prohibiting alcohol on *all* college campuses or cracking down on bars and pubs located near postsecondary institutions that were selling alcohol to students (especially those who were underage). In effect, a return to colleges and universities serving in the role of *in loco parentis* was being advocated, at least as it related to monitoring alcohol use.

CHAPTER SEVEN

The Legacy of Claimsmakers
Institutionalizing the Dark Side of the Ivory Tower

We want to briefly discuss a central presumption of the Clery Act – that students have a right to know about crime on campuses because [institutions of higher education] are potentially dangerous places. To a degree, it is difficult to argue against students having more knowledge about the safety risks of the [schools] that they are attending or may choose to attend. However, using the law to address social problems...is not cost free. It is burdensome on the [schools] to have to implement an unfunded mandate that requires them to collect crime statistics...and to publish and distribute annual security reports. In this regard, it seems reasonable to place the Clery Act in an appropriate social context about whether college and university campuses are, in fact, sufficiently dangerous places to warrant legislatively mandated oversight.[1]

The social construction of campus crime as a new American social problem began during the late 1980s and into the 1990s with claims made by four groups: Security On Campus, Inc. (SOC); campus feminists; student crime victims and their families; and public health researchers. Collectively, their claims created a damning picture of the "new reality" of the dark side of the ivory tower. Each group claimed ownership of a particular aspect of the campus crime problem and legitimatized ownership of that component. With the help of electronic and print media, each group spread its message to the public about the problem it had identified. Eventually, each group had its claims institutionalized, and through individual and collective efforts, the legislative and judicial branches of government established new mandates

---

[1] Bonnie S. Fisher, Jennifer Hartman, Francis T. Cullen, and Michael Turner, "Making Campuses Safer for Students: The *Clery Act* as Symbolic Legal Reform," *Stetson Law Review* 31 (1, 2002): 79.

and rulings designed to attack the problems of violence, vice, and victimization on college campuses. Administrators at postsecondary institutions responded, in turn, by implementing new campus-based policies or programs aimed at complying with the mandates.[2]

Claims about crime occurring on American college and university campuses and the spread of these claims occurred despite historical evidence showing that violence, vice, and victimization had existed on American college and university campuses for nearly 300 years. Yet, within two decades, four activist groups had convinced not only the parents of college-age children but the American public as well that campus crime was a "new and dangerous threat" to the health, safety, and well-being of millions of American college-age students. As the public demanded action, state legislatures and then Congress became involved and created new policy mandates concerning how higher education would respond to the "new" problem of campus crime.

To this point, we have examined in detail the claims made by each of the four groups and how each group was able to capture the public's attention with those claims, as well as the new policies and programs that arose in response to them. Taken together, the four groups and their claims were influential in helping construct campus crime as a new American social problem. In effect, "campus crime" consisted of several integrated pieces, each of which was claimed by one of the groups. Each group then took its piece public by coming forward, taking ownership of its specific problem, expanding the domain in which the claimed problem existed, identifying new victims and villains associated with the problem, and then influencing policy responses to their particular problem. Ultimately, each group was able to institutionalize its particular claim about campus crime as a new problem. Thus, while the groups themselves focused their attention on getting the public to accept their specific claims, ultimately those claims

---

[2] One beneficiary of these changes has been college and university student affairs personnel. Over the past 15 to 20 years, they have become increasingly involved in designing and implementing campus-based sexual assault and sexual harassment education and prevention, underage drinking prevention, and violence prevention. See, for example, Florence A. Hamrick, Nancy J. Evans, and John H. Schur, *Foundations of Student Affairs Practice: How Philosophy, Theory, and Research Strengthen Educational Outcomes* (San Francisco: Jossey-Bass, 2002).

formed the basis for a much larger claim: campus crime was a new and dangerous threat to millions of American college students.

In this final chapter, we focus on several commonalities we believe exist among the claimsmakers, beyond the activities in which the groups engaged that resulted in elevating campus crime to a new social problem. These commonalities ultimately created a loosely coupled network of claimsmakers relating to campus crime who were ultimately responsible for socially constructing it as a new social problem. We also examine the legacy of each group to the social construction of campus crime and explore issues that arise in attempting to determine whether campus crime really is a threat to millions of college students and their families. Finally, we describe how our study contributes to understanding how complex societies identify and respond to their social problems.

COMMONALITIES AMONG CLAIMSMAKERS

As one analyzes the activities of the four claimsmakers during the past two decades, one begins to see commonalities among the strategies they used to help establish campus crime as a new social problem. First, each group used what we call a "triggering event" to catapult the group (and its claims) to center stage – with the assistance of electronic and print media sources. Second, these triggering events nearly always involved a particularly heinous incident involving one or more students. These incidents, according to the claimsmakers, constituted the new reality of life on college campuses. For example, the brutal rape and murder of Jeanne Ann Clery illustrated the new reality of how violent and dangerous college campuses had become because of lax security and uncaring college administrators. Third, there was overlap in the audiences to which the claims were directed and which ultimately helped to strengthen the individual claims made by each of the groups. Fourth, even if one of the groups had failed in its efforts to legitimize and institutionalize its specific claims, the remaining groups were still active and could pick up the slack and thus reduce the chances their claims about campus crime could be deconstructed or have campus crime fail to be labeled as a new, pressing problem. In effect, the four groups constituted enough of a critical mass of claimsmakers that the absence of one or even two of them from the collective would not have changed the final outcome. Finally, in their claims, each group targeted postsecondary administrators as the new villains associated with the problem that the group brought to the fore. In so doing, claimsmakers put a human face and name on the new evil they had brought before the public, including parents, students, researchers, and policy makers. Putting a face on the new villains would ultimately inspire parents, students, and other groups to mobilize and pressure state and federal policy makers to take appropriate steps to address the urgent problem of campus crime.

Triggering Events

A triggering event can be described as an incident that occurred on or near a college campus and around which a group of claimsmakers rallies itself. This event then becomes the basis for future claims made about the particular problem in which the group expressed an interest. For example, the 1986 rape and murder of Jeanne Ann Clery in her dormitory room at Lehigh University was clearly a triggering event for Connie and Howard Clery (and, ultimately, Security On Campus, Inc.). Their daughter's death sparked the Clerys to begin their crusade to make college campuses safer for all college students and provided them all the evidence they needed to claim that colleges and universities were unsafe and violent. Further, the settlement the Clerys received from the lawsuit they had filed against Lehigh for their daughter's death provided them the necessary financial resources to start SOC. The settlement also provided the Clerys with evidence they could use to support their claims about postsecondary administrators' turning a blind eye to the lax security, which, the Clerys touted, "caused" their daughter's murder. Ultimately, Jeanne Ann Clery, both literally and figuratively, became the "poster child" for the problem of unsafe and violent college campuses. SOC then used this to its political advantage to rally others – parents who had lost children to campus violence, victims' rights advocates, and campus counselors dealing with the aftermath of student violence – who shared SOC's and the Clerys' sentiments.[3]

---

[3]   Literally, in the sense that Ms. Clery's image is prominently featured throughout the SOC Web site.

Campus feminists also experienced a triggering event: publication of Mary Koss's national study on the extent of rape and sexual victimization among college women. Before the release of Koss's study, there had been little empirical evidence to support feminists' claims concerning the frequency of rape experienced by women more generally and by college women in particular. With publication of the Koss study – combined with the coverage *Ms.* magazine afforded it – campus feminists now had empirical data to support their claim. Koss's "one-in-four" estimate then became the rallying cry for campus feminists seeking to have new policies and programs developed to reduce the high incidence of date and acquaintance rape annually committed against college women on campus, be those campuses large or small, public or private, secular or religiously affiliated.

Claimsmakers comprising student victims of campus crime and their families likewise had a triggering event: the point at which civil lawsuits brought against colleges and universities over on-campus victimizations first started being won by plaintiffs in the mid-1980s.[4] The successes of those lawsuits then became a rallying call to *other* student victims and their families to pursue litigation against postsecondary institutions for *their* victimizations as well. Clearly, the call was heard, as the number of lawsuits filed against colleges and universities during the late 1980s and into the 1990s rose to numbers heretofore unseen.[5] As these lawsuits became more common, victim-litigants – particularly those who were successful – used the specifics of their cases to support their claims that campus security was lax. The claims were then broadcast by a variety of local, regional, and national media outlets.

Finally, public health researchers saw their triggering event occur in 1992 when the CORE group at Southern Illinois University released results of its study of college students' drinking behavior. That study paved the way to what became a torrent of research into collegiate alcohol abuse and acceptance by the public health and medical establishments – along with federal health agencies (e.g., National Institute

---

[4] Michael Smith, "Vexatious Victims of Campus Crime," pp. 25–37 in Bonnie S. Fisher and John J. Sloan III (Eds.), *Campus Crime: Legal, Social, and Policy Perspectives* (Springfield, IL: Charles C. Thomas, 1995).

[5] Ibid., p. 25.

of Drug Abuse; Office of the Surgeon General) – of not only the concept binge drinking but the standardized measure for it (the "5/4 rule").

Heinous Events

Beyond triggering events, each of the groups used a particularly heinous crime-related event to support its specific claim. In the case of SOC, the rape and murder of Jeanne Ann Clery was the event; for campus feminists, graphic stories of gang rapes of college women perpetrated by members of college fraternities or student-athletes showed the "normality" of date and acquaintance rape on college campuses. Crime victims used events such as running gun-battles in campus dormitory parking lots at the University of Southern Colorado or the rape of a student in a practice studio at American University to show that campus security was lax to nonexistent. Finally, public health researchers used events such as drunken-driving-related deaths of students and alcohol poisoning deaths of members of campus fraternal groups to show that binge drinking was the norm on college campuses. In each case, the heinous nature of the event chosen increased the impact factor of the group's claims on its target audience, which included policy makers and the public.

Audience Overlap

Further, as the groups made their claims, there was overlap in the audiences to which the claims were being directed. When SOC spoke of the death of Jeanne Ann Clery as indicative of the unsafe and violent nature of college campuses, it obviously was speaking to parents who had also lost a son or a daughter to campus violence. Campus feminists speaking out on the problem of campus date and acquaintance rape were directing their claims especially at college women and their parents. Student victims and their families who successfully litigated their claims against postsecondary institutions likewise were speaking to those who had experienced the trauma of victimization because of lax campus security. Finally, public health researchers spoke to both parents and students, those whose lives had been touched by alcohol abuse, especially binge drinking.

Beyond those narrow audiences, we believe that messages from claimsmakers were also reaching *each others' audiences*. For example, SOC's message about the heinous rape and murder of Jeanne Ann Clery likely reached those who had experienced any type of on-campus victimization and who believed that lax security caused the event. College women and their parents, concerned about violence against women on campus, no doubt heard SOC's message too. Parents with children in college, while hearing public health research-ers' messages about the dangers of collegiate alcohol abuse and binge drinking and its link to criminal victimization and drunken driving, also heard SOC's message about unsafe and violent college campuses. In short, claimsmakers' messages did not reach only their narrowly defined respective audiences – those who could relate either directly or indirectly to the claim being made. A much broader audience was likely to put the claims together and realize that the dark side of the ivory tower now included a *variety* of threats against the health and safety of young people, who either had already matriculated at various colleges and universities around the country or were contemplating doing so.

Because of audience overlap, it becomes plausible to argue that claimsmakers were able to easily mobilize public action on the pol-icy front. For example, when representatives of SOC testified before Congress on what had happened to Jeanne Ann Clery, campus femi-nists, crime victims or their families, and alcohol researchers could have been sitting on the dais as well, telling *their* stories and making *their* claims before policy makers. This spurred state legislators and then members of Congress to make their assessments about specific responses to the problem by taking into account *all of the claims made* about the looming threat posed by campus crime. If representatives of SOC testify before Congress that Jeanne Ann Clery's murder was due to lax security that university officials knew about but failed to act on, followed by the grieving mother of a student murdered in a campus parking lot who testifies to the same thing, a more coherent picture emerges for policy makers to consider: college and university campuses have become unsafe and violent places. If this testimony is followed by alcohol researchers speaking to the consequences of collegiate binge drinking as including violent victimization of college students by other students, even *more* evidence has been piled on to support SOC's basic claim. Thus, although the *specific claims* by the groups varied, when taken as a whole the public and policy makers were presented with a coherent picture. That picture spurred them to take action to address the supposed imminent threat to the well-being of college students that was posed by the "dark side" of the ivory tower.

Strength in Numbers

One of the more interesting commonalities involving the four claims-makers was that even if some of the groups had somehow faltered in their ability to convince the public and policy makers of the legitimacy of their claims, the remaining groups were *still there* to move forward with *their* claims and ultimately help construct campus crime as a new social problem. Because multiple groups were involved, each bringing its own claims about campus crime to center stage, eventually a loosely coupled *network of claimsmakers* evolved.[6] The creation of this network was also facilitated by the overlapping interests of the target audiences of the claimsmakers. For example, had SOC's drive to make college campuses safer eventually stalled, there were still *three other groups* bringing forth claims about campus violence, campus safety, and campus drinking to parents, students, postsecondary administrators, and policy makers. SOC's claims about unsafe and violent college campuses could easily have been integrated into or piggybacked onto claims made by one or more of the three remaining groups. Further, doing so would not have diluted its specific claim. For example, campus feminists could easily have used Jeanne Ann Clery's rape and murder to illustrate the on-campus dangers that college women face. Finally, student victims who sued their schools for damages arising from on-campus victimizations could easily have integrated the one-in-four estimate from the campus feminists into their claims about lax security leading to victimization.

---

[6] We were unable to find any specific evidence the groups *deliberately* coordinated their efforts for the purposes of enhancing the impact on policy makers or the public of the individual claims made by each group.

The four groups thus appeared to constitute a loosely coupled yet critical mass of claimsmakers that was large enough to survive, even with the loss of one or more of the groups from the core. Because the claims being made complemented the others' claims, for one group to have taken up the claims of the other groups would not, in our opinion, have changed the overall dynamic the groups were responsible for initiating. We believe the critical mass was so powerful and the messages so passionate and persuasive that they captured different audiences' attention and that even had one or more of the groups fallen apart, campus crime would *still* have been elevated to the level of a new social problem.

Campus Administrators as New Villains

Finally, while each claimsmaker identified new villains associated with the problem it was bringing to center stage, in all four instances administrators at American colleges and universities were named by the groups as the new villains, who were at least partly responsible for the new problem of violent and dangerous campuses, of campus date and acquaintance rape, of lax security on campus, and of college students' binge-drinking behavior.

An analogous situation would be the naming of gangs such as the Crips and Bloods as new villains who were responsible for gun-related crimes occurring in large American cities. As Best describes it, once the new villains are named, they can then be dealt with through such institutions as the legal system, which mobilizes local prosecutors and police departments to address the new threat. Out of such mobilizations, special gang units are created by the local police and known Crips and Bloods members are targeted for surveillance and, ultimately, arrest.[7] In the case of college and university administrators, once named as the new villains they became targets of legislation passed by the states and by Congress and in court rulings concerning postsecondary institutional liability. Mobilization occurred via congressional passage of the *Campus Security Act* (and its subsequent

---

[7] Joel Best, *Random Violence: How We Talk about New Crimes and New Victims* (Berkeley: University of California Press, 1999), suggests this in his discussion of institutional changes that occur in response to new social problems.

amendments) and enforcement of the legislation's mandates. Mobilization also occurred via new court rulings, which appeared to revitalize the legal principle of *in loco parentis* and thus redefined the relationship between college and student. Through formal and legally binding actions, the scope of the threat posed by the new villains – and, by implication, the new problem for which they were being held responsible – would be reduced.

By explicitly naming the new villains associated with their particular problem, the four groups of claimsmakers were able to show parents, students, and other activists just "who these people were" that were responsible for threatening the health and safety of American college students. Claimsmakers relating to the media the sworn statements of a vice president for student affairs from a particular school who testified in a civil trial relating to a liability claim over an on-campus victimization, or putting that person (or someone of similar stature) "on trial" in the media, allowed them to put a "real face" on the villains responsible for the new evil of campus violence, date and acquaintance rape, lax security, or binge drinking. Claimsmakers could then potentially motivate members of the public to support "the cause," since the public had now seen these new villains and could hear their "feeble attempts" to deflect the claimsmakers' criticisms directed at them over their (in)actions and resulting compromise of the safety of millions of college students each year.[8]

Once evil has had a face put on it, claimsmakers' ability to mobilize the public against that evil becomes much easier. Concurrently, public pressure on policy makers to pass new laws targeting that evil becomes greater. For example, the crime of "carjacking" – the unlawful taking of a motor vehicle by force or threat of force[9] – has *always* existed in

---

[8] SOC, in particular, has hammered away at college and university administrators as the "new villains" by tracking and updating instances of *Campus Security Act* noncompliance and posting that information to its Web site.

[9] At federal law, carjacking is defined in the *Anti-Car Theft Act of 1992* (18 U.S.C.A. § 2119). Specifically, carjacking is defined as: "Whoever, possessing a firearm with the intent to cause death or serious bodily harm, takes or attempts to take a motor vehicle that has been transported, shipped or received in interstate or foreign commerce from the person or presence of another by force and violence or by intimidation." Punishment for this offense ranges from fines and imprisonment, to death if someone is killed during the commission of the offense.

criminal law as armed robbery. Apparently, however, the label "armed robbery" was not enough – it failed to capture the "true evil" of having one's car stolen at gunpoint. So, to separate the specific evil associated with having one's vehicle taken by force and intimidation at gunpoint from "ordinary" armed robberies, a new class of federal and state offenses involving illegal taking of motor vehicles by force or threat of force became warranted because of pressure from interest groups and the public. Thus, carjacking was born. In the present context, claimsmakers were so successful in their activities that policy makers created entirely new sets of legislative and judicial policy designed to force the new villains to change their behavior or to risk either having their respective schools' images tarnished or facing sanctions for non-compliance, or both. Creating new policies that targeted the villains, such as the new crime of carjacking, was then supposed to reduce the threat posed by the new evil.

Thus, in examining the social construction of campus crime as a new social problem, certain commonalities among the claimsmakers can be identified. The first is a triggering event, which each of the four groups used to launch its set of claims into the public arena and then to serve as a rallying point to generate public attention. Such triggering events are commonly found when examining new crimes or criminals,[10] and they provide an entryway into capturing the public's attention. Once this was accomplished, members of the four groups could then seek the public's assistance in convincing policy makers to act on the threat posed by that problem. Ultimately, those claims were institutionalized, and new social policies and postsecondary institutional programs were created to help thwart the threat posed by campus crime.

Further, the claimsmakers focused on particularly heinous incidents to help illustrate how serious a threat their particular aspect of campus crime had become. Although the claims made were directed toward relatively large but narrow audiences, there was eventually overlap in the audiences receiving their respective messages because the four groups were, in effect, talking about the same phenomenon: campus crime and the threat it posed to the safety and well-being of college

[10] See Best, *Random Violence*, for discussion.

students and their families. The critical mass that the four groups
constituted guaranteed the dissemination of their messages and, we
believe, the social construction of campus crime as a new problem. In
addition, by naming postsecondary administrators as the new villains
at least partly responsible for a variety of ills on college campuses, the
claimsmakers put a face on the new evil of campus crime and helped
mobilize the public to rally around their claims and to press policy
makers for change.

THE CLAIMSMAKERS' LEGACIES

If the new reality of campus crime consisted of separate but interlock-
ing claims made by four groups of activists, each group ultimately took
ownership of a claim and moved its claim forward toward institutionalization. Through the mass media and with the help of the network
of claimsmakers, the public fit the claims together, which then formed
a clear image: the dark side of the ivory tower threatened the health
and well-being of millions of students enrolled at American colleges
and universities. Each group's claims became a component of a larger
story being told, and the legacy of each group lies with its claims.

SOC claimed that college campuses were unsafe and violent places.
SOC and its representatives then used Jeanne Ann Clery's rape and
violent death as *the* ultimate illustration of that point and gathered
and disseminated similar tragic stories to lend credence to its claim.
SOC then spent years working the media and other interested parties,
such as campus law enforcement officials, to publicize the claim. They
also spent years lobbying multiple states and then Congress to pass
laws intended to reduce campus violence. Once the *Campus Security
Act* was passed in 1990, SOC successfully worked to have the legislation amended to address additional concerns it had with victims'
rights, sex offenders on campus, and timely warnings in the event a
major threat to campus safety or security arose. Along the way, it also
appointed itself a "watch group" for institutional compliance with
federal legislation. It then closely monitored postsecondary institutions for evidence of noncompliance, and when such evidence was
found, SOC broadcast that fact to the public via mass media and on
its Web site. Finally, SOC also assumed the role as "the trainer" for

postsecondary officials responsible for compiling *Campus Security Act* information and submitting that information to the U.S. Department of Education. Clearly, the *Campus Security Act* and its subsequent amendments are the single greatest legacy of Security On Campus, Inc.'s involvement in the social construction of campus crime.

Campus feminists also have a legacy in the social construction of campus crime as a new social problem: the one-in-four estimate relating to campus date and acquaintance rape. Regardless of the *substantive* accuracy of that figure, it nonetheless became the rallying cry for people who were concerned about sexual violence perpetrated against college women. The figure inspired college women to try to do something about campus sexual violence, which resulted in such campus-wide activities as the Clothesline Project and annual Take Back the Night remembrances. The one-in-four figure likewise pressured postsecondary administrators to develop campus-based programs to help college women avoid "becoming a statistic," while also putting college men on notice that improper sexual advances would no longer be swept under the rug. The one-in-four figure helped pressure Congress to take action, resulting in amendments to the original *Campus Security Act* that created new rights for student victims of sexual assaults occurring on campus. With SOC serving as the watch group for *Campus Security Act* compliance, campus feminists could rely on SOC to monitor whether postsecondary institutions were taking the necessary steps to protect college women from the horrors of sexual assault. Should evidence of noncompliance be uncovered, they could join SOC in broadcasting that fact to the public. From our perspective, the one-in-four figure is the clearest legacy of the campus feminists who came forward during the late 1980s and assisted in socially constructing campus crime as a new social problem.

Student victims and their families also leave a legacy with the social construction of campus crime. During the 1980s, it was they who sued colleges and universities for damages arising from their on-campus victimizations and, importantly, won some of those cases. Before the 1980s, very few of these lawsuits ever made their way into court, and among those that did, fewer still were successful. Beginning in the early 1980s, state courts began seeing more of these suits and, by the late 1980s, began ruling *against* postsecondary institutions in these cases. Some of the student plaintiffs (or their families) recovered not only compensatory damages but, in some cases, punitive damages as well. Because of a willingness to litigate liability for on-campus victimizations and damages arising from those incidents, crime victims, their families, and their attorneys put colleges and universities on notice that lax security could result in large jury awards for monetary damages. Thus, their legacy became that of convincing the courts either that existing law relating to civil liability *was* applicable in these cases or that a quasi *in loco parentis* interpretation of the relationship between institution and student was warranted.

Finally, public health researchers studying collegiate binge-drinking behaviors also left a legacy regarding the social construction of campus crime as a new social problem. They created the term "binge drinking" to describe collegiate alcohol abuse and convinced the public health and medical establishments and government agencies such as NIAAA of the validity of the concept, the validity of measures for it, and the negative toll the behavior was taking on students. Had these researchers not created a term to capture the essence of their claim and quantify it, collegiate drinking could have remained postsecondary education's "dirty little secret." However, in creating both the term and standardized measures for it, which they incorporated into their surveys, public health researchers – particularly those with highly regarded reputations such as those affiliated with the Harvard School of Public Health – significantly impacted the way college administrators, dormitory advisors, freshman orientation counselors, and researchers *conceptualized* college students' drinking behavior. Binge drinking ultimately became a monster that needed slaying, and it fell on postsecondary administrators to design and implement new programs that would do so. Thus, the discovery of collegiate binge drinking is the strongest legacy of public health researchers in the social construction of campus crime.

In constructing campus crime as a new social problem, each of the four groups we profiled left a legacy of involvement. From SOC being almost single-handedly responsible for pressing Congress to pass the *Campus Security Act* and serving as a self-proclaimed watchdog for institutional compliance, to the Harvard Alcohol Study group's invention of the term binge drinking, each of the groups has a legitimate claim to having left a significant legacy in elevating campus crime to a new social problem.

CONCLUSION

The creation of social problems involves ongoing processes that appear to repeat themselves over time and occur *regardless* of the substantive nature of the problem or its actual threat. The same processes occur whether one is examining unsafe drinking water, random violence in the city, terrorist sleeper cells, or campus crime. The processes begin when individuals or groups, "claimsmakers," come forward and claim the existence of some new and serious threat to the public's health and welfare. Claimsmakers then convince the public and policy makers the problem they have identified is indeed worthy of being elevated to the status of a new social problem and worth their time and energy to develop reasonable responses to that particular problem.

We have now presented four separate but interrelated case studies of how groups of claimsmakers came forward and convinced the American public and policy makers that campus crime was a new problem; that the problem threatened the health and safety of every college student in America and, by extension, their families; and that immediate steps had to be taken to reduce that threat. We showed how each group, although making distinct and separate claims, used the media and engaged in similar activities to get their message out and convince the American people the dark side of the ivory tower now overshadowed almost all of the supposed positives that had long been associated with higher education. We also showed how the groups convinced policy makers, at least from the perspective of the claimsmakers, to take necessary steps to address the problem. These steps occurred either through new legislation targeting campus crime or via court rulings involving postsecondary institutional liability.

Whether campus crime is *actually* a threat to the health and well-being of millions of college students and their families has not been settled. Are college campuses unsafe and violent? Do college women have a high risk of experiencing a date or acquaintance rape while in college? Is security at postsecondary institutions lax? Is collegiate binge drinking as dire a threat as some would have us believe? And, perhaps most important, to what extent have the policies and programs implemented in wake of the claims we have chronicled actually had any sort of impact on the problems raised by the claimsmakers?

Consider, for example, SOC's claims about America's college and university campuses being unsafe and violent. The first issue this claim raises is rather straightforward: unsafe and violent *compared to what?* Surrounding communities? Cities of similar sizes? Further, if we are concerned about violent crimes committed against college students, would we not want to compare *their* rates of violent victimization with those of *nonstudents* of similar ages to determine if students experience higher, lower, or similar levels of violent victimization?[11] A related issue involves deciding *by what metric* is "unsafe and violent" to be determined: a rate per some unit population (e.g., the number of assaults per 1,000 students), or a rate that statistically controls for (i.e., removes the effects of) factors such as geographic size, size of student body and its demographic characteristics, location of the campus (e.g., urban, suburban, or rural). Simple *counts* of the number of incidents occurring on college campuses, which are what colleges and universities release in compliance with the *Campus Security Act* mandates, do not tell us very much. For some people, even a *few* violent incidents on a campus where thousands of students are enrolled would lead them to say that *particular* campus is violent and unsafe, while others considering the same evidence would rejoice over the fact the campus had such *low* levels of violence.

An additional issue here is that campus crime data released by schools in compliance with federal law *include only offenses reported to campus police or other campus authorities.* Why is this important? We know from studies of criminal victimization in society more generally that people, for a variety of reasons, do not always report their victimizations to

---

[11] The Bureau of Justice Statistics has examined this issue by comparing the violent victimization rates of college students ages 18 to 24 with those of nonstudents in the same age group during the period 1995–2002. Generally, college students' overall violent victimization rates were lower than nonstudents' rates, and their overall violent victimization rates fell more steeply than did rates for nonstudents during the period. See Katrina Baum and Patsy Klaus, *Violent Victimization of College Students, 1995–2002*, NCJ 206836 (Washington, DC: U.S. Department of Justice, Office of Justice Programs, 2005).

police.[12] We also know from victimization surveys that college students do not always report their victimizations to campus authorities, and thus crime statistics compiled under the *Campus Security Act* omit such incidents.[13] Thus, publicly reported campus crime statistics available under *Campus Security Act* mandates likely undercount, perhaps by a significant amount, the true volume of crime occurring at postsecondary institutions. Also important here is the fact that, although postsecondary institutions have been reporting their crime statistics since at least 1992, per the mandates of the *Campus Security Act,* one key offense omitted from these statistics is larceny or theft. This omission is problematic because several studies have shown that larceny or theft is *the* single most commonly occurring offense on college campuses.[14] Yet, because federal law does not require it to be reported, few schools voluntarily include larceny or theft in their crime statistics. Once again, we are left with the problem of available data undercounting the true volume of campus crime.

Further, SOC argued that once Congress passed legislation mandating colleges and universities to publish their campus crime statistics annually, such data would raise the awareness about campus crime not only of students already in college but of prospective students and their parents. In particular, SOC assumed that prospective students – and their parents – would use campus crime data available under the *Campus Security Act* as part of their decision-making process when choosing a school. The problem is that scientific evaluations of the impact of the *Campus Security Act* on student awareness about campus crime – the role such data play in helping students decide on which school to attend, and on the extent of institutional compliance – are largely nonexistent.[15]

---

[12] See James P. Lynch and Lynne A. Addington (Eds.), *Understanding Crime Statistics: Revisiting the Divergence of the NCVS and UCR* (Cambridge: Cambridge University Press, 2007).

[13] See Fisher et al., "Making Campuses Safer for Students," for discussion.

[14] See, for example, ibid.

[15] For example, see Dennis E. Gregory and Steven M. Janosik, "Research on the *Clery Act* and Its Impact on Higher Education Administrative Practice," pp. 45–64 in Bonnie S. Fisher and John J. Sloan III (Eds.), *Campus Crime: Legal, Social, and Policy Perspectives,* 2nd ed. (Springfield, IL: Charles C. Thomas, 2007). Gregory and Janosik found only a handful of published studies that have examined *Clery's* impact on higher education. According to Gregory and Janosik, the few surveys that

What about claims concerning women and their risk of experiencing a date or acquaintance rape while in college? Several issues arise here as well, perhaps the most important being how rape is operationalized. For example, if rape is limited *only* to penile penetration of the vagina, then all *other* forms of vaginal penetration involving fingers or objects, *must* be excluded because they are outside what is meant by rape. Additionally, there is the issue of determining what exactly constitutes consent on the part of the victim. If, for example, the victim initially consented to nonpenile penetration of the vagina but then declined to allow penile penetration, is this still rape? What about if consent was given, but the victim was under the influence of alcohol or drugs? Is consent *automatically* negated at that point? At what point might alcohol intoxication lead to an inability of the victim to give her legal consent to engage in sexual intercourse? According to most states, a blood alcohol concentration of .04 or .05 renders one legally intoxicated for purposes of operating a motor vehicle.[16] Should such a standard be established concerning whether, after achieving a certain level of blood alcohol content, a victim can no longer give her legal consent?

What about claims that security at most colleges and universities is lax at best? If a particular college or university devotes 10 percent of its total operating budget to campus security, does that mean it still has lax security? What about the role that students may play in contributing to security breaches in college dormitories and other on-campus facilities? If campus police or security officers at a particular campus routinely patrol dormitories *on the hour* to ensure that students have not propped open doors or otherwise tinkered with or defeated locks or other security devices, yet a student is assaulted in the laundry room of one of the dormitories, is security at the school still lax? Is there a need for some kind of national standard concerning campus security that takes into account the complexity of operations of a particular campus?

have asked students and their parents about knowledge of the *Clery* Act and whether information the statute mandated affected college choice decisions found that only a small minority even *knew* about *Clery* and an even smaller minority actually used *Clery*-based information when making college choice decisions.

[16] See, for example, http://www.totaldui.com/state-laws/default.aspx, retrieved April 29, 2010; http://www.progressive.com/vehicle-resources/blood-alcohol-calculator. aspx, retrieved April 29, 2010.

What about claims concerning the binge-drinking behavior of students? Because almost all of the evidence shows that large numbers of students drink and many of them regularly binge-drink, what about students who do both yet do not suffer the dire consequences routinely reported in the literature? How many are there? How do they avoid these consequences? Further, what are the *long-term* trends in collegiate alcohol use and abuse? Because surveys have been tracking levels of collegiate alcohol use and abuse for at least a decade, have levels remained relatively constant or have they significantly changed one way or the other? If use and abuse levels *have* changed, what may account for the change?

Other questions remain as well. For example, how *effective* have postsecondary institutional efforts been in addressing the concerns raised over college students' criminal victimizations, date and acquaintance rape victimizations, lax security, and binge drinking? While many colleges and universities have implemented various prevention programs designed to address campus crime, date and acquaintance rape, or binge drinking by incorporating such programs into new student orientation or creating stand-alone programs aimed at a particular problem, published evaluations of how *effective* these efforts have been in helping students avoid victimization or reduce levels of alcohol abuse are lacking and are often little more than case studies undertaken at a few schools.

The evidence raises potential doubts concerning the validity of the claims that have been made about campus crime. That being said, our purpose in raising the evidence was *not* to dispute the claims, settle possible disputes among the claimsmakers, or settle disputes between claimsmakers and critics. Rather, from a social scientific standpoint, what *is* important is understanding *how* violence, vice, and victimization – behaviors that have existed on American college campuses for more than 300 years – suddenly, in the span of about two decades, became *institutionalized* as new social problems in American society, worthy of legislative and judicial intervention, and which prompted dutiful responses from postsecondary institutional officials. To identify and to understand these processes and to see them at work in varying contexts of social problem creation, whether in the areas of public health, crime, housing, education, or the economy, contributes to a better understanding of how complex social arrangements, involving millions of people and multiple institutions such as education and families, move in one direction as opposed to another. We believe that chronicling how campus crime came to be defined as a new social problem provides such insight and helps us to understand more fully not only how societies define their social problems but ultimately how they respond to them.

Index

academic performance, 2–3, 169–170, 179

Accuracy in Campus Crime Reporting Act (HR715), 66–67

acquaintance rape. *See* date/acquaintance rape

administration (university administration). *See* higher education

Alabama A&M University, 40–41, 67

alcohol abuse: academic performance and, 2–3, 169–170, 179; accidental injury and, 2–3, 141–142, 179;alcohol poisoning, 147–151, 158–159; binge drinking preventive measures, 147–148, 173, 176–177; broadening of scope of, 149–150; campus crime and, 165–166; campus "party culture" and, 139, 140–141; culture of drinking, 143, 155–156, 161–162, 164–165, 169–170, 176; date/acquaintance rape and, 92, 198; drinking age laws and, 142–143, 145–146, 163–164, 177; early twentieth-century drinking traditions, 13–14; freshman orientation initiatives against, 25; institutionalization of problems

and, 175–178; media depiction of, vii, 139; as "new problem," 143, 151, 179; in nineteenth-century institutions, 10; Prohibition era drinking, 15–17; public health research and, x; sexual victimization and, 2–3, 86, 141–142, 152–153, 165–166, 169–170; statistics and history of campus alcohol use, 141–143; student drinking games, 145; student pro-drinking attitudes, 167–170. *See also* binge drinking

Americans for Effective Law Enforcement (AELE), 58–59

American Society of Industrial Security (ASIS), 113–114

Amethyst Initiative, 143

Amherst University, 11–12

Animal House, 170–172

Annual Conference on Campus Violence, 94–95

Antioch College, 107–108

antiviolence activism: anti-date-rape activism, 91–92, 105; public promotional initiatives, 76–77; redefinition of campus violence, 27–28, 33; Security On Campus, Inc., ties to, 64–65. *See also* Security On Campus, Inc.

Argosy University, 6